LEGITIMATE LEADERSHIP

by

Wendy Lambourne

First publication 2012

ISBN 978-1482569049

Author:
Wendy Lambourne
Tel +27(0)82 800 4188
wendy@schuitema.co.za

Published by:
Rogue Works LLC
info@rogue-works.com
www.rogue-works.com

Design, typesetting and layout:
Lisa Borman
Tel +27(0)82 990 2983

Editing and proofreading:
Valda Strauss
Tel +27(0)82 686 4483

Dedication

To the three men in my life: Teigue, Nicky and Morgan.

Biography

Wendy Lambourne has an MA in Industrial and Organisational Psychology (University of Cape Town) and is a Registered Psychologist with the South African Medical and Dental Council.

Much of her early career was spent in the South African chemical industry. In the 1990s she was employed at what was then the biggest explosives company in the world. The company was beset by productivity, quality and safety concerns, at the core of which was a failure in leadership. In a senior organisational development role she worked with her leadership colleagues to transform the organisation, the golden thread being Schuitema's Care and Growth leadership model.

Convinced from first-hand experience of the power of the model, she joined Schuitema Associates and is a partner in the company.

Over the past 18 years she has become an internationally-recognised authority on practically achieving transformation in an organisation using the Care and Growth model. Her implementation experience is in diverse contexts, across many industries, and in many countries.

She is married to Teigue and lives in Johannesburg. Her interests include reading, music, hiking, travel, white wine and red setters.

CONTENTS

Foreword

Over the last twenty years Wendy has applied her exceptional professionalism to a set of ideas that we have come to refer to as the 'Care and Growth Leadership Model'. In the process she has assisted a very broad range of clients on four continents to fundamentally transform the calibre of the leadership in their organisations. These organisations were also very diverse, including government departments, NGOs, and enterprises in the banking, insurance, retail, manufacturing, information technology, hospitality and mining industries.

This book represents the wisdom distilled from this experience.

This book's major contribution is to be a very well thought through answer to the question 'So what do I do?', which is what leaders often struggle with after they have been exposed to the basic principles of the Care and Growth model. This is not to suggest that the book is a paint-by-numbers set of recipes. Rather, Wendy has blended a very insightful grasp of the abstract principles of Care and Growth with an impressive range of application areas.

These application areas range from the issue of where the leader spends his time, to how to deal with issues of structure and system. In each case Wendy provides practical, principle-based advice, which is the product of years of struggling with the task of enabling leaders. This book should be viewed as a key text for anyone who is really interested in human excellence and the role of leadership in enabling it.

The Care and Growth model requires the leader to shift his or her attention from results to process and people. The tools which it provides enable leaders to do so and, simultaneously, deliver the results required. This, therefore, provides an essential handbook for balancing the many irreconcilable interests operative in a corporate job.

Etsko Schuitema
Originator of the Care and Growth Model

Introduction

Etsko Schuitema developed the Care and Growth model from research into conflict and trust in South Africa's gold mines that he did in the late 1980s, under the auspices of the South African Chamber of Mines.

He introduced his model to my colleagues and I at what was then the biggest commercial explosives factory in the world, in the early 1990s. The basic tenets of his model provided the golden thread for the transformation of a company beset by productivity, quality and, above all, safety concerns – at the core of which was a failure in leadership.

At the time my colleagues and I gained two key insights. Firstly, that as leaders we were there to serve our people, not the other way around. Secondly, that in the process of leading others, you grow. You realise your full potential as a human being.

Over the past 20 years, working with both individual leaders and leadership teams to implement the Care and Growth model, in various parts of the globe, I have remained convinced that the following is true: *there is an inextricable link between an individual's personal maturation as a human being and the successful leadership of others*.

The platform for this book is Etsko Schuitema's book *Leadership, The Care and Growth Model* (2004) and the readers of this book are encouraged to read *Leadership* to gain a fuller understanding of the model. I have quoted freely from *Leadership* but have not attempted to cross reference all of the passages since that would have disrupted the flow of this text.

Etsko encouraged me to write this book as a guide to the leaders of enterprises who embark on the challenging journey of translating the Care and Growth framework into practice.

The book seeks to answer two questions:

1. *What is required of the leadership of an enterprise to gain the trust, willingness, and loyalty of its employees, without which the delivery of exceptional results is not possible?*

2. *What enables the personal maturation of those in command roles? How can leaders use the opportunity, which leading others affords them, to grow as human beings?*

The book is organised into five sections. Section One provides a synopsis of the Care and Growth model by reiterating the key principles upon which the model is built. It also delineates how leaders are tested, and in the process grow, in their everyday interactions with direct reports.

The following three sections, the body of the book, deal with the enablement of employee contribution. They address the three key variables that facilitate contribution – the provision of Means (Section Two), the enablement of Ability (Section Three), and the cultivation of Accountability (Section Four).

The final section is concerned with the practicalities of implementing a Care and Growth intervention in an organisation. It is a distillation of the lessons learnt with client organisations over the last two decades, what leads to failure and success.

The book will have served its purpose if the collective experience of those who have worked with the Care and Growth model as described in this book, is helpful to those concerned with successfully leading others and transforming themselves in the process.

SECTION ONE

The Care and Growth Model

The Care and Growth model originated out of primary research done in the area of management-employee conflict in the South African mining industry in the late 1980s, under the auspices of the South African Chamber of Mines Research Organisation.

The initial research led to the development of a framework for understanding the leadership conditions under which the management of an enterprise is trusted by those in their charge. What the research demonstrated unequivocally is that managers, individually and hence collectively, are accepted or rejected on the strength of their perceived interest in the wellbeing of their employees. Trust is granted or withheld, leadership is seen to be worthy of support or not, primarily on this basis.

Since then it has consistently been shown that, in any group, there are two populations – an anti-establishment and a pro-establishment group. These groups will always exist. The size of the positive group, however, is directly determined by employee perceptions of the leadership's intent.

When leaders of an enterprise have benevolent intent they are there to give or serve their people. This giving is not a giving of *things*, so much as a giving of *self*. Employees work willingly for those who exercise authority over them, only when they deliver on two drops of essence. In the first instance those in authority have a genuine concern for those in their charge, as human beings, not human resources. Further to this, they enable their people to realise the very best in themselves.

The right to demand delivery, in other words, is earned. Not by paying a wage but by subscribing to the criteria of Care and Growth.

What has become known as the Care and Growth model promotes an alternative approach to the leadership of people in modern organisations. It is an approach which views leadership as not about achieving results or getting the work done through others, but rather as using the results and the work to be done to cultivate exceptional people.

In **Beyond Management** (Chapter One), the different ways in which the Care and Growth model challenges conventional managerial assumptions and customs are presented. For each challenge, alternatives are posited, which collectively constitute the four core principles which underpin the Care and Growth model. Lastly, the practical implications of each of the Care and Growth principles are defined.

Intent, or being here to serve, evidences itself in the typical command situations that leaders face on a day-to-day basis, as they perform their leadership roles. In **Living the Care and Growth Values** (Chapter Two) the intent test, inherent in each of these command situations, is defined. Thereafter, what is required of leaders in each command situation to pass the intent test, and consequently solicit the trust, willingness and loyalty of their people, is demonstrated.

Beyond Management

Almost twenty years ago Etsko Schuitema issued a warning, in his book *Beyond Management* (1994), regarding the dire consequences of the continued perpetuation of current management customs. He went on to posit what seemed back then to be a radical set of alternatives to the norm. Taken collectively these alternatives constitute the core principles which underpin the Care and Growth leadership model.

THE NATURE OF THE RELATIONSHIP BETWEEN EMPLOYER AND EMPLOYEE

The nature of the relationship between employer and employee is usually viewed as a buying and selling relationship; as an exchange of X kilojoules of labour for Y units of money. The key issue in this relationship, as is the case in any trading relationship, is price.

On the face of it, this appears to be true. The deal which is struck between the two parties is formalised in an employment contract which specifies the rights and obligations of both parties.

Secondly, as with any trade, it would appear that the one commodity (money) is handed over in return for another commodity (labour). This thing called 'labour' has a commercial value and hence people are referred to as 'our greatest asset'. They are also labelled 'human resources', which along with other resources, are unfortunately a cost to the business and must be managed.

Thirdly, the market forces of supply and demand clearly also apply to a labour market. Where labour is plentiful, it is cheap and hence can easily be dispensed with. Where labour is in short supply, it gives rise to a 'war for talent' and to spiralling costs as employers scramble to outbid each other for acquisition and retention of this precious resource.

▷ Challenges to Conventional Wisdom and the Alternative

There are however two ways in which the assumption of a buying and selling relationship can be challenged.

- *It is not possible to buy and sell labour.*

In the first instance the notion that labour can either be bought or sold is a fallacy. A product or service can be traded but people cannot – at least not since the abolition of slavery.

It is simply not possible to acquire human effort and expertise independently from the person in whom they are vested. Whether organisations like it or not, along with labour comes a human being.

- *The two parties are not equal.*

Secondly, what is implied in a buying and selling relationship is that the exchange that takes place is between two equal parties. Even if the agreed price is affected by the relative bargaining power of the two parties, neither one is subordinate to, and hence has to answer to, the other.

In the employment relationship, however, the two players are not equals. This is because employers have the right to ask employees to do things; to exercise power over them. In return for a guaranteed sum on a predetermined date in the month, employees have to submit themselves, on a daily basis, to a boss's instruction, to a person who has authority over them.

The relationship between employer and employee, therefore, is not a buying and selling relationship – it is a relationship of power.

What is at issue in a relationship of power is not price, it is *legitimacy*. It is the acceptance, or otherwise, of the authority of the superordinate by the subordinate.

Axiom 1:

What is at issue between employer and employee is not the price of a commodity called labour, it is the legitimacy of a relationship of power.

 Implications of Axiom One

The prime implication of the first principle is the understanding that for command to happen there has to be acceptance of command. Those in command in the workplace can only lead if, and when, they have mobilised the consent of the majority of employees to their doing so.

Of the two parties in the relationship it is employees, not management, who ultimately decide to what degree they are prepared to be led. In the final analysis, managers have only as much power as their employees permit them.

Management knows where it is positioned, at any point in time, on a scale from 'total rejection' to 'total acceptance' of their authority by the general climate which prevails among employees.

When those in authority are accepted, their visibility outside the boardroom is welcomed. Employees take their concerns to them rather than to their employee representative or to the human resources function. They abide by managerial decisions and, if disciplinary action is taken, do not rail against it. The average employee does what is expected and more.

The key challenge facing anyone in authority, therefore, is that of establishing and then maintaining the legitimacy of that authority.

In summary then:

THE NATURE OF THE RELATIONSHIP BETWEEN EMPLOYER AND EMPLOYEE	
Convention	**Challenges**
• The relationship is a buy and sell relationship. • The issue is price.	• It is not possible to buy and sell labour. • The two parties are not equal. • The issue is legitimacy.
Axiom 1	**Implications**
What is at issue between employer and employee is not the price of a commodity called labour, but the legitimacy of a relationship of power.	• For command to happen there has to be acceptance of command. • The key challenge for leadership is therefore establishing and maintaining legitimacy.

THE LEGITIMACY OF A RELATIONSHIP OF POWER

There are a number of assumptions and beliefs currently held about what the manager's job is and what is required to be successful in it.

The commonly held view of the job of those in authority at work is that it is to achieve a *result*, a *vision*, or an *outcome* through people. By definition managers don't do the work themselves, they get the work done by others. That managers perceive their role in this way is not surprising given that managers in general are measured and rewarded for the *results* they get out of their people.

Further to this, managers believe they have the right to demand delivery because they pay people and/or because of their position in the hierarchy. When employees sign up with the company they become contractually bound to perform as agreed in the employment contract. If employees do not arrive at work and do their jobs, management is within its rights to terminate the contract.

Finally, managers generally believe that the way to achieve results is through the skilful use of a host of management tools at their disposal – ranging from targets, deadlines, budgets, direct instructions and performance ratings through to inspiring vision statements, public recognition, incentives and good verbal communication.

The possibilities are seemingly endless. They boil down, however, to using either compulsive or persuasive means to achieve the desired results. There is a 'hard' way and a 'soft' way to get employees to do what management wants them to.

The most effective managers are those who are most skilled in the deployment of these management tools or strategies. They know the best strategy to use in a given situation and are therefore versatile in their approach. Hence the popularity of the so called 'situational leadership' school of management.

Managers who are most successful, however, allegedly rely more on persuasion than compulsion. This is simply because, in the long term, they know that persuasion works better than compulsion.

When it comes to the motivation of employees, therefore, it is a combination of intellect, personal charisma, interpersonal skill and style which accounts for success.

 ## Challenges to Conventional Wisdom and the Alternative

There are a number of fundamental challenges to be raised.

- *There are inevitable consequences to the use of 'sticks' and 'carrots'.*

People can be driven to perform in response to both the 'hard' and 'soft' approach. What is not openly acknowledged, however, is the inevitable consequences, in the fullness of time, of the use of both the 'stick' and the 'carrot'.

All forms of compulsion essentially motivate through fear. People understandably feel that they are being forced, coerced, even bullied, into doing things. They comply, but only in order to avoid the negative consequences for them of not doing so. The coercive means engender resistance. They breed an attitude of 'I will do exactly what you say and I hope that it fails'. Eventually there is only apathy and a lack of commitment.

Carrots, on the other hand, appeal to the greed in human beings. Employees make the desired response but only in order to get what they want. Contrary to popular belief, the 'soft' approach often leads to a worse reaction than the 'hard' approach. No matter the skill of the persuader, those who are being persuaded or positively influenced, are not fooled. They sense that they are being manipulated and because of this their response goes beyond resistance to retaliation, to getting their own back.

Over time persuasion leads to hostility and to conflict, rather than harmony, in the relationship between the two parties. Both protagonists are only in the relationship to maximise their own self-interest, to get as much as possible for giving as little as possible.

In response to both the 'stick' and the 'carrot', employee reaction is predictable. This is because all people are hardwired to resist coercion and to retaliate when they feel manipulated.

- *There is a limit to what 'sticks' and 'carrots' can deliver.*

Coercion and persuasion do work. There are many examples of dramatic improvements in productivity through the use of penalties and incentives.

The gains from both options are, however, limited. The reason is obvious: employees are doing what is required of them because they 'have to' not because they 'want to'. In the face of coercion they give what is required out of fear of punishment. In response to some form of enticement, they give in order to get.

Both strategies get movement but not willingness. Employees will only give if either the 'stick' or the 'carrot' is present. In the absence of the 'stick' or the 'carrot' they are inert.

- *It is not the 'what' or the 'how' but the 'why'.*

Contrary to popular opinion, whether a management tool works or not is neither a function of the 'what' nor the 'how'. A positive result does not arise because the 'right' management tool was chosen, nor because the tool was executed with sufficient skill. The determining factor is something else entirely; it is the 'why' which sits behind the 'what' and the 'how'.

The core variable for success as a manager is not behaviour, it is *motive*. This is because, as human beings, we respond in any interaction not to the other person's behaviour per se, but to what we perceive to be the *intent* behind the behaviour.

The reason we willingly submit to the surgeon's knife but resist that of the robber is because we read their intent as different. We know that the knife-wielding assailant is there to do us harm, but we trust that the pain and discomfort that the doctor is putting us through is in order to heal us.

In essence, intention is about *whose interests are being served*. Malevolent intent is about the pursuit of self-interest; it is self-serving. Benevolent intent, on the other hand, is action taken in the other's best interests.

Employees will only trust those in authority at work, therefore, when they are convinced that they have their best interests at heart. That is, when they perceive management as being in the relationship to *give* them something, not to *get* something out of them.

When this is the case, those in command have power and are truly powerful. In the absence of power, managers only have control.

- *The right to demand delivery is earned, not by paying a wage, but by subscribing to certain criteria.*

What those in command have to give to their people, what earns them the right to demand delivery, distils down to only two drops of essence. In the first instance managers have to have a genuine concern for those in their charge. They have to care for their people as human beings, not as human resources which help their bottom line to grow. Further, they have to enable their people to realise the very best in themselves.

The price to be paid before employees will be truly willing to deliver on command, therefore, is not money. It is care and growth. This is what makes the power which is exercised by those in authority legitimate.

This is equally true of anyone in authority – religious leaders, police and army officers, doctors, parents, teachers and even sports coaches. Any relationship of power is legitimate only if the aim of that relationship is the care and growth of the subordinate in the relationship.

- *The product of leadership is not a result, it is an exceptional human being.*

The leader's job is not to get results through others. Leaders do not produce results; they produce extraordinary people.

A coaching analogy is useful here. It is the players, not the coach, who play the game and put a result on the scoreboard. How the game is played and the resultant score are not irrelevant to the coach. Both the game and the score, however, are not the coach's job. They are the coach's tools, the vital information the coach needs and uses to enable the players.

Axiom 2:

Any relationship of power is legitimate if the aim of that relationship is the care and growth of the subordinate in that relationship.

▶ **Implications of Axiom Two**

Axiom Two has three key implications:

- There has to be a fundamental change in the boss-subordinate relationship from being *boss-centred* to being *subordinate-centred*. Subordinates are no longer there to serve their superiors. Managers are there to serve their people. What is traditionally a *reporting relationship* must become a *coaching relationship*. No less than a total inversion of the line of service is required from up the line to down the line.

- Legitimate relationships of power have to exist at every level in the hierarchy. Each person in a command role is required to care for and grow those who report to him directly. Each manager therefore has as many pieces of leadership work as he has people reporting to him directly. The line of command will only be strong when everyone in the line pays the price of legitimacy. Failure to do so, by any manager anywhere in the hierarchy, will create a point of weakness in the line and jeopardise the legitimate authority of others in the hierarchy.

- What those in leadership roles are measured on, and rewarded for, has to change. Managers should not be measured and rewarded for what they get out of their people, but rather for what they give to them. The primary criterion against which leaders should be judged is not personal or business achievement. Rather it is the calibre of the people in their charge; the degree to which they have set up their people for success.

In summary then:

| THE LEGITIMACY OF A RELATIONSHIP OF POWER ||
Convention	Challenges
<ul><li>The manager's job is to achieve results through others.</li><li>Managers have the right to demand delivery because they pay people or they are the boss.</li><li>Intellect, personal charisma, interpersonal skill and style account for success.</li></ul>	<ul><li>The leader's job is not to achieve results but to cultivate exceptional people.</li><li>The right to demand delivery is earned by subscribing to the criteria of Care and Growth.</li><li>The core variable for success as a manager is not skill or behaviour, but intent.</li></ul>

Axiom 2	Implications
Any relationship of power is legitimate if the aim of that relationship is the care and growth of the subordinate in that relationship.	• A change in the relationship from being boss-centred to subordinate-centred is required. • There must be legitimate relationships of power at every level in the hierarchy. • The primary criterion against which leaders should be judged is the calibre of their people.

EMPOWERMENT/GROWTH

The Care and Growth model is once again at odds with the conventional view when it comes to both the meaning of 'empowerment' and what the empowerment process itself entails.

It challenges the notion that empowerment is synonymous with both employee participation and democracy, that it is possible to empower overnight and to separate empowerment from accountability.

▷ Challenges to Conventional Wisdom and the Alternative

• *Empowerment is not the same as employee participation.*

Participative management has been in vogue for many years. It arose out of management's recognition that there was a reservoir of good ideas among those lower in the ranks which was largely untapped and hence unavailable to the business.

The way to access this collective wisdom was through the implementation of employee involvement programmes, quality circles and the like. In this sense, the empowerment of employees meant sharing information with them, which had been the sole domain of management, and then listening to employee views and opinions on the data which had been given to them.

Employee empowerment, however, is much more than employee involvement. Real empowerment requires leadership to go beyond asking people for their opinions, listening to them and only then deciding. It means *letting them decide and living with their decision*, even if it is contrary to the decision that the leadership would have made.

By definition, then, it is simply not possible to give up *authority* but to still hold on to *control*. When authority is handed over, so is control. To truly empower literally means to give up power. The corollary to the enfranchisement of employees is the disenfranchisement of management.

- *Empowerment is not the same as democracy.*

Democracy is when the people make the decision. Furthermore, in a democratic system where there is 'one person, one vote', everyone is equal.

A precondition for *empowerment*, however, is *inequality*, not equality. For those in authority to give up authority they have to have it in the first place. Before power can empower and thus be legitimate, there has to be inequality between the subordinate and the superordinate.

This is true of any person in authority – parents, teachers, coaches or managers. Without the requisite authority to do so, they cannot enable those in their charge.

When teachers lose the authority to discipline, then students can no longer learn because the teacher can no longer teach; she is too busy trying to restore a vestige of order in the classroom. Similarly, if parents were to be prohibited from spanking their children, they would breed monsters rather than young adults fit for society.

Empowerment, therefore, is not about replacing autocratic behaviour with democratic behaviour since there is room for both in any legitimate relationship of power.

This can be clearly seen when one considers the boss one works for willingly. The 'want to' boss can behave in a soft and democratic manner by listening, being approachable, supportive and sympathetic. Equally, she can act in an autocratic way by setting direction, assigning responsibility, taking disciplinary action and so on.

Those on the receiving end of the 'want to' boss's autocratic behaviour are nevertheless prepared to accept this behaviour without question. This is because they intuit that the reason for the autocratic behaviour is related to their empowerment. The boss is being tough with them with their highest self-interest in mind.

Autocratic behaviour in other words can be entirely legitimate but only when it is seen to be subordinate to the intention to empower.

- *Empowerment is not an instantaneous process.*

There is a misconception that people are either empowered or they are not. In other words, that control either sits in one person's (the manager's) hands or in another person's (the subordinate's) hands. The handover of control is somehow instantaneous. Nothing could be further from the truth.

At one extreme the imposition of control, coupled with an intention to never let go, is clearly disempowering. It is akin to insisting on always holding the infant's hand. The child will never learn to walk. At the same time, the instantaneous and total suspension of all control is also disempowering. Letting go of the child's hand and standing in the far corner of the room, even though he cannot yet walk on his own, is equally disabling.

In both cases the child will be rendered unable to walk independently.

What is enabling in this context is for the adult to start holding the child's hand, then to let go but stand close by, finally stepping back to let the child walk alone. That is, not an instantaneous, total suspension of control, but an incremental suspension of control in order to empower the subordinate.

This recognises what we know from nature – that growth does not happen overnight. The seed cannot transmute into a mature plant in a matter of hours. Similarly in humans, adulthood takes at least twenty-one years to get to.

The level of control which is exercised in a legitimate relationship of power, therefore, must be commensurate with the maturity of the subordinate in the relationship. The starting point is the current level of maturity of the person being empowered. As the person matures the amount of control lessens, becomes less stringent.

Control is simply a tool in the empowerment process; it is a means, not an end.

- *There are three variables which affect empowerment, not two.*

Empowerment is a process for enabling contribution; for cultivating 'givers'. People can't make a contribution if they don't have the 'means' to do so; literally, they are not allowed to give. In an organisation, empowerment means providing people with an enabling environment in which to perform by giving them the requisite tools, resources, information, authority, support and standards.

Equally for contribution to happen, people must have the 'ability' to give. They need to know from their manager both 'how' to do what is required of them and 'why' they should do it.

Generally, managers believe that having addressed the two variables of 'means' and 'ability' to contribute, their empowerment job is done. To use the analogy of empowering a man to fish, the process entails providing him with the tools and bringing in an expert to teach him to fish. Suitably equipped and able, the man is now fully empowered to feed himself and his family by fishing. Or is he? No, he is not. What is missing is the third critical variable in the process – the issue of 'accountability'. At some point the fisherman has to be told: 'If you don't catch the fish, very sorry but starve.'

What engages people's will to contribute is accountability. Through the centre of accountability runs a standard. A person's contribution can either be above standard or below standard. When a person's contribution is above standard, either the person is going the extra mile, in which case it is appropriate to *reward* the person, or the person is careful to meet the standard and should be *recognised*. Similarly if the person has the means and ability but is below standard, it is for two kinds of reasons: either the person is careless and should be *censured* or she is malevolent, which requires that she be *disciplined*.

To empower someone means to address all these three aspects of the empowerment process. Unless due consideration is given to all three – in the order of means, ability and then accountability – empowerment has not happened.

Axiom 3:

Empowerment implies an incremental suspension of control in order to enable the subordinate.

Implications of Axiom Three

Axiom Three has implications for the whole issue of authority and control within an organisation. If we define control as 'the intent to manage predictable outcomes', it is clear that in any organisation there are a myriad of mechanisms that serve this purpose. Collectively these mechanisms make up the systems and structures which constitute the organisation.

What happens to structures and systems with the implementation of Axiom Three is not that they cease to exist or that there is a wholesale obliteration of all the controls in the business. This would be tantamount to a deconstruction of the organisation itself.

Rather, when management applies the principle of an incremental suspension of control, the following happens incrementally over time.

- Decision-making authority that is vested at the centre and up the hierarchy is devolved progressively away from the centre and to lower levels in the hierarchy. Allied to this, a series of small finite adjustments to the organisational design lead, over time, to a flattening of the hierarchy.

- There is a gradual relaxing of rules and procedures, replacing them with broader policies and guidelines. There are fewer, not more controls, in the processes within the business.

- The role of staff functions changes, as they are weaned off their auditing and compliance function, to rechannel their time and effort into *empowering* the line.

These changes happen, not as once-off projects, but continuously. There is no final solution in terms of either the organisation's structures or systems. They remain fluid, with small, discrete changes being made as circumstances change and people grow.

The Third Axiom also has implications for the whole issue of accountability in organisations. To empower means both handing over control and replacing *control* with *accountability*.

In practice this implies, firstly, that whenever authority is given, so too is accountability. Before people are given the freedom to operate without control, a tight link must be forged between autonomy and accountability (both positive and negative).

Secondly, this implies that when there is a deviation from standard, the appropriate action is to find out who is accountable for the deviation and hold them appropriately accountable, rather than impose a control on everyone.

Only when managers act consistently with this insight is it possible for the real product of the empowerment process to be realised – namely, people who focus on doing the right thing and who are accountable for what they do.

In summary then:

EMPOWERMENT/GROWTH	
Convention	**Challenges**
• Empowerment is synonymous with employee participation and democracy. • It is possible to empower overnight and to separate empowerment from accountability.	• Empowerment is not the same as employee participation. • Empowerment is not the same as democracy. • Empowerment is not an instantaneous process. • Empowerment is not possible without accountability.
Axiom 3	**Implications**
Empowerment implies the incremental suspension of control in order to enable the subordinate.	• A devolution of decision-making authority and flattening of hierarchy. • A shift from being procedure to being policy driven. • Fewer, not more, controls. • Empowering support functions. • Replacement of control with accountability.

MATURATION AND MATURITY

When leaders successfully implement the first three axioms of the Care and Growth leadership model their people change – they grow or mature.

In today's corporate world, employee growth, it is believed, is reflected in positive changes in their fame, fortune or facts. In other words, as employees mature they 'get' more knowledge, power, status, reward and so on.

The Care and Growth model proposes an alternative view of maturity and the maturation process, which has far-reaching implications for the leadership of organisations.

 Challenges to Conventional Wisdom and the Alternative

- *The process of maturation is the process of the maturation of intent to give unconditionally.*

By definition a mature person is the very opposite of an immature person. Maturation is about moving from one state (immaturity) to another state (maturity). It involves a transformation in the person from 'taking' to 'giving'. Immature people are here to take. Mature people are here to give.

The difference between 'taking' and 'giving' is that of intent. When a person gives but has no intention to give, she is not giving but is being taken from. When a person gives with the intention to get something back she is similarly not giving; she is making an investment. Only when a person gives, neither wanting nor expecting anything in return, is she actually giving. Giving is only giving when it is unconditional.

Immaturity is about continuously seeking and desiring to 'get' more. Maturity is about an increasing determination and preparedness to 'give' unconditionally.

- *There is a connection between intention and attention.*

The difference in intention between an immature and mature person is reflected in what they give attention to. Faced with the same situation, the immature and mature attend to different things.

The immature person focuses on what is in her best interests in the situation. Her actions are expedient. The mature person focuses on what is correct, even when it is neither convenient nor in her immediate best interests. This does not mean that the mature person does not have needs; it means she can suspend her needs and act for reasons higher than self-interest. Her actions are values-driven, rather than needs-driven.

The immature person attends to her own expectations rather than to what the situation requires of her. The mature person concerns herself with what she should be contributing; what she should be giving in the situation. The mature person views her expectations objectively, weighs them up against what she should be contributing and acts accordingly. She reflects before she acts.

The immature person focuses on her 'rights'; on what she believes she is owed or entitled to. The mature person attends to her 'duties'. When the immature person does not get what she believes she is owed, she blames others or forces outside of herself. The mature person takes accountability for the circumstances in which she finds herself.

The immature person focuses on the end, on the desired outcome or result. She endeavours to control the other person or the situation in order to get the outcome she wants. The mature person, on the other hand, is less concerned with the outcome. Her concern is with means or with process, not ends.

- *Where a person's attention is focused has consequences for him and his relationship with others.*

There is an inextricable connection between immaturity and weakness which is obvious when one considers the consequence to oneself of being 'here to get'. What a person 'gets' clearly does not sit in his hands; what one gets comes from 'other' to 'self'.

An immature person, because he always wants something, is always needy and controlled by the other's ability to withhold that which he wants. The immature person is manipulable by others.

The immature person, moreover, has an external locus of control. As a consequence of focusing on that which he has no control over, he is weak. He feels and behaves like a victim.

The immature person essentially views other people as a means to his end. He is generally discourteous, disrespectful and demeaning. He is concerned with his own significance and is therefore viewed as selfish and arrogant.

His pursuit of self-interest causes others to resist him. His inherent competitiveness makes for conflict and disharmony in his relationships with others. In time, the immature person destroys others as well as himself.

Maturity on the other hand is associated with strength. This is primarily because the mature person focuses on the source of his power; what sits in his own hands and what is in his control. Since he cannot be manipulated, he cannot be controlled and hence he is free. This enables him to be proactive and to be a master, rather than a victim, of his situation.

The mature person is able to exercise restraint; to delay gratification. He listens to others and is therefore seen by them to be reasonable, rational and objective. He relates to others in a manner which is courteous, humble and respectful. As a result others respect him. His relationships are cooperative rather than competitive. Consequently his relationships work, they are constructive and mutually affirming.

- *Giving is not about being nice, it is about being appropriate.*

A person who is 'here to give' does not necessarily give away all her worldly possessions to charity, nor allows herself to be constantly taken advantage of by others. Giving is not about always being nice, it is about being appropriate.

In essence, 'giving' means doing what the situation requires unconditionally. As such 'giving' presents itself in two forms as *generosity* or *courage*. Both of these involve taking a risk.

When a person acts generously she is risking things associated with herself. When a person acts courageously, however, she is risking herself; she is putting self, not things, on the line. Of the two forms of giving, courage is clearly harder, because the price which may be paid is much higher.

In any situation, then, a person's maturity is not a function of what she has got out of the situation, but what she has put into the situation unconditionally.

Axiom 4:

Maturity means being here to serve, or acting with generosity and courage.

 Implications of Axiom Four

The process of aging is mandatory but the process of maturation is voluntary. Whether an individual is generous and/or courageous is a matter of choice. Anyone can be a 'giver' or a 'taker' right now.

In any workplace, therefore, one finds both mature and immature souls. There are 'givers' and 'takers' throughout an organisation and at all levels in the hierarchy. Employees who are mature are intent on serving. They are loyal, trustworthy, dedicated and willing to give unconditionally in pursuit of the organisation's objectives.

Mature leaders are similarly intent on serving their people. In doing so, they are not always nice. This is because they have no tolerance for mediocrity and will do whatever is necessary to push their people to realise the very best in themselves. A leader who is truly here to serve has benevolence in the heart but steel in the hand.

In an organisation where those in leadership positions act consistently within the spirit of the Fourth Axiom they do the following:

- They spend significant time with and give attention to their people because they care about them.
- They trust their people and entrust them with more as they grow.
- They set high standards both for themselves and for their people.
- They clarify, assess, review and reward their people for their

contribution, not for the results.

- They deal with exceptions by addressing the leadership causes for the exception, not by instituting a control.
- They confront victim behaviour by encouraging their people to take accountability for their situation.
- They use the task as a means to grow the person rather than use the person as the means to get the job done.
- They teach their people both 'how' to do what is required of them and 'why' they should do it.
- They provide a line of sight between each individual's contribution and the overall performance of the enterprise.
- They do the right thing, rather than the expedient or popular thing, in every situation.

At an organisational level, Axiom Four requires the organisation's systems, structures and processes to be reconfigured to align with the Care and Growth criteria. Ultimately even the company's mission or purpose has to change from one of making a profit for the shareholders to one of serving the customer.

In summary then:

MATURITY AND MATURATION	
Conventional Wisdom	**Challenges**
• Maturity is about being 'here to get' – be it in terms of facts, fortune, fame or fitness. • Getting is what strength is all about.	• Maturity is about being 'here to give' unconditionally. • There is a connection between intention and attention. • Strength is a function of giving, not getting. • Giving is not about being nice but about being appropriate.

Conventional Wisdom	Challenges
Maturity is about being here to serve, acting with generosity and courage.	• Employees are here to serve customers. • Leaders are here to serve their staff. • The organisation is here to serve, to add value to people's lives.

At the root of the Care and Growth model is the intent to serve. As individuals and organisations who have embraced this model have demonstrated, it is the intent to serve which ultimately accounts for both organisational and personal excellence.

Living the Care and Growth Values

The initial turnaround that the Care and Growth model enables is an understanding by those in positions of command that they are there to serve their people, not the other way around. Leadership is about giving to one's people, not getting something out of them.

A further, and more dramatic, insight however is that ultimately, leading others has less to do with the care and growth of those being led than it has to do with the growth of the leader himself. In the process of leading others, those in leadership positions are given a unique opportunity to grow, to unleash the best in themselves, to realise their full potential as human beings.

THE ISSUE OF INTENT – THE 'WHY'

'Have to' or 'Want to' kind of boss

'Have to' boss	'Want to' boss
Gets people to do what he wants by coercing them.	Can behave in soft, persuasive ways.
In which case they feel bullied and resist over time.	By listening, being approachable, helpful, sympathetic – behaviours that are about CARE.
Or gets people to do what he wants through persuasion.	Can behave in hard, compulsive ways.
In which case they feel manipulated and are in conflict with him over time.	By being fair, honest, giving feedback, being visionary, giving direction, allowing freedom and therefore accountability – behaviours that are about GROWTH.

The key difference between the 'Have to' and 'Want to' boss is not their behaviour because both kinds of bosses can act in a soft/persuasive and hard/compelling manner, but in how their intent is experienced and perceived by their subordinates. Intent is not about what the leader does (behaviour) or how he does it (style or approach), but why he does it.

41

In Care and Growth workshops we use what we call 'the pen example' to illustrate this. Assuming that two delegates, Yunus and Jabu, have forgotten to bring a pen with them to the workshop, the facilitator gives each of them a pen. To Yunus, she says, 'you need a pen, have mine'. To Jabu, she adds, 'but I want you to agree with everything I say today.'

The Pen Example

"Yunus, you need a pen, here have one of mine."

"Jabu, you need a pen, here have one of mine – but I want you to agree to everything I say today."

The facilitator gives (her behaviour) both Yunus and Jabu a pen. *Why* the facilitator gave the pen to the two individuals is, however, very different. She gave Yunus the pen because he needed it. She gave Jabu the pen to get something back from him.

Only with the first interaction is the facilitator actually giving. The 'giving' of the pen in the Jabu case is an investment she is making to get out of him what she wants. Giving is only giving if it is unconditional.

Assume I am very knowledgeable in a job that both Fred and Joe have to do because I did that job in 1980.

- "Joe, in 1980 I did what you have to do and what I did worked, don't argue with me. Do what I did."

- "Fred, in 1980 I did what you have to do and what I did worked. It may be helpful to you. Take a look."

Further, the essence of the difference between giving (benevolent intent) and taking (malevolent intent) becomes apparent when one considers who the beneficiary is in any transaction. The Joe and Fred example makes this point very clearly.

In the Fred interaction, Fred is the beneficiary because the intent of the boss is to teach Fred something, to enable him.

In the Joe interaction, the boss is the beneficiary. The boss's intent is to get the job done, with Joe as the means to achieve that end.

Success as a boss requires the boss to act in the best interests of the subordinate in every situation. Only when this is the case, is the intent of the boss perceived as benevolent.

THE INTENT TO GIVE

The intent of the boss to give is not necessarily about the boss being nice or acquiescing to everything that the subordinate wants. It is about the boss being appropriate to what the situation demands.

Giving in fact presents itself in two categories. There is the giving of things associated with the self, which is called generosity. Then there is the giving of self, which is termed courage.

Both forms of giving imply a preparedness to put oneself at risk, potentially to lose. Generosity suggests that one is willing to rise above a fear of loss of things; courage necessitates rising above a fear of loss of self.

In the context of a boss-subordinate relationship, generosity is not only a giving of money or resources. It includes inter alia a giving of time, assistance, support, concern, understanding.

Acting courageously may include the giving of constructive feedback, making unpopular decisions, holding someone accountable as opposed to instituting a control, and the disclosure of sensitive information.

Taking, on the other hand, means that in a given context, one acts inappropriately. If the situation requires generosity, but the leader behaves in a so called courageous way, then he is not giving but taking – he is being selfish. When the situation requires courage, but the leader responds with generosity, he is again not giving but taking. This kind of taking is called cowardice.

When a boss is himself under pressure for results, and he demands delivery rather than asking 'what can I do to help?' he is being selfish. When he should dismiss someone for poor performance, but instead entices the person to leave by way of a handsome retrenchment package, he is evidencing cowardice.

To say that a leader should act consistently with the generosity or courage that is applicable in a given situation is, however, not sufficient. This is because 'generosity' and 'courage' are too abstract. Everything to do with courage is not necessarily confrontational. It takes courage, for example, to tell someone that his life partner has been killed in an accident on the way to work, but the leader's behaviour would hardly be confrontational. Similarly, not everything to do with generosity is sweet and accommodating.

Between generosity/ courage and behaviour there is a set of criteria which more specifically indicates what giving appropriately means. These criteria are 'values'. Giving in fact means to act consistently with the value that is operative in any given situation. It means to do what is transactionally correct, even if it does not appear to be the most expedient or workable thing to do at the time. Only when a leader does this is he giving appropriately. When he fails to do so, he is taking.

In a disciplinary situation, for example, the value which is operative is fairness. Giving here means being fair, not nice. When the leader breaks the golden rule of discipline and acts unfairly, he is taking. The value which is operative in the case of the employee's partner, who died, however is not fairness. The criterion which makes this a 'giving' rather than a 'taking' transaction, is compassion or care.

PUTTING INTENT TO THE TEST

Every interaction that takes place between a boss and a subordinate puts the former's intent to the test. The boss's real intent becomes apparent, is revealed. This is true in both a seemingly trivial interaction and one which is highly significant – what could be termed a defining moment in the relationship between the boss and the subordinate.

This is because, in any interchange between the two parties, the boss's behaviour can be informed by only one of two things – by his needs or by the correct thing to give in the interaction.

If the boss acts on the basis of his needs he is essentially putting his self-interest first. When he behaves on the basis of the value which is operative in the situation, he acts for reasons higher than his self-interest. He is concerned with doing what is right rather than expedient.

This does not mean that a boss does not have needs. He wouldn't be human if he didn't have needs. In fact, our instinctive reaction as human beings, our default position, is to act on the basis of our needs.

Having benevolent intent means that, in the moment, one is capable of rising above one's needs. This only happens at work if the boss *makes a deliberate and conscious choice to put what is in his immediate self-interest second.*

The choice that the boss makes reflects directly on his level of maturity as a person. When his choice is based on what he wants to get, even if he is willing to give something in order to get, he is being immature. His maturity comes to the fore only when he is unconditional; he gives what is required, wanting nothing back.

Consciously or otherwise the subordinate makes a call on the boss's intent in every situation, by applying a simple rule of thumb.

The rule is this: *to what degree is the boss able to suspend his agenda for mine – or, more accurately, for what is right?*

When things go well, who gets the credit? Conversely when things go horribly wrong, who gets the blame? Does the boss support me, even if it means putting his career on the line? Whose agenda is being served here, his or mine?

Anyone in a command position is continuously on stage. The choices that leaders make never go past unnoticed. What those in charge choose to make significant to themselves, more than anything else, determines their success or failure over time.

Whether a boss really cares or not becomes apparent whenever she has to deal with an employee's personal problem. When she communicates, her honesty is put to the test. The degree to which she is prepared to coach, to give everything she knows away, is indicative both of her generosity and courage.

TESTING THE LEADER'S INTENT

SITUATION	TEST FOR THE LEADER
Personal problems	Care
Communication	Honesty
Coaching	Enablement
Discipline	Fairness
Reward	Gratitude
Consultation	Humility
Teamwork	Respect
Empowerment	Trust

While praise and reward depend on the gratitude which sits in her heart, her capacity for fairness is tested in a disciplinary context. The degree to which the leader is prepared to listen is a measure of her humility. In team relationships the issue is respect, both amongst members of the team and between the leader and the team. Finally, trust in the other is fundamentally tested whenever a boss empowers a subordinate.

PERSONAL PROBLEMS – THE CARE TEST

An employee's commitment to a superior, and hence to the organisation, rather than to the pursuit of money and power, or even to a chosen profession, is largely a function of the superior's interest in the employee as a human being.

More than perhaps at any other time, the sincerity of the boss's interest is put to the test when the subordinate has problems of a personal nature. When a genuine personal problem arises – the death of a loved one, a divorce, a serious illness – does the boss notice and does he care?

What the boss should and should not do in these situations is a matter of debate. Should the boss approach an employee who has a personal problem but doesn't want to talk about it or would this be an intrusion on the person's privacy? When is the best time to broach an issue? How should a sensitive issue be tackled? Is it ever appropriate to talk to someone else about the employee's problem, especially if the person has expressly asked the boss to keep the concern between the two of them?

To none of these questions is there a clear answer. The really critical question in fact relates, not so much to the 'when', 'where' and, 'how' of the problem, but to the 'why' the boss is concerned.

In Care and Growth workshops we talk participants through the following true story:

> *'The Sales Director, Sales Manager and Sales Representatives from a particular company are at an out-of-town venue for their annual bosberaad (conference). One of the Sales Representatives openly and single-handedly drinks an entire bottle of brandy on both nights of the conference. Despite this, he does not become abusive or embarrass the family in any way. He presents himself promptly for each of the working sessions and participates fully.'*

The initial response, especially with sales audiences, is 'only one bottle?' Jokes aside, very few participants feel at this point that, if they were the person's manager and saw this, they would talk to him about it. There is nothing in the Sales Representative's behaviour which would cause them to do so. In any case, it is not uncommon for people to let their hair down at an event such as this.

47

> *'The Sales Representative,' we then say, 'happens to be the ace salesperson in the business. He is very experienced and his customers love him. This is reflected in his sales figures. However he regularly invites clients for a drink at the end of the day. A bottle of brandy later, he is wise enough to book himself into a hotel rather than drive himself home or continue on to his next appointment.'*

Participant responses, at this point, are often quite horrifying. Has a client ever complained about this? Who is paying for the brandy? Does the company pick up the tab for the hotel? Only a small number of delegates say that they would talk to him. Even fewer would do so out of concern for his family life or the impact his drinking may have on his health.

> *'What eventually happened was that the Sales Director, not his immediate manager, elected to talk to the man. He put what he had witnessed at the bosberaad on the table. The Sales Representative was very defensive. "Why are you talking to me about this? Do you have a problem with my sales performance?" The Sales Director responded as follows: "Not at all. The reason I am raising this issue with you is because I care about you."'*

The above tale challenges the prevailing view of what the employer–employee relationship is actually all about. It is not a buying and selling relationship, an exchange of X kilojoules of labour for Y units of money. If it was, whatever was happening in an employee's personal life would only be of issue if and when it impacted on the person's work performance.

When a boss talks to a subordinate because the subordinate's personal problem is affecting delivery, she is revealing her intent. What the boss really cares about is not the person but what she is getting out of him. The person's personal problem and the person's work performance should be separate issues which are not conditional on each other. Care is only care when it is unconditional, when it is de-linked from the issue of work performance.

It can be argued that the modern organisation is in many ways increasingly inhumane. In the relentless pursuit of results, sometimes impossible demands are made on employees, causing severe stress and fatigue. Success at work is achieved, but takes a huge toll on many employees' physical and mental health and personal lives.

Personal Concerns

VALUE / GOLDEN RULE

CARE

SUBRULE 1

Care is only care if it is unconditional

When times are tough, or even simply to keep the shareholders happy, loyal employees are often put out on the street with little conscience. The infamous 10-70-10 formula introduced by General Electric, where the bottom ten percent of employees are removed from the organisation on an annual basis, is evidence of hard-heartedness by many of those in charge.

The only thing worse than a lack of care, however, is feigned concern. Managers who don't really care about the personal concerns of their employees, and who wish that people would leave their problems at home, add insult to injury when they profess otherwise. Employees would rather that they were honest than lay claim to a concern which it is not there.

When compassion, rather than indifference, is evidenced by those in command the effect on employee commitment can be overwhelming. A manager of a car rental agency turned down offers at twice her current salary, from competitors, for one reason only. When she was hospitalised with a brain tumour, her boss did her job for her during the day and came to visit her in hospital most evenings throughout her convalescence. In a similar vein, when a CEO forked out a large sum of money from his own pocket to pay the medical expenses of an employee mowed down by a drunk driver, the youngster, who didn't have medical aid, pledged to give his best to the organisation for the rest of his life.

If the employee's personal problem is impacting on her work performance, what is appropriate? Now the sincerity of the leader is really put to the test because sincerity, in this situation, requires the leader to be tough, not sweet.

Once again, it is important to separate the personal problem from work performance. Being unconditional here requires the leader to still hold the employee accountable for work performance. If the person's attention is not on the job because of problems at home he should be made to understand that this is not acceptable. It may be appropriate, with agreement, to change the standard for a while, but not for ever. What is called for here is 'tough love'.

Personal Concerns

VALUE / GOLDEN RULE

CARE

SUBRULE 2

Care will only be seen to be unconditional when people are still held accountable for their performance

This was highlighted for me in a workshop on *Holding People Appropriately Accountable*. The group was given the following scenario.

One of your direct reports is having marital difficulties and is probably heading for a divorce. He is a good employee and you have offered your help by lending a sympathetic ear and offering to pay for professional counselling, but this has been politely refused. As the weeks go by his performance declines as numerous careless mistakes are made. What do you do?

a) Issue a letter of reprimand.
b) Verbally warn him about his performance.
c) Express sympathy, tell him you understand his position but that you are concerned about his performance.
d) Take no action, hoping that once he is through the divorce his performance will pick up again.
e) Find the occasional good thing he does and praise him in an effort to raise his morale.
f) Other.

At this point, one of the participants announced: 'That is me. My wife has just walked out on our marriage of twenty-seven years. She has run off with my best friend.' In the shocked silence which followed, he went on to say: 'What I want more than anything else from my boss at this point in time is for him to hold me accountable for my performance. Do you think that I want to fail at work as well as in my personal life?'

Supporting a person through a personal crisis, while still insisting that he performs at his best, is what passing the Care test here means.

COMMUNICATION – THE HONESTY TEST

Site X: What employees want to know (Top 10 items)		
1.	Nothing/don't need information	21%
2.	Money/wages	19%
3.	Promotions/job opportunities	15%
4.	Bonus system	11%
5.	Equal opportunities/discrimination	8%
6.	Safety/health	6%
7.	Pension/Provident fund	5%
8.	Salary deductions	4%
9.	Employee benefits	2%
10.	Training opportunities	2%

The first question with respect to management communication pertains to what ought to be conveyed by management to employees in a company. My view on this is based on answers given by thousands of employees who have participated in Schuitema Climate Surveys to the question: 'What information should management be communicating to you?'

On one site, shown above, the results were singularly depressing. Those who wanted to know anything at all from management, were primarily concerned with their own interests – what they could get in the situation. Not surprisingly trust in management on this site was extremely low.

Fortunately, this is not the typical response. From the following example, it is clear that employees are primarily concerned with two issues:

- How is the business doing?
- How am I doing?

Site Y: Information employees feel should be communicated to them. (Top 10 items)	
	Freq
1. Financial performance/position of company	52
2. Future of the company	32
3. What is happening/any changes	26
4. Give feedback on production and improvements	20
5. Anything that directly/indirectly affects us	18
6. More info on sales/marketing of products	17
7. Money/wages	4
8. Employee performance/what company expects of us	4
9. Performance against competition	4
10. Personal news	3

What they are not particularly interested in is what many company newsletters focus on, namely 'social news', like which department won the in-house soccer league.

A prerequisite to effective management communications is, therefore, that what is communicated is relevant to employees. Regular communication on the company's financial performance and how well employees are contributing to the overall success of the company is the content which employees are most interested in receiving, and the content which is most enabling for them.

Further to the above, Etsko Schuitema's research in the South African gold mining industry (*Beyond Management* by Etsko Schuitema (1994)), drew the following conclusion: 'The critical factor accounting for successful internal communication is the degree to which employees trust the source of the communication.' Neither the content of the message, nor the choice of medium to convey it, are anywhere near as important as this.

When management is trusted, what it says is generally believed and accepted. When trust in management is low, employees are suspicious of everything management says, even if it is the truth.

This was clearly illustrated to me during wage negotiations at one organisation.

> The annual ritual commenced with a presentation by the managing director on the state of the business. One complex slide followed another, painting a somewhat gloomy picture. By the end of the presentation there was not a dry eye on management's side of the room. The general secretary of the union leaned back in this chair, yawned and said: 'I was thinking a fair demand this year would be X%. I am now utterly convinced that ten times X% is more appropriate.' At this point, management called for a caucus!

As mentioned previously, trust in management is a function of the degree to which employees believe that management is acting in their best interests in every situation.

Participants in a Care and Growth workshop are given the following scenario to consider in this regard.

> You have decided for business reasons to close down two out of three manufacturing facilities and run the remaining factory 24/7. The distance between the two factories being closed and the remaining one means that many people will be unable to relocate and will have to be laid off.
>
> You are only likely to act on this business decision in 12–18 months time but have chosen to communicate the decision now. Why would you communicate now when such bad news may well lead to low morale, resignations, etc? Why not wait until just before the closure of the two sites to do so?

The only reason why management would break the news now, despite possible disadvantages to itself, is that not to do so would be dishonest. Honesty means speaking the truth, even when it appears not to be in one's best interest at the time. Only when management does this, sharing both the good and the bad news, is it trusted over time.

Honesty is the golden rule, the value which is operative in any communication. It overrides both utilitarian and consequential justifications for deception, even though in the real world this is not always easy to do.

The Johari Window

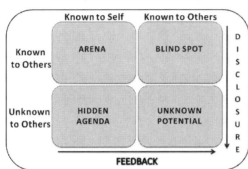

Drawing on Harry Ingham and Joseph Luft's theory of communication from the 1950s, honesty, in the first instance, means not telling a lie. When a manager lies this has a devastating impact on trust, either immediately or at some time later when the deception is discovered. When managers lie they destroy trust. They create the condition that, going forward, their people can no longer take them at their word. As Frederick Nietzsche said so succinctly: 'What upsets me is not that you lied to me, but that I can no longer believe in what you say.'

Honesty, however, means more than not telling lies. It means openness, disclosure and the giving of accurate feedback. Without these, the arena or area of effective communication remains small.

On occasion we have experienced managers who pride themselves on their honesty and sincerity but who nevertheless score poorly on the following item on a Leadership Assessment.

ITEM	SCORE
I believe that my manager tells it like it is.	-2.8

The only explanation for this is a lack of transparency on the part of the manager. Since he does not share either his real thoughts or feelings, he is seen to be literally a 'dark horse'. His lack of self-disclosure, rather than what he says, leads to suspicion that there is some hidden agenda, something which is deliberately not being said.

It would appear that managers are only really seen to be honest when they are prepared to be open with their feelings as well as with the facts.

A further test of management's honesty is the degree to which it is prepared to practise open-book management and share the financial performance of the business with all employees. Logically, employees are only likely to commit to playing the game if the score is disclosed to them fully and on an on-going basis. Disclosure of financial information is not without risk, however. When management is reluctant to share this information it is generally out of fear that what is shared will be used against them, either by employees in wage demands or by competitors should they gain access to the numbers via disaffected employees.

In a low-trust relationship it may be suicidal for management to expose itself in this way. However, experience has shown that employees rarely break the trust that is extended to them. What is unwise, however, is to disclose information without understanding. Dulux South Africa went so far as to train all 450 employees in the business to understand the numbers prior to sharing them with them.

Communication

VALUE / GOLDEN RULE

HONESTY

SUBRULE

Openness, disclosure and feedback

Often the biggest failing in a company's performance management system is not the system per se, but the lack of honest feedback to subordinates on their performance. Jack Welch, in his book *Winning* (2005), refers to a lack of candour by managers as 'the biggest dirty little secret in business'.

Contrary to common belief, employees want to know what the boss really thinks about them. Employees want more critical feedback and less of the positive stuff.

The honesty of those in charge is, in essence, measured by the degree to which they are prepared to be open, disclose and give feedback.

COACHING – THE ENABLEMENT TEST

In the Schuitema Individual Leadership Assessment subordinates are asked to mark with an X where they currently experience their manager to be against a number of criteria which pertain to the issue of coaching or the enablement of others.

ENABLEMENT

Keeps knowledge and experience for self.   Shares knowledge and experience freely.

0	1	2	3	4	5	6	7	8	9	10
						X				

ENABLEMENT

Disables others/ prevents potential being realised.   People 'blossom'/ the best in others is realised.

0	1	2	3	4	5	6	7	8	9	10
				X						

ENABLEMENT

Holds on to/safeguards own position.   Deliberately makes self replaceable.

0	1	2	3	4	5	6	7	8	9	10
		X								

It is rare for managers to score well on all three criteria. As the sample above shows scores are typically higher on the first criterion (*sharing knowledge*) than on the other two (*realising the potential of the subordinate* and *deliberately making self replaceable*). Needless to say those rare bosses who score well across the board have subordinates who will go to the ends of the earth for them.

Delivering on this aspect of the leadership role is exceptionally taxing for a leader. Coaching, possibly more than any other of the care and growth activities, tests a manager both in terms of courage and generosity.

Even at the basic level, coaching a subordinate in the skills required to do his job calls for generosity on the part of the boss. Unlike the provision of means or accountability, the enablement of a subordinate takes considerable time and patience. Much of the time, as most mothers will testify, coaching for competence is simply boring.

A manager once described to me what a boss did who excelled in this coaching activity. The boss used to come out and visit him for a couple of hours at a client site. Rather than telling him what was wrong with his contract and how to fix it, he would get the subordinate to think through what he thought needed attention or did not meet the company standard. Only then would he suggest areas that the subordinate had missed and invite him to come up with solutions to the problems. Each visit, the subordinate reported, left him feeling that he had learned an immense amount.

Coaching

VALUE / GOLDEN RULE

Enablement

SUBRULE

Make yourself replaceable

The greatest test for the leader which coaching provides, however, is one of courage rather than generosity. Giving away what the leader knows tests the leader's own feelings of insecurity. It takes courage to deliberately put one's own job at risk, to give away the crown jewels and allow a subordinate to be better than oneself.

Coaching, therefore, ultimately puts the leader's own significance to the test. One manager summed it up when she said 'it is the athlete, not the coach, who gets up on the podium'. The employee is the star, the manager is only the agent.

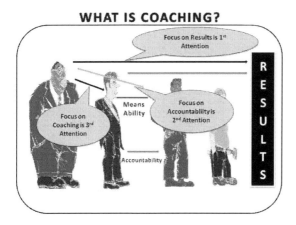

WHAT IS COACHING?

Coaching is truly a giving activity. When a boss focuses on the results he is only concerned with what he is getting out of the subordinate.

When a boss focuses on holding a subordinate accountable for what the subordinate is doing, he is giving to get. The boss in essence is saying: 'I have given you the means and ability, now do what I require of you.'

Only when the boss coaches the subordinate is he finally giving unconditionally. This is because the deliverable in a coaching relationship is growth or change in the subordinate, rather than a result or a job that is done. Growth in the subordinate has now become an end in itself.

The test for the boss, when coaching, is the degree to which he is capable of delaying his own gratification. As such, coaching truly puts the boss's maturity to the test.

RECOGNITION AND REWARD – THE GRATITUDE TEST

When people are held accountable for their contribution, there is a different consequence for those who meet the standard compared to those who fail to do so.

Further, the positive outcome for those who consistently exceed the standard should be significantly greater than for those who only do what is required of them.

Employees who are careful in the execution of a task should be praised for doing so, while those who evidence benevolent intent, by consistently going the extra mile, ought to be rewarded for their greater contribution. This is because differentiation, in tangible ways, between satisfactory and excellent performance is not only fair, it cultivates excellence over time.

Not all managers in organisations agree with the above. Some argue that praise is not necessary. After all, the person is being paid to do what is required of them. Generosity (praise/reward) should be reserved for those who really deserve it, for when results are achieved and not before.

In fact, failure to praise for a job well done has negative consequences for those managers who fail to do so.

A friend of mine, a superb chef, resigned from a well-paid job for just that reason. His job at an advertising agency was to cater for client functions, but also included providing a tasty lunch for the directors on a daily basis.

He handed in his notice after he had captured in a little black book every comment made to him by one of the directors over a two-week period. Apparently the longest sentence uttered to him was 'what dining room are we in today Jeremy?' He said that even one 'thank you, that was a very nice lunch today' might have led him to stay.

We often hear employees say, 'I wasn't asking to be paid overtime; all I wanted was for my extra effort to be noticed, to know that what I am contributing is appreciated.' In many employees' eyes few bosses would go to their deathbed regretting having praised too much! In the absence of praise, employees feel exploited. They feel that they have been taken from.

When a manager praises is not as important as *why* she praises. There are typically two responses to the question 'why praise?' The first, and more common, response is 'because doing so motivates or encourages the employee'. The other reason given is 'acknowledgement or appreciation by the manager for what the employee has given'.

Praise / Reward

> VALUE / GOLDEN RULE
>
> ### Gratitude
>
> SUBRULE
>
> Praise for carefulness, reward the extra mile

Of the two, only the latter reason is unconditional. The motivational reason is a giving (praise) in order to get (a continuation of, or even better, performance). Genuine praise without wanting anything back is in fact simply good manners. It is about saying 'thank you' for what was given.

The value/golden rule which is operative when praising and rewarding people, is gratitude. It is fullness in the heart which enables generous giving. Conversely a lack of gratitude is what causes the other to withhold.

I experienced a case of generosity prompted by gratitude at OR Tambo International airport recently. The computers were down and several passengers were taking out their frustration on the staff, who were trying to manually produce boarding passes as quickly as possible. When it was my turn I found myself saying, 'I have noticed how unbelievably gracious you have remained throughout this mayhem, thank you very much.' The lady smiled and gave me my boarding pass.

It was only when I arrived at my destination that the effect of my comment was realised. The second bag to emerge on the carousel was mine due to the first class ticket the grateful book-in agent had, against all the rules, attached to it. What she didn't know was how big a favour she had done me. My suitcase travelled first class for six months before someone picked up on the 'error' and removed the first class sticker!

Once again sincerity is at issue. If a leader's attitude is that he does not have to praise because people are paid for what they do and then, suddenly out of the blue, he praises, his sincerity will be doubted.

Also, if there has never been praise but now there is a celebration – the attitude will be 'what does he want from me now?'

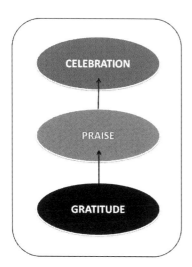

I witnessed this once in a factory. The managers there generally took their employees' efforts for granted. However, after a particularly good month of record production they decided to celebrate with a braai (barbeque). Of course everyone arrived. However, to a man, they grabbed a few beers, put a piece of wors (sausage) under their arm and left. What the management from hell then had to say about their workforce was libellous.

The intent behind managers' actions is all-important. When a manager's praise or reward comes from a place of gratitude his attention is on the past, on what was given. When he praises or rewards in order to incentivise employees to do more, his attention is on the future – on what he can get out of employees tomorrow. The effect of the latter over time is devastating. Employees' reaction to being bribed in this way is to weigh up every request by management to do something in terms of 'what's in it for me?' They give grudgingly and only when they perceive the carrot which is being offered as worth their while. Consequently management truly reaps what it has sown.

A question often raised is what one should do if one's praise is sincere but the response from employees is not to give? The answer is obvious: don't cease to praise. If history has given rise to scepticism, employees are unlikely to leap forward with instant generosity. In any case, their response is not the manager's issue. He is only accountable for what he does. His only concern should be to do what is appropriate. How employees choose to respond sits in their hands.

DISCIPLINE – THE FAIRNESS TEST

In any disciplinary context, the value/golden rule which is operative is fairness. Both in the case of misconduct or when performance is below standard, fairness dictates that a manager takes the time to find out why this is so before she acts.

Moreover, being fair means to act without prejudice or favouritism. Action taken should apply equally irrespective of race, gender or position in a company. What is good for the goose should be good for the gander.

Fairness should not be compromised for reasons of friendship or personal connections. Family members should not be given special treatment. Employees with exceptional talents should not be treated any differently from those who are less gifted.

Discipline

VALUE / GOLDEN RULE

Fairness

SUBRULE

Consistently censure carelessness and punish deliberate malevolence

More importantly discipline is only appropriate for reasons of carelessness or deliberate malevolence. Discipline is not appropriate when poor behaviour or performance is due to either a means or an ability issue.

An employee who fails to do the right thing due to a lack of means should be remediated through the provision of the necessary means. When a lack of ability is the issue, corrective action typically means formal training or on-the-job coaching. If the person lacks the capability to do the job, then fairness dictates that the person is removed from the role and redeployed into a position which is in line with his capability.

Negative Accountability

Discipline is notably not about re-mediation; it is about justice. The purpose of disciplinary action is to punish, not to correct behaviour. Its function is to hold a person account-able for his actions. Failure to do so creates the conditions whereby no one is accountable.

The disciplinary action imposed should be consistent with the intent behind the action. When a person has been careless or negligent, a ver-bal reprimand or censure is appropri-ate. In cases of deliberate malevo-lence, formal disciplinary action up to and including dismissal is required. Repeated carelessness should be treated as malevolence, since there is a point where on-going careless-ness is no longer a mistake, it is deliberate.

A manager's capacity to discipline is a real test of his leadership. General Electric's Jack Welch sums it up when he says: 'Anyone who cannot bring themselves to fire someone cannot lead. At the same time, anyone who enjoys firing someone cannot lead.'

Disciplinary action tests the leader's courage; the leader's capacity to confront. Those in positions of command who need to be liked too much find the taking of disciplinary action inordinately difficult to do. They are operating from a position of 'get', rather than 'give' because their actions are conditional, based on their need to be liked.

An incapacity to confront can constitute a fatal flaw in a leader's make-up. As Manfred Kets de Vries (2001) comments in *Leadership Mystique*:

'I don't have an exact formula for success but I know a sure formula for failure, and that is trying to please everyone.'

In most instances, dismissal decisions are neither unjustified nor premature. A CEO of one company spoke the truth when he said: 'I have never fired or transferred someone too soon.' Sadly the reason why some employees find themselves out on the street is because managers fail to take appropriate action when poor behaviour or performance first occurs. They delay, hoping to avoid conflict, until they can do so no longer.

> I will never forget a conversation I had with an employee when I was in a human resources role. The individual, a man in his early fifties, had just been retrenched. He told me that he knew in his heart of hearts that the reason he was leaving the company was because no one really wanted him to stay. In the twelve years he had been with the organisation he had done enough to get by but no more than that. 'What really burns me up,' he said with tears in his eyes 'is that no one I reported to in all these years cared enough about me to challenge my mediocre performance and to hold me accountable for it.'

Finally, disciplinary action should never be taken in anger or to get one's own back. More than anything else, if a leader takes frustration or rancour into a disciplinary situation, he will not be fair.

CONSULTATION/LISTENING – THE HUMILITY TEST

In a Care and Growth workshop we challenge participants with the following scenario:

> A subordinate approaches you with what is seemingly a crazy idea. Why should you listen?

The first reason that participants give for consulting with or listening to employees' ideas is a pragmatic one. Managers should listen to and consult with employees because they will then feel that they have been listened to and will therefore be committed (to what we as management want to do).

Clearly, if you really want to alienate people, you should go through the motions of consulting with them and then tell them what the right answer is. This is the height of manipulation and employees, quite rightfully, will respond with hostility once they have realised what is going on.

Managers, however, should not confuse keeping people informed about a decision which they have made with genuine consultation. Individuals should not accept a command position if they are not prepared to make and then stand by decisions they make.

Keeping subordinates informed of management decisions should not, however, be confused with a genuine intention to consult. Leaders should only consult when they are sincerely prepared to listen to their subordinates' views. By 'listen' is meant *entering the consultation being prepared to change their own views and opinions*.

The second reason that participants give for listening to employees' ideas is that the idea may not be so crazy after all. There may just be a nugget of gold hidden in a pile of dirt. This reason is however conditional. The danger lies in *who decides when an idea is just too crazy to be listened to?* When managers make the call, they typically stop listening when they perceive an idea as just not workable or outside the boundaries of what is feasible.

Listening to Ideas

VALUE / GOLDEN RULE

Patience/Humility

SUBRULE

Accept that someone else may be right

The unconditional reason for listening to employees' ideas is a function of the leader's humility. Humility means not only paying attention to what is being proposed, but being prepared to suspend one's own judgment, to really hear what is being said.

Listening/consultation tests a leader's arrogance. It requires a leader to accept that someone other than oneself may be correct. It requires the leader to be sufficiently secure within herself to acknowledge that nobody has all the answers and that saying 'I don't know' is alright.

The humility which is called for does not mean *thinking less of oneself*, but *thinking of oneself less*. It means being fascinated at least as much by the other as by oneself.

A leader who is humble is prepared to grant more significance to others than to herself. She does not need to take all the credit but rather prefers to give credit to others, to acknowledge the contribution of those other than herself. Jim Collins, in his book *Good to Great* (2001), expresses this sentiment when he says 'great leaders look in the mirror to account for failure but look out of the window to account for success'.

TEAM RELATIONSHIPS – THE RESPECT TEST

Successful Groups

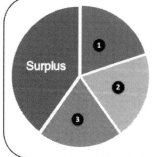

- We measure the success of the group by the size of the surplus
- A surplus is only produced when people are collectively giving more than they are taking
- The degree to which the group is successful is the degree to which the members of the group are unconditional in pursuit of the group's objectives

A successful group is one which produces a surplus. Further to this, a surplus is only produced when members of a group are collectively giving more than they are taking.

A powerful team, in essence, is one where its members give more than they take. A weak team is one where its members take more than they give. The final arbiter of whether a team is giving, is making a meaningful contribution, is of course the team's customers. A team which does not give or serve its customers (be they internal or external) will cease to exist.

Typically when there is conflict within a team, the team shifts its focus from the customer to the conflict within. This internal wrangling, whatever its cause, has the potential to destroy the team. The job of the leader in this situation is to rise above the conflict, to intervene and do whatever is necessary to stop it. In an extreme case, the leader needs to evince the courage to eject one or more members of the team. This may come at a price – the loss of talented individuals, for example. But it is a price which sometimes has to be paid for the team to survive.

In really successful teams the interests of the team are put before individual interests. Team members' capacity to do so is put to the test when times are tough. Rather than blaming each other, team members encourage and support other team members. They put personal interests aside to ask 'how can I help?'

The real hallmark of a powerful team, however, is respect, both amongst members of the team and between the leader and the team.

Respect, in the first instance, means not belittling others, not trivialising people or being dismissive of them. When a leader witnesses any lack of respect within the team, he needs to assert himself and stamp it out. He needs to demonstrate courtesy himself and insist on it from others. Where courtesy is absent, the team becomes divisive and eventually falls apart.

Teamwork

VALUE / GOLDEN RULE

Respect

SUBRULE

Cultivate a spirit of cooperation rather than competition

Mutual respect exists when team members are moreover accredited for what they bring to the team. An appreciation and celebration of the different strengths within the team makes the team powerful. A lack of respect leads to differences becoming a liability rather than an asset.

A key role for the leader of a team is to cultivate a spirit of co-operation rather than competition between members of the team. Internal competitions, especially those where 'the best wins' or the 'winner takes all' are divisive, cause low motivation (what about the guy who comes second?), and can lead to a wide range of undesirable behaviours, including cheating.

EMPOWERMENT – THE TRUST TEST

... THE UNIVERSE IS A FRIENDLY PLACE ...

Care and growth is about pushing people to realise the best in themselves

Empowerment is about unleashing the capacity in the subordinate to give. A leader's cultivation of givers is not about being nice. Nor is it about tolerating taking or accepting mediocrity. It is about pushing people to realise the best in themselves – whether they like it or not. As such, it requires an absolute unconditionality on the part of the leader.

Empowerment is associated practically with an incremental suspension of control. Whenever control is suspended over a subordinate there is a greater degree of trust and entrustment of the subordinate by the leader.

Giving up authority or handing over control, is once again a measure of a leader's generosity and courage. When a leader holds onto authority rather than handing it over, she is being selfish. She prefers to do the thing herself. Holding on to power gives a leader a sense of her own significance. It justifies her current status or position in the hierarchy. On other occasions, lack of humility is the issue. 'If I really want it done well, then I must do it. They (whoever they are) will never be as good at this as I am.'

When a leader avoids empowerment she also displays a lack of courage in that she is not prepared to take the risk, which is always associated with letting go of control.

Her fear is typically based on two things. Firstly, that she will hand over authority to someone who cannot do the task/who lacks the requisite skill and will therefore 'screw up'. Secondly she fears that she will hand over authority to someone who is untrustworthy, who can't be trusted to do the right thing.

The risks associated with empowerment can be minimised by following the golden rules with respect to handing over control. In the first instance the process should be incremental. Further to this, the means and ability issues involved need to be addressed before handing over the authority and accountability which goes with it. Finally, whenever control is removed, it must be replaced by accountability.

Failure by a leader to empower others typically says more about the leader's fear than it does about the subordinates' incompetence or untrustworthiness. For a person to demonstrate her trustworthiness, she has to be trusted in the first place. Only when a leader rises above this fear will subordinates be empowered.

From all of the above it is clear that in every command situation the leader's generosity and courage is tested. Only when a leader is consistent with the golden rule or value, which is operative in any command situation, does he pass the test which is inherent in the command situation. Only then does he realise the best in himself, does he grow.

SECTION TWO

Providing the Means

A precondition for employee contribution is that employees are provided with the MEANS to contribute. Without the Means to do so, employees are literally not *allowed* to make the contribution required of them. The Means do not sit within individuals, but rather in the environment in which they operate. One of the key functions of leadership, therefore, is to provide an enabling environment for those who report to them.

Organisationally, this suggests that everyone in an organisation needs to be given, inter alia, the following:

- The *resources* to do what is required of them – those things people add value to.

- The *tools* to do what is required of them – those things that people add value with.

- An *organisational* design – providing people with an enabling formal context in which to contribute.

- *Information* – a scoreboard that points people to what they need to do to make a contribution and also tells them how well they are doing so.

- *Time* – both a reasonable workload as well as sufficient time and support from their boss.

- *Authority* to execute their responsibilities – both for those who impact directly on the results and those whose job it is to enable them to do so.

- *Clarity of expectations* – specification of the results to be achieved and what is expected of each individual as their unique contribution to the results.

Clearly the Means, in terms of tools and resources, differ from organisation to organisation. There is, however, a set of Means that is at issue across all organisations since this relates to a leader's capacity to care for and grow subordinates.

The first of these Means is an enabling organisational structure. In **Designing Enabling Structures** (Chapter One) three core beliefs about the role of structure in enabling employee contribution are given, followed by a specification of the conditions which make a structural change appropriate. Thereafter, five principles for good organisational design are outlined. Finally a seven-step process for designing an organisational structure, which delivers 'head room' for individual growth and development, is provided.

The next chapter, **Humanising the Scoreboard** (Chapter Two) deals with the issue of the numbers. Specifically, it deals with how to use the results as a means, not an end. It is argued that leaders who successfully use the numbers on the scoreboard to enable employee contribution, not only believe, but also act, on five key insights. What those insights are, and how to use them to realise the true power of the numbers, is the focus of this chapter.

Clarifying Contribution (Chapter Three) is concerned with the Means issue which most people in organisations believe, if addressed, would most enhance their contribution to the organisation. This chapter demonstrates that it is possible to define an individual's unique contribution both at the level of the role and for the next reporting period. Also that it is possible to clarify both direct contribution to the results to be achieved, as well as a leader's contribution to the enablement of others.

The next Means issue relates to what leaders put their attention on and where they spend their time. The argument which is made in **Care and the Issue of Time and Attention** (Chapter Four) is that leaders who generally care for their people make time for them; they suspend their own agenda for the agenda of their people. This chapter provides practical advice on what a leader should give attention to and how to focus attention appropriately. It is demonstrated that a shift in time and attention, sometimes a radical shift, is imperative for the implementation of Care and Growth.

The last chapter in this section, **Growth by Handing Over Control** (Chapter Five) addresses the twin issues of control and authority in organisations. Clearly, it is not possible for leaders to care and grow their subordinates if they are not given the authority to do so. More generally, a key measure of the growth of any individual is that which is entrusted to him. That is, what decisions an individual can make independently of his manager, and ultimately what he is held accountable for. This chapter provides principles and methodologies for dealing with authority and control in organisations.

Designing Enabling Structures

Enter an organisation's portals and you are likely to find that management is busy restructuring. If not currently in the process of restructuring, it will have just completed a restructuring or be about to embark on one. Restructuring, it seems, has become a way of life in the corporate world.

Given the sensitivities inherent in any restructuring exercise, it is unlikely that executives will ever totally escape criticism by their employees for their efforts in this aspect of leadership. There will, inevitably, be those who remain resolutely wedded to a structural option other than the one sanctioned by management. In addition, there will almost certainly be employees firmly of the view that the process of implementing a given structural option has been mismanaged or badly done.

Nevertheless, there are some clear dos and don'ts regarding both the design and implementation of enabling organisational structures. As far as implementation is concerned, adherence to good change management practices and principles applies as much to restructuring as to any other change initiative in an organisational setting. In terms of design, there is no foolproof formula for organisational design. Possibly this is because in modern, complex organisations, one does not exist. There is, however, a set of design principles which collectively constitutes a good design.

THREE BELIEFS

The Care and Growth design principles are underpinned by three beliefs or propositions:

- Any structural initiative cannot, on its own, deliver organisational excellence.

- The perfect organisational design does not exist.

- Structural changes of any magnitude should be undertaken only when absolutely necessary.

Belief One: Structural Excellence Is Not Synonymous With Organisational Excellence

It is generally acknowledged that to transform an organisation requires intervention at a number of levels. At the strategic level, the organisation's purpose, its mission, vision and strategy need to be defined. At the structural level, the work processes, as well as the necessary formal organisation and resources, need to be put in place.

At an organisational culture level, desired employee values and behaviours need to be cultivated and become a way of life throughout the organisation. Finally, at the level of professional competence, employees need to be given the knowledge and skills to perform at the point of application.

THE ROUTE TO EXCELLENCE

PURPOSE
Vision, Mission, Strategy
STRUCTURE
Work Processes, Structure, Resources
CULTURE
Values, Behaviour, Motivation
PROFESSIONAL COMPETENCE
Knowledge, Skills

Despite essentially sound structures, organisations can and do fail. This is because weaknesses, which have nothing to do with structure – an ill-advised business strategy, a malignant culture or sheer people incompetence – can all lead to organisational demise. An elegant organisational design, in other words, is a necessary, but not sufficient, requirement for organisational transformation.

This does not mean, however, that structure does not have a very specific role to play in the transformation of an organisation. A good structure provides an enabling formal context in which people can contribute. Its unique value-add is that it creates the head room for individual growth and development to actually happen. Any organisation should be designed with this eventuality top of mind.

Belief Two: The Perfect Design Does Not Exist

In any organisation which is more than a one-person concern, several structural options will be possible, from the multitude of organisational types that exist.

WHICH TO GO FOR?

> **FUNCTIONAL**
> **DIVISIONAL**
> **MATRIX**
> **PROJECT**
> **NETWORK**
> **VIRTUAL**
> **ETC**

Previously the organisation type of choice was the functional organisation comprising of a number of departments made up of employees with similar professional expertise. Later, divisional structures become popular. The divisions were based on criteria such as clients, customer groups, products, markets, geography and so on. Then the matrix, with its dual reporting lines, came into vogue. Even more recently, organisations have experimented with various 'new age' structural forms – the network, the boundary-less structure, the virtual organisation and so forth.

Each successive organisational type has, unfortunately, failed to provide the ultimate organisation design. Each has both advantages and disadvantages. These are all well documented and can be substantiated simply by speaking to those who work in a particular organisation type.

Given the above, a quest for the perfect design is not a fruitful exercise.

A far more productive use of managerial energy is to divine the basis on which the organisation wishes to differentiate itself from other players in the field. Whatever the preferred competitive edge – market specialisation, technical excellence, innovation – it should be reflected in and promoted by the structure. The organisation structure, in other words, should be indicative of the organisation's strategy and vice versa. The one should inform the other.

Belief Three: Don't Change Organisation Structure Any More Than You Have To

To say that a company should restructure or reorganise only as a last resort, is clearly too extreme a standpoint. Nevertheless, a senior executive once told me that the best decision he made in his last job was 'to change nothing'. He had inherited a particular organisational structure and deliberately chose to live with it. Although he made many changes in the five years he was in the position, what he didn't alter was the essential arrangement of jobs, workgroups and reporting lines, which were in place when he stepped into the role.

FREQUENT RESTRUCTURING

- **Disrupts the business**
- **Focuses a company inwards**
- **Undermines legitimate authority**
- **Stalls people development**

Resisting the temptation to change the shape of an organisation reduces the disruption to the business that a restructuring of any significance causes.

By definition, an internal reorganisation focuses a company inwards. It soaks up enormous amounts of managerial time and energy. It also gives rise to feelings of insecurity, which in turn lead to turf wars and power games. From the first rumour of a restructuring to when the dust finally settles, and people get back to the business of the business, productivity suffers and morale dives.

Structural changes also tend to undermine the legitimacy of those in authority. This is because the price of legitimacy, the care and growth of the subordinate in the relationship, is limited in a context of constant alterations in reporting lines.

When a boss-subordinate relationship is 'temporary' managers are reluctant to invest too much in their people. They are able to avoid giving the care and growth that their staff require, because they don't have to live with the consequences of their failure to do so. Why bother, because another reorganisation is bound to be just around the corner and, in all likelihood, everyone will be moving on shortly.

Clearly a sizable reorganisation does become a necessity in certain circumstances. It becomes essential in the face of significant changes in business conditions, when there is a move to a new business model or there is a major shift in strategy.

RESTRUCTURE WHEN

- Business conditions change
- Strategy changes
- Structure is fundamentally disabling

A reorganisation is also imperative when the existing structure is fundamentally disabling. In other words, when the structure so contravenes the principles of good design that it effectively disallows employee contribution.

Aside from these circumstances, managers should leave the structure alone and rather focus their energies on the empowerment of their people. They should work at increasing individual accountability through an incremental handing over of control.

In doing so, small but finite structural adjustments will take place naturally. There will be continuous growth in people without the need to kick-start growth by means of a structural change injection. In the fullness of time, because the empowerment of people is on-going, major restructuring exercises can become what they should be – the exception rather than the norm.

ORGANISATIONAL DESIGN PRINCIPLES

A good organisational design is one which adheres to the following organisational design principles.

PRINCIPLE 1: Build the structure around the work to be done, not the people

There is a great temptation, when creating a structure, to try to accommodate the needs and aspirations of all the people within it. In a political context, this is classically the case whenever there is a change of government. Similarly, in business, what would be a sensible structure is often compromised to meet personal ambition, to avoid offending certain individuals or to compensate for a lack of people capability.

What an organisation should be built around is not its people but the actual work to be done. The work is prime, because it is the work which turns organisational inputs into outputs or outcomes. Everything else – technology, systems, layout, hierarchy, information flows and so on – are all secondary to the work itself and therefore subordinate to it.

PRINCIPLE 2: Minimise handovers

Any handover in a work process disrupts the flow of work and slows it down. Every time a piece of work is put down, before it is picked up by another person, there is a delay.

HANDOVERS CAUSE

- Delays
- Lack of accountability
- Finger pointing/blaming

MINIMISE HANDOVERS

- Assign complete work
- Gather connected outcomes together in one workgroup

Each handover also undermines or reduces accountability. This is because there is now more than one person involved, more than one person accountable. The minute there is more than one person accountable, no one is accountable.

The likelihood of blaming and finger pointing also increases. People complain that they can't do their jobs properly, not because of themselves, but because they have been 'let down' by someone else.

The work that was handed over to them, they say, was substandard, was late, or both and therefore they couldn't do their job properly.

I experienced all of the above first hand when I tried to 'hurry up' a bond registration within a financial institution. I finally gave up after being passed on from the twelfth person to a fifth department in a third locality. Everyone claimed to have done their bit, but the registered bond still had not emerged from the process. Too many handovers, in effect, lead to frustration, conflict and poor outcomes.

The elimination of all handovers, from one person to another within a workgroup and from one workgroup to another workgroup, is clearly not possible. Handovers can be minimised, however, in the following ways.

- Assigning responsibility for complete pieces of work. In other words, by giving individuals a job to do from beginning to end rather than a fraction of the job. No one in an organisation should have a job where the activities performed by the incumbent do not produce at least one value-added outcome. When this is the case, jobs are more demanding, simply because people are more accountable, but they are also more meaningful and worthwhile.

- By housing together a number of separate outcomes within a single workgroup, thereby reducing the number of workgroups. This is important simply because coordination and communication between people are greatest within workgroups, and least between workgroups.

What determines which outcomes belong together and therefore need to be the collective responsibility of a particular workgroup, depends on the number and strength of the links between separate outcomes.

Two or more outcomes

OUTCOMES AND WORKGROUPS

may be linked by the need for coordination and communication between those responsible for achieving them or because the quality of one outcome impacts positively or negatively on the quality of other outcome(s). A strong connection may also exist between outcomes because the means to produce them (skills, resources, standards, systems) are similar or shared. Finally, the potential for mutual learning may create a link between outcomes.

Whatever the rationale for linking outcomes, the sum effect of 'clustering' a number of outcomes together within a workgroup, is that the frequency with which work has to cross workgroup boundaries is reduced.

- By including auxiliary tasks, which directly support the outcomes of the group, as part of the responsibility of the group. Sales Administration, for example, can be incorporated into a single team made up of sales executives and sales administrators. Similarly, schedulers, engineers and QC specialists can belong to one Production Team, rather than being accommodated in various functional departments outside of production.

PRINCIPLE 3: Optimise span of control

ORGANISATIONAL HIERARCHY

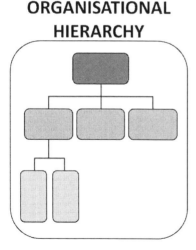

The size of a workgroup and hence the number of people who should report to a manager has been a matter of much debate. The two extremes – very small groups and very large groups – are both problematic.

As a rule of thumb, a group comprised of fewer than four people is too small. Two or three individuals, one could argue, do not even constitute a group. That aside, the effect of having groups of fewer than four produces an organisational hierarchy with one on two or one on three reporting relationships.

The effect of this is an overly hierarchical organisational structure with too many levels. As a result, managers tend to interfere, both in the work of those reporting to them, and in the work of their colleagues. This is because they don't have enough managerial and leadership work of their own to keep them occupied. Groups that are too large, as opposed to too small, have a different set of problems. Experience shows that both efficiency and motivation are negatively affected. Large groups often also split up, not formally but informally, into subgroups or cliques.

Most importantly, when a group is too big it becomes difficult, if not impossible, for leaders to perform their Care and Growth role effectively. This is simply because there is a practical limit to the number of people that anyone in a leadership role can care and grow, no matter how talented and committed he is.

SPAN OF CONTROL

The maximum number of direct reports should never exceed 25

What that actual limit is will depend on factors of geography, work complexity and the independence/task maturity of direct reports. Nevertheless the absolute maximum number of direct reports should be 25, while at senior levels the number should be much fewer.

When the span of control is too wide the only option is to reduce the number of direct reports. In a call centre environment teams of about 35 were reduced to 25 (maximum) with more capable team leaders being assigned bigger teams. In a global manufacturing business, the operations director appointed a site manager for the local manufacturing facility and effectively reduced his span of control by eight people. In both cases, optimising the span of control led to an improvement in leadership excellence.

PRINCIPLE 4: Insist on unique accountability

When roles within a workgroup (horizontal) or roles at different levels in a hierarchy (vertical) overlap, there is confusion and a duplication of effort. Moreover it becomes difficult to say who exactly is accountable for what. In large organisations this is especially the case the higher up the line one goes.

Lord Creosote   The Boss   The Overseer   The Worker

Roles need to be distinguished, not only by virtue of area of responsibility, but also by their particular set of accountabilities. What differentiates one job from another, both horizontally and vertically, needs to be crystal clear.

Further to this, no management level in a hierarchy should exist only for reasons of managing and controlling the work of the level below. Each level in the hierarchy needs to add its own unique value, distinct from the value being added by the level above or below it. In one organisation, for example, the *head of African operations* had, as his core purpose, the development and implementation of a strategy to grow the African business. He was not responsible for the profitability of any country/regional area within the continent since that was the accountability of each of the *regional executives* who reported into him.

The principle of unique accountability also pertains to the issue of Care and Growth. The response to the question, 'who is your boss?' should not be 'I don't know, X, Y and Z' or 'someone up the line'. It should be 'the person I report to directly, my immediate manager'. Similarly, a question to anyone in a managerial role, 'whose care and growth are you responsible for?', should evoke a list of specific individuals.

For each individual in an organisation, in other words, there should be someone designated to provide that person with Care and Growth. That person should preferably be the person's immediate manager. If this is not the case, the person who is responsible should nevertheless be clear both to the person who is charged with the Care and Growth of an individual and the recipient of that Care and Growth.

Unique accountability, as it applies to leadership, lastly means that the different aspects of Care and Growth (Care, Means, Ability and Accountability) are carried out by the same person rather than divided up and distributed among two or more managers. This is because all the aspects of caring for and growing people are highly interdependent.

Splitting the accountability for Care and Growth between two or more people can work but it is not optimal. Generally it causes confusion and obfuscation of accountability.

PRINCIPLE 5: Get the right balance between core and support

Over the years the number of jobs which are outside of actually developing, making/doing and selling an organisation's products/services to its customers has increased. The sum effect of this quiet revolution has been that the number of people engaged in an organisation's core functions, relative to the number of employees in non-core functions, has decreased. At one company this has taken the organisation to the point that, as someone put it, 'we now have so much scaffolding that we can no longer see the building'.

The 'too much scaffolding' problem is addressed by righting the balance between the number of employees assigned to the core and non-core functions of the business. It is also addressed by taking action to ensure that 'the dog wags the tail' rather than its inverse.

There are a number of options for dealing with the 'scaffolding problem':

- Strip the organisation down to its bare essentials and do away, altogether, with certain support functions and specialist roles. For example, entirely shut down head office, or take all the industrial engineers off the payroll. Drastic surgery of this type should however be reserved for dire circumstances only. This is because most support functions and roles have the potential to add both short and medium term value to the organisation. Better, at least in the first instance, to work at enabling them to do so rather than impetuously shutting them down.

- Outsource a support function to experts, to those who make the function (payroll administration, facilities management and so on) their core business. This, however, needs to be thought through very carefully. Many organisations have rued the day that they contracted out, when keeping the support function in-house would have been the better way to go.

- Judiciously prune the number of people in support roles. This can be done by declaring certain jobs which do not produce a value-added outcome of their own – 'middleman' type jobs – redundant. In addition it can be done by 'restocking' the core functions, by putting support staff back in the line where the making, doing and selling actually happens.

- It also may be useful, as a fourth option, to simply put a ban on any new non-core jobs, especially those which drive initiatives like quality, transformation, learning, etc, throughout the organisation. Rather than creating new company-wide specialist roles, it may be better to task line functions with effecting these initiatives in their own areas and providing them with the dedicated staff to do so.

- The final option is to reduce the 'power' of non-core functions. After all, functional expertise should be there to enable, not as an end in itself. An engineering function, for example, only exists because there are things to be made. Similarly, a marketing function has a role only because what is being made is being sold. When functional departments become an end in themselves, they, in effect, become 'the tail that wags the dog'.

In addition to this, there is a structural means of discouraging the tail from wagging the dog. It is to have support staff report into the line. In the event of dual reporting lines the straight line should always be into the *core* and the dotted line into the *support* function. Clarity around who is here to serve whom and how specifically the support function can add value to the core function that it is there to support can also be helpful.

GOOD DESIGN PRINCIPLES

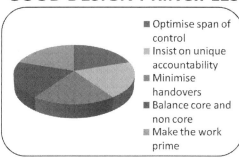

- Optimise span of control
- Insist on unique accountability
- Minimise handovers
- Balance core and non core
- Make the work prime

Each of the design principles outlined above work in unison with each other. A good organisation design, in essence, is one where the structure is built around the work to be done, where handovers within and across workgroups are minimised, where spans of control are optimal, where there is unique role accountability and where the ratio of core to non-core staff is appropriate.

THE DESIGN PROCESS

Given the above, the question which still remains is how to actually construct an organisation, bearing in mind the three beliefs and five principles outlined above. Should one begin top down or bottom up? Is the place to start with the design of individual jobs or the delineation of workgroups? At what point in the process should support functions be considered? And so on.

From experience, an organisational structure should be constructed by completing a number of steps in the following sequence.

Step 1: Start with the overall architecture of the organisation. This is devised on the basis of what needs to be done by the organisation to achieve its strategic intent and meet the key needs and wants of the organisation's customers. The 'what needs to be done' determines the core segments of what the organisation should be. What is created is an overall framework like an umbrella with each member of the executive team representing one of the spokes of the umbrella.

With the core segments defined, the structure within each segment of the organisation can then be designed, but now from the bottom up rather than from the top down.

Step 2: Within each core segment of the organisation, the different work processes need to be identified and analysed. Doing so makes it possible to pinpoint where in each process value is actually added and an outcome achieved. Some examples of value-added outcomes in different segments of an organisation include 'contracts signed' (sales segment), 'components assembled' (manufacturing segment), 'prototypes developed' (research and development segment), 'goods delivered to customer' (distribution segment) and so on.

The outcomes themselves then need to be clustered or grouped together based on the degree to which they are connected to one and other. Outcomes which cluster or belong together should then ideally be performed by the same workgroup.

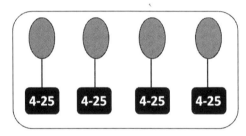

Step 3: Having determined the key value adding outcomes and the strengths of the relationships between them, the next step is to ascertain how many people are required for each workgroup. This will depend on the number and type of skills required to achieve each workgroup's defined outcomes. The matching of people to groupings of outcomes needs to, as far as possible, be in line with Principle Three (right sized workgroups) but still keeping, as far as possible, outcomes which belong together in the same workgroup.

Step 4: The next step is to build an organisational hierarchy to support the core work to be done. This is achieved by assigning the leadership responsibility for Care and Growth to one person per workgroup. The management structure, above core workgroups, is then constructed by keeping workgroups rather than outcomes, which belong together, reporting into the same manager.

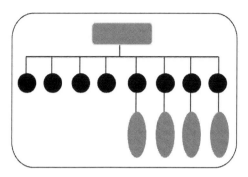

Step 5: Only at this point can individual specialists or even functional teams be incorporated into the management workgroup. This should only be done on condition that the optimal span of control at each level in the hierarchy is not compromised.

Step 6: Individual jobs, both within core workgroups and at different levels of management, can now be designed in more detail. Each job should be distinguished by the value-added outcome(s) which constitute the core job. In addition jobs can be made more 'whole' by making a number of enhancements to the core job. By, for example, tasking the person in the job with planning and evaluating, as well as doing the work that needs to be done.

Step 7: Finally, as part of the design process there should be a determination of the necessary means to ensure that the organisation functions as more than a collection of stand-alone parts. Various structural mechanisms can be used to enable cohesion between parts of a structure. They include, among other things, formal meetings with participants drawn from each part of the structure as well as information systems which promote coordination between different elements in the structure. The inclusion of formal arrangements like these in the organisational design is imperative if what has been finally created is to function as a cohesive whole, rather than exist as a series of silos or independent parts.

Good organisation design requires adherence to the three beliefs, five principles and seven steps outlined above. Organisational design will, however, always remain far more of an art than a science. For this reason, a good design takes due consideration and time to emerge. Like the implementation process, the design process should neither be too protracted nor completed with unseemly haste.

Humanising the Scoreboard

In some people's minds the Care and Growth model suggests that 'results don't matter'. This is absolutely not true. We are surely not playing the game devoid of any desire to win it!

The Power of Process over Outcome

When you put your attention on perfecting the process the outcome comes to you.

The results, however, are a means not an end. They are a tool for perfecting the process on which the desired outcome depends. The results do this for us in two ways. Firstly, they provide the context within which the contribution necessary to deliver the desired results can be clarified. Secondly, the results serve to provide feedback on contribution made. As such, the results inform those making the contribution what they should be doing differently in the future, in order to realise a better result going forward.

Many organisations, however, do not capitalise on the results in this way. They produce scoreboards, initially, to align everyone in the organisation to a set of goals. Thereafter they use the scoreboards, primarily, for evaluative purposes. They use the actual results achieved, in other words, as a means of assessing and rewarding past performance.

Those organisations, on the other hand, which have really benefited from their scoreboards have understood and acted on the following five insights:

1. Scoreboards have limitations and can be misleading.

2. Scoreboards should primarily serve the needs of employees, especially those in the front line of the business.

3. What you elect to measure is critically important because what you measure is what you get.

4. People will only be committed to achieving the results when they are co-designers of the results.

5. The 'why' behind the score is far more important than the score itself. It is only when the 'why' is understood that improved performance is enabled.

None of these insights is rocket science – they are common sense. Taken together though, they ensure that the real purpose of any scoreboard is realised, namely to enable employee contribution.

SCOREBOARDS HAVE LIMITATIONS AND CAN BE MISLEADING

Scoreboards are limited by the fact that the actual scores on a scoreboard, the results achieved in a given timeframe, are by definition a measure of history. They are a combination of what was done in the past and factors outside of people's control. What the actual scores don't tell is what is happening out there now, which will only evidence as a score on the scoreboard at some later date.

This was brought home to me when I walked into the office of a section manager, an ambitious young MBA graduate. Every inch of the walls in his office was covered in graphs and diagrams. 'Wow!' I said to him, 'this is impressive! But why don't you just walk 200m down to the plant if you want to get a grip on how things are going?'

Scores on a scoreboard can also be misleading, as seen in the following example.

> *A regional sales manager, running an area where the customer's sales revenues were exceptionally good, decided to visit one of his best customers. The customer's response to the technical support she received from his company was lukewarm at best. She felt that there was considerable room for improvement in responsiveness, technical expertise and frequency of customer visits.*
>
> *It turned out that the technical representative in question was a keen surfer, who spent more time on the ocean waves than with his customers. He had had little, if anything, to do with the customer's excellent sales performance.*

For both these reasons a scoreboard can never be a substitute for 'watching the game', for getting out there to see what is really going on, and therefore, what needs to be done to fix or improve it.

A useful analogy in this regard is coaching. The coach goes to the game on Saturday but his eyes are not on the scoreboard, as interested as he may be in the score. His attention is on the players, on how well they are playing the game and the effect that this is having on the score on the scoreboard. This is the vital information that the coach needs for the next week's practice session, when he does his real job of developing the team to play a better game on Saturday.

Good leaders are like good coaches. They spend considerable time, not in their offices, but out in the field where the products are made, the services are delivered and potential customers are engaged. They use the scoreboard, but only as a pointer for what they should go and look at or ask questions about. They do this because they know that the scoreboard never tells it all.

SCOREBOARDS SHOULD PRIMARILY SERVE THE NEEDS OF EMPLOYEES

The simple reason for this is that the people who need to know the score, more than anyone else, are those who put the score on the scoreboard. The following story illustrates the point.

I was invited to a cement factory where I was told that an excellent performance management system had been installed. The first meeting I attended was a shift handover at 05h30. The meeting consisted of the operators reporting back the numbers from the night shift to management – volumes, efficiency, quality, etc. At 06h00 I witnessed a similar ritual but this time in the engineering workshops, where again management took note of the metrics.

I was then ushered into the operations room and given a cup of tea while members of management fed the numbers into their computers. The subsequent management meeting was a repeat of those earlier. It was essentially an exercise in gathering up the numbers.

At this point I requested a meeting with the site manager. His response: 'I can't speak to you now, I have to get the figures through to head office before their 09h00 meeting!'

The image I was left with was that of a vacuum cleaner, sucking up the numbers rather than the dust from the floor. What, I wondered, did the people at head office actually DO with the information that hit their computer screens at precisely 09h00 each morning?

And this is not an isolated example. I know many managers who are stuck in their offices feeding the insatiable information needs of those higher in the hierarchy. What 'they' do with the information is often a mystery. It reminds me of the wonderful 1988 film *Pascali's Island* in which Pascali, a spy for the sultan, diligently sends monthly reports through to Constantinople for 20 years that nobody reads.

A recent experience I had at Johnson Matthey ECT in the United Kingdom could not have been more different. Management have invested considerable time and energy in installing an information system on each production line. Information pertaining to all the critical measures are there on the screen, in real time. What the system gives the operator is the means to make immediate changes to the process the instant he needs to do so.

> *The shift leader also has access to what is happening on each production line, as it is happening. This enables him to intervene on his shift where and when he can to add the most value to those running the process.*
>
> *Interestingly, the person who designed the system is a talented industrial engineer with a bent for information technology. In the true spirit of service he worked with the operators to really understand and deliver on their needs.*
>
> *As for the production manager, it is a simple matter for him to collate the trends from the real time information on a weekly basis.*

WHAT YOU ELECT TO MEASURE IS CRITICALLY IMPORTANT

How you score a game most certainly influences how the game is played. In rugby, for example, if the points awarded for a drop goal were twice those given for a try, the game as we know it would be very different.

The same is true of organisations, both at the level of the overall score and with respect to team/individual scoreboards. In all instances, what you measure has a significant impact on what you get.

 Measure of business performance

The overall score which should be used as the principle score for measuring the performance of an organisation is the Value Added Statement (VAS). The VAS is one of four approved accounting statements; the others are the Income Statement, the Balance Sheet and the Cash Flow Statement.

The VAS (tongue in cheek) originated with the first business known to mankind.

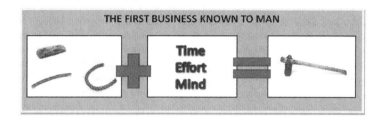

THE FIRST BUSINESS KNOWN TO MAN

A Neanderthal man found a stick, a stone and a piece of fibre from which he furnished an axe – which he possibly then used to find himself a wife!

The difference between the stick, the stone, the piece of fibre and the axe represents what the Neanderthal contributed. It denotes the value which he added to his raw materials – namely his time, his effort, and his mind.

A slightly more modern example is that of a little old lady who went to the market to buy a ball of wool, knitted the wool into a jersey and sold it. She paid R100 for the wool and was paid R200 for the jersey. She, therefore, added R100 worth of value by her knitting.

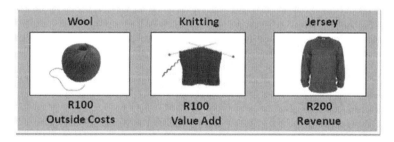

Wool	Knitting	Jersey
R100	R100	R200
Outside Costs	Value Add	Revenue

The basic elements of the VAS, true of any business, are therefore:

TURNOVER	200
What the customer is prepared to pay based on the perceived value of the product/service.	
OUTSIDE COSTS	**100**
What is paid to the external suppliers.	

VALUE ADDED	100
The difference between turnover and outside costs. The measure of wealth created.	

Value Added is, in essence, a measure of what was given or contributed. As such, it puts into quantifiable terms what we believe to be the benevolent intent of any enterprise, namely, to make a contribution to a customer.

This is in sharp contrast to the conventional measure of business performance which is Gross Profit derived from the company's Income Statement or Profit and Loss Statement. Profit is a measure of what the shareholders get.

To believe that measuring success in terms of ROI (return on investment) will motivate the employees in a business is at best naïve, and at worst it renders them hostile to the business. And so it should, because it highlights the inherent inconsistency in calling on a person to make an unconditional contribution to a customer, and then principally measuring the performance of the business on the basis of the interests of the shareholders.

The VAS, however, measures both wealth creation and how the wealth created was distributed among those who contributed to the value added. The percentage of value added which accrues to each contributor varies, but in a sustainable enterprise the typical distribution would be as shown here.

EMPLOYEES	60%
Salaries, wages, training and benefits.	
RESERVES	20%
Retained income and depreciation. Legally they belong to the shareholders but are in all parties' interests because they enable future trading.	
TAX	12%
For the provision of infrastructure which enables trade to happen.	
DIVIDEND	8%
The return on investment to the shareholders.	

Noteworthy, in the first place, is the fact that what employees receive is not accounted for as a cost, but as a portion of value-add. In most organisations, employees take the largest share of the value added, which is a just reflection of the fact that they are the biggest contributors to it.

Secondly, the VAS places the interests of the shareholder in perspective. It confirms the inappropriateness of measuring the success of the business on the basis of those who get the smallest part of the cake.

The problem with making the shareholders' interests prime is that it makes the company 'bottom line-driven'. It encourages a focus on cost reduction through, for example, employee retrenchments. In order to protect the shareholders' interests, the interests of the other stakeholders are compromised.

The VAS, on the other hand, makes the company 'top line-driven'. It creates a common purpose among all its stakeholders of adding more value by selling more, getting a better price or by reducing outside costs. A healthy value-add ensures a place in the sun for everybody, including the shareholders.

Not in all cases, but in some companies, a consistent sharing of the company's performance using the VAS, has led to the increased maturity of its employees. It solicits contributory behaviour because what is measured is just that – contribution.

In one instance, evidence that the shareholder was not being paid a dividend gave the union insight into why the business was under threat of a hostile takeover. The union played a key role in persuading the Competition Tribunal to rule against the purchase of the company.

In another company, employees showed concern for their disproportionate size of value added (85%). They provided valuable input to management and worked with them on ways to both increase revenue and reduce outside costs.

Most companies, however, are seemingly reluctant to use the VAS as the primary measure of enterprise performance. If they do use the VAS, it is often as an addendum to the balance sheet and the income statement in the company's annual report. There could be many reasons for this. Perhaps they see the VAS as too simple, even though it is constructed from the same figures as the profit and loss statement. Perhaps they are not comfortable sharing the wealth distribution part of the statement. This was certainly our experience with a client in India. Or perhaps, although their mantra to employees is that 'we are all here to serve the customer', their true belief is that 'we are here to maximise the return to the shareholder'. Old habits die hard!

Measures for teams and individuals

VALUE ADDED SCOREBOARD

Wealth Creation Subscores			Wealth Distribution Subscores
MPS	TURNOVER	100	TRAINING
OEE	OUTSIDE COSTS	50	PROGRESSION ON PROJECTS
FAILURE RATE			BBBEE
QUALITY INDEX	VA	50	EFFLUENT RECOVERY
PRODUCTIVITY			
OTIF	EMPLOYEES	30	SAFETY
RM SHORTAGES	RESERVES	18	SUPPLIER DEVELOPMENT
STOCK ACCURACY	TAX	6	INDEX
	DIVIDEND	4	
OVERTIME			

There are various methodologies for determining appropriate measures or key performance indicators for a team or individual scorecard. The Balanced Scorecard methodology is one of these. The method we prefer is a simple one, which uses as its spine the company's VAS.

The wealth creation subscores pertain to the results which, if achieved, will positively impact on the value added of the company. The wealth distribution subscores, on the other hand, relate to the key variables that affect the sustainability of the organisation.

The value of deriving subscores in this manner is that they produce a clear line of sight or golden thread between contribution and, ultimately, the overall performance of the organisation. They enable a scheduler of delivery vehicles, for example, to see quite clearly how a poor schedule impacts on OTIF (on time in full) delivery, which in turn increases delivery costs and ultimately could lead to a loss of customers and hence reduction in turnover.

CRITERIA FOR GOOD SCOREBOARDS

❖ Linked to vision and strategy.

❖ Aligned top to bottom.

❖ Include measures that the team / individual can directly influence.

❖ Balanced – addresses the needs of all stakeholders, short term and long term.

❖ Few in number to provide focus.

❖ Visual – available for all to see.

❖ Simple – easy to understand.

❖ Valid – up to date and accurate.

❖ Useful – facilitates comparison to past and future benchmarks.

A well designed scoreboard satisfies all of the criteria for good scoreboards as shown here.

Unfortunately though, many of the scoreboards that I have been shown contravene one or more of these criteria. Often, there are just too many measures. In an attempt to cover all the bases, the 20% of the results, which make 80% of the difference, get lost in the multitude of metrics.

Many of the measures are also too complex. They are derived using complicated formulae (TRIR or the Quality Threshold Model Index) which, when you probe a little, are often not fully understood by those who must improve on them.

Lastly, there is a tendency to contravene the rule 'that which is measured is only what the team/individual can directly influence'. It is clearly disempowering to hold people accountable for something they can do nothing about.

But the key weakness that I see in most scoreboards is the predominance of measures of output, to the detriment of input measures.

According to Johan Southey, a keen cyclist, there is only one output of importance in cycling and that is average speed. The cyclist with the highest average speed wins the race. What determines average speed however is a combination of watts and cadence exerted by the cyclist's legs on the pedals. Serious cyclists track watts and cadence. Average speed is measured at less frequent intervals, purely to make decisions on whether or not to make changes to these determining inputs. Clearly, if what improves outcome is process, then what you need to measure is not only outcome but also process.

AEL Mining Services did just that to effect a dramatic improvement in safety performance. Traditionally it had measured and reported on the 'number of serious accidents', 'fatalities' and 'disabling and lost-time injury rates'. It kept these output measures but added others like 'reduction on risk scores of specific tasks', 'adherence to housekeeping standards' and 'time spent by management on the floor'. This is where its primary attention was focused. This is what gave it the desired improvement in Total Reportable Injury Rate (TRIR).

PEOPLE WILL ONLY BE COMMITTED TO ACHIEVING THE RESULTS WHEN THEY ARE CO-DESIGNERS OF THE RESULTS

The design process itself is a further critical factor in the successful use of scoreboards. The early generation of balanced scoreboards were often designed remotely by consultants. Managers did not trust, and so failed to engage with and use, the measures. They simply viewed them as being created by people who lacked in-depth knowledge of the organisation and managerial responsibility for the results.

In a big retail bank, a central unit was set up tasked with the design of scoreboards for its branch banking network, using a sophisticated linkage model. All branches across the country were measured on the same set of metrics and ranked according to a numerical total score. This provided management with a single ruler to compare branch performance across all the branches in the business.

One branch manager complained bitterly to me of the imposed target that she had to meet for student loans. Her branch, you see, was situated in an industrial area, kilometres away from the city's educational institutions.

Similarly, managers on a mine were severely demotivated by annual targets given to them by head office. Their failure to achieve the stretch targets that they had been given meant that they had not received a bonus in the last three years. The metal recovery rate, the key measure, was, in their view, a function of over-optimistic projections by geologists when the mine was initially started. Nevertheless, they continued to work against targets, which experience had shown were well beyond their reach. No wonder they were lacking in motivation.

GOAL ALIGNMENT PROCESS

1. Decide on the year's goals and communicate them to staff via email.
2. Determine the goals and then communicate them via a series of road shows in which the staff can ask questions.
3. The management team goes away for a couple of days to review last year's performance and agree targets for the year ahead. They get ratification up the line before dissemination to staff.
4. Staff are provided with detailed information on the state of the business. Their input on what the targets should / could be is taken into consideration before deciding.
5. Each team comes up with its own targets and management lives with these proposals.

One could argue that the appropriate process for establishing a set of measurable goals for a defined period should be a function of employee maturity. The more mature the people, the more empowering the process that should be used. The diagram above depicts various process options from least to most empowering.

Nevertheless, it is clear that the more those tasked with delivery of a set of results are co-designers of the results, the more likely they are to be committed to their achievement.

One company instituted an annual planning or goal alignment process which followed the format shown below.

The process took some time and involved everyone in the management hierarchy. Thereafter, all team leaders took a further day with their teams to finalise the plans for their sections. Interestingly, the proposed and agreed targets were often not the same. In some instances, the information exchange led to a less-than-initially-proposed target. In other instances, the often very heated debate led to a target more challenging than initially proposed.

GOAL ALIGNMENT PROCESS

Summary of last year's successes.

Context of the company's strategic objectives.

Review of performance against last year's targets (didn't meet/met/ exceeded).

Proposed target for the year with rationale per goal (input per team).

Agreed target after debate.

Establishment of specific plans for the achievement of each target per area. Each team presents and takes ideas from the bigger group.

What impressed me most about the process, however, was the follow-through in terms of specific plans for the achievement of each target. Targets are all well and good, but without clarity on what has to happen to achieve them they remain empty goals. For example, setting a new goal for a marathon time and yet following the same training programme as last time is an unlikely recipe for success.

THE 'WHY' BEHIND THE SCORE

To make the spine of the team/individual review process the scoreboard is absolutely correct. From my experience the critical step of establishing the 'why' behind the scores, however, is often missing or poorly done in both team and individual review meetings.

 Operational Team Review Meetings

An example which springs to mind is of a food company in South Africa whose products adorn the shelves of most major supermarkets.

> *A major food processing company in South Africa has instituted a review process, which it calls Invocoms, at both its mills and bakeries. At every level the meeting follows a very structured format: a looking back (what results were achieved) and a looking forward (what results are needed going forward). Depending on level, the meetings are daily, weekly or monthly.*
>
> *At the start of the meeting the actual performance achieved since the last meeting is displayed and good/bad performance denoted by icons on the board (green or red faces). The results required between now and the next meeting are also clarified and improvements which need to be made emphasised.*
>
> *There are other agenda items but this is the essence of the meetings.*

Effective operational meetings need to follow the steps shown below.

A report back on next steps from the previous meeting (REVIEW) must happen but should be sharp and to the point. Was the agreed action done by the person accountable for doing so – yes/no? Should the next step not have been done, and yet the person had the means and ability to do it, he should be held to account. The temptation to simply roll the action over for completion at the next meeting should be avoided, since this breeds a culture of non-accountability and mediocrity.

Not every score should be reviewed at every meeting since the frequency of review should vary depending on the nature of the score. The focus should, in any case, be on the 'outliers' – *both* the positive and negative exceptions. For each exception WHAT accounts for the score needs to be clear. For example, a poor FTR (first time right) score was the result of two batches which were delayed for 48 hours in the bulk plant.

The WHAT also needs to include the effect of the score on other scores on the scoreboard (for instance, the effect of a reject batch

THE OPERATIONAL REVIEW MEETING FORMAT

Review of next steps from previous meeting.
(REVIEW)

Communication and understanding of the scores.
(WHAT)

Clarification of the reasons for the scores.
(WHY)

Determination and assignment of ACTIONS or next steps.

highlighted in the quality score on other scores like delivery and productivity). It also needs to include the impact that the score has on the value added statement (for instance, the effect of the reject batch on sales and outside costs). Time spent on the WHAT is not wasted. It provides an increasingly clear line of sight between contribution/what is done and its effect on wealth creation and organisational capability.

Clarification of the reasons for the scores (the WHY), however, should be the 'meat' of the operational review meeting. This should be reflected in the amount of time dedicated to the WHY in the meeting. As a rule of thumb 20% of time should be spent on review of previous steps and communication of the scores and 80% on understanding the why and agreeing future actions.

DEALING WITH EXCEPTIONS

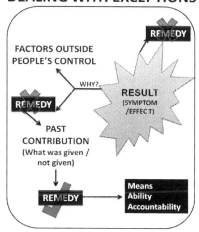

The members of the team who have exceptions in their area of responsibility (significant negative or positive scores) should deliver a diagnostic on the score at the meeting.

The diagnostic (the WHY) should get behind the score (the WHAT) to ascertain what was done/not done which caused the exception. A further questioning of the WHY behind what was done/not done reveals the root cause(s) for the exception categorised as means, ability and accountability reasons.

103

Failure to get to the WHY behind the score leads to remedial actions, which deal with the symptom rather than the cause. As a consequence of this the exception inevitably comes back and the score repeats itself.

The agreed ACTIONS should then be focused on, addressing the means, ability and accountability issues identified during the reflective part of the meeting. Each action needs to be assigned to a specific individual with an agreed completion date.

Finally, it is useful to add an additional agenda item (FOCUS REVIEW) at the end of specified operational meetings, which ensures that the team breaks out of its on-going review cycle at appropriate intervals. While the routine operational review meeting provides the opportunity to review progress against the team's objectives, the FOCUS REVIEW provides designated occasions during which the team can change its mind with regard to what its objectives should be.

The Focus Review discussion should lead to a determination of what is now important and, therefore, what the team needs to give attention to in the future. Thereafter, it should lead to agreement on which scores/measures on the scoreboard need to change to reflect the change in focus.

Both the scores on the left and the right of the Value Added Statement (VAS) need to be reviewed asking the following:

- Are we focusing on improvements which, if successful, will enable us to increase sales, increase prices and reduce costs? (wealth creation)
- Are we focusing on improvements which will build organisational capability and ensure that the legitimate expectations of all stakeholders are met? (wealth distribution)

Clearly, the outcome of the review will be unlikely to lead to a totally new set of measures. This is because many of the issues will continue to be important and to require attention on an on-going basis. Unless some new or different measures are determined, however, the team will become frozen in time, out of touch with changes in its environment, and it will stop growing.

 **Individual Review Meeting**

Similarly, in the individual review discussion, it is the WHY which often gets short changed, as the example below illustrates:

> *The review that I sat in on took place between a manager and a sales supervisor at Old Mutual Group. An updated scoreboard was on the table between the two parties. Sales revenue was good but the manager's concern, highlighted in red, was the policy lapse rate. Apparently policies were sold, payments made for a few months, and then payments lapsed, which in effect rendered a percentage of recorded sales redundant. The manager made it clear that the current lapse rate was unacceptable and that something needed to be done urgently to address the problem. Before he shifted attention to another score I asked the following:*
>
> - *'WHY is the lapse rate so high?' 'Because the sales people sign up clients, knowing that they can't afford the policy, in order to make their monthly targets.'*
> - *'If the team leader knows this WHY does she not intervene?' 'Because she is too soft and doesn't want to confront her sales people.'*
> - *'So WHY don't you make her accountable for holding her sales people accountable, and review this at your next meeting?'*
>
> *'That's a good idea,' he said.*

The outcome of any individual review discussion should be agreed-upon actions which enable the subordinate's enhanced contribution, growth and accountability going forward. The WHAT that has been achieved, both in terms of results and contribution, should have been established beforehand. 80% of the meeting should be on the WHY (means, ability, accountability issues) which sit behind the WHAT (results/contribution). The discussion will then deliver a set of actions which will address means deficiencies, enhance ability or, in the example on the previous page, cultivate accountability.

HOW A COMPANY HUMANISED ITS SCOREBOARDS

Over the years there is one company, Dulux South Africa, which stands out for me as having successfully used the results as the means to the end of enhanced employee contribution. This company had not performed well for several years. Its continued existence relied on the fact that it made a contribution to group overheads, and, despite efforts, no buyer for the company had come forward with an acceptable offer.

The company had also never shared business information with all employees on a regular basis, below the level of senior management. It was decided that this was one of the things that needed to be changed to engage employees' willing contribution to improving the state of the business.

The process began with the CEO sharing the finances of the business with all 450 employees. He did this in groups of 40-50 employees at a time, and the format he used was the Value Added Statement.

Attendance at these sessions was voluntary and the first attempt realised minimal interest. The CEO returned to the locality and tried again. With each subsequent quarterly session, attendance and participation increased as employees began to ask questions.

After several months Value Added Workshops were run for everyone in the business. These sessions served to explain to employees how wealth was created and distributed in their company. The workshops were facilitated by senior managers, not by the training function.

As employees' understanding of the numbers increased, they began to contribute ideas for improving the state of the business. The lukewarm response of employees to the numbers at the outset was totally understandable: 'They are telling us this so that we will accept low increases at year end or, worse still, to prepare us for retrenchments.' Employees began to really trust the figures, and the management that shared them with them, only when the business broke even, then made a profit and the sharing of the numbers continued.

Scoreboards were put in place and operational review meetings were instituted. I attended a meeting on the sales side of the business. The sales figures had been sent out 24 hours before the meeting to everyone who was attending. There was a brief period allowed at the start of the meeting for clarification of the figures. Thereafter each team member explained the reasons for exceptions in his area and asked colleagues for their ideas on how to improve the results under review.

Not only was everyone in the meeting engaged throughout, but there was a most useful exchange of learnings among participants. The focus of the meeting was on using the history, reflected in the scoreboard, to improve the way forward. The outcome of the meeting was a definite sense of accountability by each member. For the leader of the team, the meeting served an additional function. It informed him as to the 'watching the game' activities that he needed to carry out before the next meeting.

Getting operational review meetings to really serve the needs of those attending them takes practice. I knew that the company had really been through the learning curve when I eavesdropped on a morning meeting in one of the plants. One of the operators presented the numbers on a flipchart. She pointed to the low production figure and announced that this was primarily due to absenteeism. She then addressed an individual in the group saying 'and you are the key problem ... until you sort yourself out, this poor result will continue!' The man in question hid his face in shame.

Interestingly, the foreman was not present at the meeting. When I asked him why this was the case he said: 'These are their results not mine. I pop in once or twice a week, but as an observer, not to run the meeting.'

There is indeed great power in the numbers. Whether the power in the numbers is realised, however, is a function of how the numbers are used. Only when the primary purpose of the numbers is to *empower* those who the business depends on to produce the numbers, is the full potency of the numbers achieved.

Clarifying Contribution

Most managers can be persuaded that people in organisations should be held accountable for their contribution/for what they *give* rather than the results/what they *get*. They nevertheless balk at the prospect of actually applying this dictum in practice.

The reason is primarily a *how to* problem. They know how to set targets, measure people's achievement against target and calculate an increment/bonus amount aligned to the actual results produced. They do not necessarily know how to specify, assess and reward people for their contributions in the context of the results to be achieved.

Means

- Tools/Resources
- Processes/Systems
- Time
- Authority
- Clear Expectations
- Information/Feedback

Clarity of contribution is a critical enabler of contribution. It is the *means* issue which most people in organisations believe, if addressed, will most enhance the value they can add to the organisation.

Clarity of contribution is, moreover, a precondition for *holding people accountable for their contribution*. This is because it is not possible to fairly assess and reward people for their contributions if their contributions have not been clarified and agreed upon in the first place.

CONTRIBUTION VS RESULTS

Contribution is different from *results*. Contribution is about giving, about what a person puts into a situation. Results, on the other hand, are about getting. Results have to do with outcomes.

Contribution, moreover, refers to what is done or delivered, which is of added value to someone else. As such, contribution sits squarely in the hands of the person making the contribution.

A farmer, for example, adds value by what he does – he ploughs, fertilizes, plants and harvests. How well he carries out these tasks, and whether he is below/on/above standard, describes the nature of his contribution.

Similarly, the value added by a debt collector is a promise to pay by the debtor. Debt collectors who perform above standard are those who are able to convince a significantly higher proportion of debtors to pay than the average debt collector.

While contribution is against a standard, actual results are relative to desired or anticipated results. Any result can therefore be below/on/above target.

Results are in part a function of contribution but are also affected by external factors. Whether the farmer gets a bumper crop or not is partly dependent on the weather. Similarly, whether a debtor actually pays off his debt can be due to reasons other than the debt collector's powers of persuasion. The debtor may, for example, have received an inheritance and decided to use this windfall to get out of debt.

	CONTRIBUTION (Below/On/Above Standard)		RESULT (Below/On/Above Target)	
1	On/Above Standard	☺	On/Above Target	☺
2	Below Standard	☹	On/Above Target	☺
3	On/Above Standard	☺	Below Target	☹
4	Below Standard	☹	Below Target	☹

The difference between contribution and results outlined above does not suggest that the two are independent of each other. On the contrary, the complex interplay between the two produces one of four possibilities at any point in time.

The First Possibility arises when both the contribution and the results are on/above requirement. The Second and Third Possibilities are the inverse of each other. The Second Possibility occurs when contribution is below standard but the result, at a point in time, is nevertheless positive. With the Third Possibility, contribution is exemplary but the results, as reflected on the scoreboard, are less than desired. With the Fourth Possibility, both the contribution and the results are poor.

Clarification of contribution is therefore not something which should be divorced from and separate from the results. In clarifying contribution, what is determined and defined is what needs to be done or delivered, now and going forward, in order to impact positively on the desired results. In other words, contribution should be clarified in the context of the results to be achieved.

CLARIFYING CONTRIBUTION AT THE LEVEL OF THE ROLE

The most common means of delineating expectations of individual performance in an organisation is via some kind of scorecard or performance contract. The scorecard typically specifies the results to be achieved in each of a number of key result areas.

The example shown is for a Business Area Leader Process on a platinum mine. Job incumbents are required to deliver results in five areas: Volume/Quantity, Quality, Cost, People and Safety.

Within the Quality Key Performance Area shown below, there are a number of key critical measures/targets, each of which is weighted in terms of its importance. Levels of performance against targets are stipulated in numerical terms. Actual performance achieved (level 1 through 5) is then converted into a performance rating.

Quality		Weight Rating	Weight 100 %	Performance Scale					Actual Achieved	Rating 1
				1	2	3	4	5		
1	Concentration Grade	L	6.5 %	30 %	90 %	100 %	110 %	120 %		1
	Measure — 157g/ton									
2	Concentration Recovery	H	80.6 %	80 %	83 %	87 %	88 %	90 %		1
	Measure — 85.8%									
3	Information on time and correct (reporting)	L	6.5 %	6.5 %	70 %	80 %	90 %	100 %		1
	Measure — % Compliance to internal audit									
4	Appropriate Policy Implementation	L	6.5 %	6.5 %	90 %	95 %	98 %	100 %		1
	Measure — % Compliance to internal audit									

Performance scoreboards, like the one shown above, have merit. They serve to align everyone in the organisation to the same set of goals. They also provide the context in which contribution can be made. What they don't do, however, is clarify what an individual's unique contribution to the achievement of desired results in each key performance area actually is. They do not elucidate what the individual needs to effect as his unique contribution to the achievement of any of the score(s) on the scoreboard.

Where organisations do attempt to clarify contribution as well as the results, the vehicle they typically use is the job description or job profile. The problem with most job descriptions, however, is that they are written primarily for job evaluation purposes. Consequently they are often voluminous documents in which the essence of the role is lost among all the 'padding' written with the job evaluation committee in mind.

Job descriptions also tend to focus on the scope and scale of the job rather than on its unique 'give' or value-add. In a financial institution, for example, the job specifications at three levels in the hierarchy were all identical. The only difference was in the job title (Branch Manager, Area Manager, Provincial Executive) and the area/scope of responsibility.

From a Care and Growth perspective, clarification of contribution at the level of the role is most useful when it achieves the following:

- It makes explicit the unique purpose of the job.

- It distinguishes the role from other roles, both horizontally and vertically, in the hierarchy.

Role clarification, moreover, is not something which should be done off-line by the human resources function. Rather it should be an interactive process involving at least the job incumbent and his/her immediate manager, and preferably also representatives of roles which relate in some way to the role being defined.

The ensuing discussion and debate between the parties should give rise to a one-pager which spells out the sole reason why the role exists and its key accountabilities or tasks. The one-pager needs to be a live document which is in the possession of the individual fulfilling the role, not the human resources function.

Responsibility & Accountability

Contribution

From experience, there is a simple but very useful question to ask to distil out the essence of a role. It is: *what am I paying you for?* The answer to this question should be expressed in a single sentence. The role of a Schuitema consultant, for example, is 'to enable client organisations to shift the focus of their attention from taking to giving'. A role which does not have a unique purpose or value add should not exist.

The key accountabilities which, taken together, fulfil the role's purpose also need to be unique. The best way to ensure that this is the case is to build accountabilities from the bottom up. That is, to start with the role(s) which directly contribute to the result(s) to be achieved (for instance Sales Representative, Business Analyst, Rock Drill Operator) and thereafter to progress up the line from one level of management to the next.

There are two golden rules to be followed when doing a role clarification exercise. Firstly, there must be no duplication of accountability. The accountabilities at one level in the line must be distinctly different to those at the level below and above that level. Secondly, included in the accountabilities of those who lead others must be accountabilities which relate to the Care and Growth of direct reports. Accountabilities extracted from the roles of Team Leader, Production Manager and Manufacturing Manager at Snackworks biscuit factory illustrate quite clearly that each of the incumbents, at the three levels in the manufacturing hierarchy, are required to make very different contributions to the required results.

Team Leader Accountabilities	Production Manager Accountabilities	Manufacturing Manager Accountabilities
• Accountable that operators are on time, on line and on shift. • Accountable for replenishment of raw materials. • Accountable for speedy resolution of stoppages on the line. • Accountable for multi-tasking and multi-skilling of line operators.	• Accountable to provide daily support to the team leader on problems on the line. • Accountable for managing all operating costs in area. • Accountable for setting and upholding production standards. • Accountable for enabling demonstrated improvement in the contribution of each team leader.	• Accountable for identifying and prioritising continuous improvement projects for manufacturing. • Accountable for building and cultivating a mature relationship with the union on site. • Accountable for ensuring adequate service from support functions. (Engineering, Quality, etc) • Accountable for enabling demonstrated improvement in the contribution of production managers.

Note: Examples only – not a full list of accountabilities for each role.

CLARIFYING DELIVERABLES FOR A REPORTING PERIOD

Role-based descriptions of contribution define the nature of the contribution appropriate to the incumbent in the role. Any description of contribution at the level of the role is nevertheless limited in the following ways:

- Role-based descriptions are not specific enough. They do not set down what specifically needs to be delivered by an individual, to positively impact on desired results, in the next reporting cycle. Two people may be fulfilling the same role but, as a result of different external demands, may be required to focus on very different deliverables going forward. The issues facing a provincial executive in the Northern Cape province, for example, may be very different from those facing the provincial executive in Gauteng province. As a result, the nature of their contributions in the next reporting cycle would not be the same, even though they are both employed as provincial executives.

- Role-based descriptions are static. They assume the same level of task maturity of everyone in the role. Practically speaking, somebody who has only been in a role for six months is unlikely to be able to contribute in the same way that a seasoned professional, who has occupied the role for a number of years, can.

- What needs to be given by leaders in terms of the Care and Growth of direct reports tends, in role-based descriptions, to be too generic. Statements like 'regular feedback on contribution to standard given to all direct reports' or 'ensure people have the tools/resources required to do their jobs' are platitudes. They do not specify the changes in individual direct report(s), which constitute a leader's Care and Growth contribution in a given period of time.

CARE AND GROWTH CONTRIBUTION: GENERIC

CARE
1) Knows her people well and is interested in them as people, not just as employees.
2) Is there for her people, not the other way around. The line of service is down, not up, the line.
3) Spends sufficient time with direct reports in team meetings, one-on-one meetings, in the field 'watching the game'.
4) Listens to and respects the views and opinions of his/her people. Relationships with her people are characterised by mutual trust and respect.

MEANS
1) Ensures people know the mission, vision, values and objectives of the company.
2) Ensures individuals know what is expected of them and how their jobs contribute to the required results.
3) Ensures people have the tools/resources they require to do their jobs.
4) Ensures structures, systems and processes enable their people to make the contribution required of them.
5) Ensures that people have the decision-making authority to do their jobs.

ABILITY
1) Ensures formal training and development is effective in ensuring that employees have the competencies required to do their jobs.
2) Develops his/her employees' understanding of the business and how it is performing.
3) Effectively coaches direct reports both in terms of how to do their jobs and why the jobs should be done.
4) Facilitates employee growth through regular review and deliberate changes in employee accountability.

ACCOUNTABILITY
1) Holds people accountable for their contribution, not for what they are getting out/results.
2) Conducts regular reviews of contribution or feedback at an individual level.
3) Disciplines people for deliberate malevolence, and censures for carelessness.
4) Acknowledges or praises those who contribute to standard.
5) Rewards those who consistently go the extra mile.

For all these reasons the following two-step approach to clarifying contributions should be followed:

STEP ONE is the clarification of priorities/what results require focus on right now. The critical results can either be taken directly off the scoreboard or determined from the current key issues and indicators of success if they were addressed. Clarity of results provides the context for then specifying the contribution required by each person to positively impact on the results to be achieved. Without this context what people need to do could be anything.

STEP TWO is the determination of a set of deliverables per individual. That is a clear delineation of what each person needs to effect or produce, which is of added value in the next reporting period.

The reporting period may vary but should probably not exceed about 90 days. This is because it is relatively easy to see what needs to be done in the next 3-4 months. Beyond that time frame contribution becomes increasingly vague. The 90-day period also provides flexibility. If what is done does not produce the required outcome (Possibility Three in The Contribution Result matrix outlined earlier) different actions/deliverables can be effected in the next reporting cycle.

Assigned deliverables need to meet the following criteria:

- They should contribute to achieving a result. If there is no connection between an individual's contribution and a result(s), the contribution should obviously not be made. This is obviously not the case, but if for example there was no relationship between convincing a debtor to pay (the debt collector's contribution) and money in the bank (the desired outcome) there would be no reason to have debt collectors.

- They should be unique in the sense that they are specific to an individual at a point in time and in terms of his/her unique circumstances. They are also unique in that any deliverable should be assigned to one person only. As soon as more than one person is accountable for a deliverable, no one is accountable.

- They should be specific and concrete such that it should be possible to answer the question: 'Was this done/delivered? Yes or no?' If 'yes', 'was it done/delivered on or above standard?'

Criteria

- Line of sight
- Unique
- Specific and concrete
- Appropriate
- Manageable but stretching
- Time bound

- They should be appropriate to the role or level in the organisation. The deliverables of those in leadership positions, if appropriate, should contribute primarily to enabling others (through the provision of Care, Means, Ability and Accountability) rather than directly contributing to the results.

- They should provide growth for the person. That is, they should be stretching but achievable.

- They should be time bound. That is, specific to the next 90 days or appropriate reporting cycle.

BARRIERS TO CLARIFYING CONTRIBUTION

Clarifying contribution is an element in an on-going accountability review cycle, which takes place throughout the year. In all, three sets of 90-day deliverables need to be defined in a twelve-month period, following on from a review of the previous set of deliverables.

The Accountability Cycle

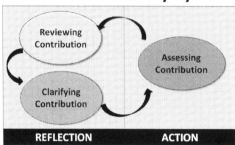

Clarifying contribution on a regular and on-going basis is not easy. From experience there are two barriers which need to be overcome if the discipline of clarifying contribution on a regular basis is to become entrenched in an organisation.

The first barrier to the scripting of 90-day deliverables is that people find this difficult to do. It takes time to learn how to do this properly. Typically three to four cycles are needed before unconscious competence is achieved. Many people are simply not prepared to go through the learning curve to get there.

The second impediment to instituting a 90-day deliverables process is that the rewards which come from clarifying contribution are not immediate. The analogy which springs to mind is that of exercise. Initially one is only aware of the toil and struggle that is being experienced. It is only much later, if one has persevered, that the benefits become apparent.

TYPICAL SHORTCOMINGS/ERRORS IN SCRIPTING CONTRIBUTION/DELIVERABLES

Result/Contribution

	RESULT	CONTRIBUTION
• Grow D3 profit variance. YTD to R170k	√	
• Hold artisans accountable for adhering to call out standards		√
• 100% rollout of quality programme		√
• Increase % of managers who are PDI to 30%	√	

From experience assisting people in organisations to clarify contribution a number of common errors are made. The most common of these are as follows:

- People confuse results and contribution. They have been schooled to think in terms of quantifiable, measurable results because that is what they have historically been measured on and rewarded for. They have difficulty identifying unique contribution or what they personally will effect, which will be their contribution to the result(s) to be achieved. What must they personally do, for example, which will aid the achievement of a profit variance year-to-date (YTD) of R170 000?

- People confuse activities with accountabilities/deliverables. People say what they are going to do, for instance, 'attend staff meetings at all contract sites', not what they are

Activities not Accountabilities

Attend staff meetings at
all contract sites

Scrutinise costs monthly

Meet with Product Houses, Segments,
Divisions monthly

going to effect/deliver by their actions. Actions/activities/effort are not, on their own, deliverables. A deliverable has only been made when something is effected or produced, which is of added value to someone else. What, for example, will be delivered/effected by the person as a result of attending staff meetings at all contract sites?

- They are too vague or generic. A deliverable has to be concrete and specific. It needs to state unequivocally what will be delivered in the next 90 days which is of value to someone else. When deliverables are too vague it is not possible to hold someone accountable (both positively and negatively) for the

Vague Deliverables

Identify any cost wastage, discuss with staff
and take appropriate action

Drive the One Chance Theme at every
opportunity

Successfully merge the cultures of X and Y
companies

Develop strategic relationship with clients

contribution that has been or not been made.

- People confuse 90-day deliverables with the day-to-day tasks which make up 80% of their jobs. On-going, routine tasks – for instance monthly billings – should not be included in a set of deliverables. What should be included are the critical few contributions which will both impact positively on desired results and provide personal growth for the person accountable for delivering them.

- 90-day accountabilities are often either overwhelming or conversely, a walk in the park. A good set of 90-day deliverables should be manageable but stretching.

- People have a tendency to duplicate the same deliverable at more than one level in the hierarchy. Someone will lay claim to a deliverable which should actually be the deliverable of his subordinate. As a result, his contribution is not appropriate to the level he occupies in the hierarchy.

- Another shortfall is to specify the 'what needs to be delivered' but not 'the standard at which it should be delivered'. Standards for tasks/deliverables are critical because they tell the person what doing the task well, or delivering to excellence, actually means.

- Finally, there is a tendency to put forward management accountabilities rather than leadership accountabilities. Words like ensure/check/monitor pertain to management. Leadership, on the other hand, is about providing the preconditions (Means and Ability) for contribution and then holding people Accountable for the contribution made.

The good news is that a set of 90-day deliverables does not have to be perfect first time round. A chance to improve on them is literally ninety days away. One manager 'fished out' his first set of deliverables, devised eighteen months previously, and said to me that he was embarrassed by their poor quality. In fact, for a first effort, they were very good. What a person needs to give in any case becomes increasingly apparent, but only with the passage of time. This is not about instant perfection.

THE BENEFITS/REWARDS FOR CLARIFYING CONTRIBUTION

Clarifying contribution enables contribution in a number of ways:

- Firstly, it provides focus both now and going forward. It helps people concentrate their efforts on those critical few things which really make a difference. It helps them remove the clutter from their day-to-day lives, to see what is really important/value adding in amongst the frenetic busyness which envelops most corporate souls.

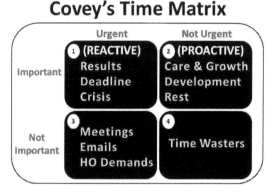

- Secondly, clarifying contribution helps a person to make the shift from reactive to proactive. Issues which are urgent (be they important or not) are those which tend to get attention. Because they are urgent they are reacted to. Issues which are important but not urgent (Covey's Quadrant Two), on the other hand, only get attention if they are deliberately planned for and people hold true to the plan. The process of clarifying contribution helps to shift people's focus to what is important; it enables people to change from being essentially reactive to being primarily proactive. It ensures that what will effect a move forward, both in terms of personal growth and improved results, actually gets done.

- Thirdly, clarifying contribution is empowering. This is because contribution, as opposed to results, sits in one's own hands/is in one's control. When people are focused on what they can do something about, they are obviously empowered.

OVERCOMING THE BARRIERS TO CLARIFYING CONTRIBUTION

All of the benefits outlined above are true. What is equally true, however, is that commitment by an individual to a set of deliverables for a defined period involves a risk. In making a commitment of this type, a person puts herself on the line far more than when she agrees to a set of targets. This is because it is always possible to rationalise away failure to achieve a target, to ascribe a below-target outcome to external factors. Failure to make an agreed contribution, however, is another matter. Contribution, as said before, sits in a person's hands. When the deliverable is not made there is no longer somewhere to hide.

Notably, it is the risk inherent in committing to a specific contribution which is initially what is apparent. The benefits of doing so, on the other hand – focus, proactivity, growth and empowerment – only become apparent over time.

For the very real barriers outlined above to be overcome requires the following:

- People need an opportunity to practise writing deliverables. They need to be given the space and time to develop competency at this task. To this end, an internal and/or external coach who helps people develop their expertise at this task can be useful.

- While people are learning how to clarify contribution, moreover, they should not be assessed or rewarded for their contribution. This is because, when assessment/reward is linked to defined contribution prematurely, people's focus shifts from genuinely seeking to make the best contribution that they are capable of to making sure they maximise their reward.

- From experience, people will only persevere with the process up to the time they begin to realise its benefits, if they are required to do so. Clarifying contribution, in other words, cannot be a voluntary process. Where organisations have successfully implemented the 90-day deliverables process, it has always been because a senior manager has insisted that the process be done. Further to this, people are held accountable for doing so.

In due course, people experience the benefits of defining contribution as far outweighing the effort involved. They wonder why they ever worked in any other way.

Care and the Issue of Time and Attention

Both the concepts of *Care* and *Growth* are often misunderstood. *Care* is frequently misconceived as a pink and fluffy thing, while *Growth* gets confused with ideas like the democratisation of the workplace or the rights of employees to advance in their careers. As one manager only half-jokingly said, 'in this organisation Care means "forgive me all of my sins" and Growth means "escalate my progress up the hierarchy".'

What Care really means, as the first of two criteria in any legitimate relationship of power and how it translates into practice in the context of leading others at work, is outlined below.

WHAT CARE DOES NOT MEAN

To understand what Care really means we need to start by debunking a number of myths about Care which still have credence in many organisations today.

Myth 1: Companies care.

The first myth pertains to the role that the company plays in Caring for its employees.

A common refrain in organisations is that 'the company (XYZ) does not care for its employees the way it used to in the past.' The 'past' may be two, ten or even twenty-five years ago. Our typical, and not very popular, response to this complaint is: 'Of course it doesn't. It never cared and never will do so. Companies don't care, people do.'

Company XYZ

To attribute a uniquely human characteristic or quality to a non-human being or an inanimate object, like an organisation, is clearly absurd. The technical term for this is anthropomorphism.

A particularly ludicrous example of this is the advent of *customer care systems* designed to do this 'care thing' on the organisation's behalf. The system conveniently generates a happy birthday message on the client's birthday, but may, also automatically, spit out a threat to close the same person's account the day thereafter.

> A 75-year-old friend of mine was so incensed by what his bank did, that he threatened to close his account of 50 years. After half a century, there was still no human relationship. He was still a number, a means to their end.

Myth 2: To Care is to look after employees' physical and material needs.

The second misconception is that Care is somehow synonymous with the work environment, with good working conditions and employee benefits. The degree to which management cares about its employees, in other words, is reflected in the company's facilities and levels of pay.

In fact this is not true. In the seminal research into trust in the South African gold mines in the 1980s, which laid the foundation for the Care and Growth model, it was found that living and working conditions on a mine did not affect in any way employees' trust in management. On a large, modern mine, where conditions were very good, trust in management was poorer than on any of the other mines, including those whose conditions were truly Dickensian.

A more recent testimony to this is a friend of mine who owns a saw-mill in Limpopo. In the three years since he has run the business, he has provided his labourers with decent accommodation on site and first-class safety equipment, while wages have increased by 120%. Despite this, the workforce is not content. They have joined a union and he is plagued by industrial relations problems.

The above does not mean that employees' physical and material needs should not be looked after by management. Legislative requirements aside, this is simply one of the costs of being in business.

Where conditions are in reality poor, employees quite rightly cite this fact as evidence of a lack of care. Mineworkers, who still use the change house facilities built for the original workforce after the mine expanded and the workforce doubled in size, clearly saw proof of a lack of care. Similarly, call centre managers residing in plush air-conditioned offices, with their agents in cramped and stuffy cubicles downstairs, were probably not unjustly seen to have limited concern for their people.

When conditions are inhumane or are such that employees' lives or health are endangered, then, in truth, management does not care. The then CEO of Anglo American, Cynthia Carroll, took unprecedented action in temporarily stopping production at some of the company's platinum mines due to their unacceptable safety performance. She was alleged to have said that 'we are killing our people because we don't care about them enough'. Harsh words, if she said them, and a bitter pill for management to swallow, but she could be right.

Even when the physical environment is pleasant, perceptions that management does not care often persist. I was once floored by a senior manager with over thirty years of company service when I asked him why he believed that the company he had worked for all of these years no longer cared. With tears in his eyes he said: 'They took away my newspaper.'

In his mind, and that of many of his colleagues, a lack of care equated with the taking away of privileges once deemed to be the just deserts of the wage slave – such as a company loan, housing support or access to company products at reduced rates.

"GOOD PAY, BENEFITS AND FACILITIES ARE NOT A SUBSTITUTE FOR CARE AND NEVER CAN BE!"

Clearly neither a continuation of paternalistic human resource policies, like those cited above, nor their modern equivalents – on site crèches, gyms or concierge services is what Care is all about.

Employee-focused policies and procedures are in fact 'caring carrots'. They bring certain people through the door and may earn a few points on a 'Best Company to Work For' survey. But good pay, benefits and facilities are not a substitute for Care and never can be.

Myth 3: Care is the job of Care specialists.

The third myth is that Care is something which could/should be done by experts in the field. It is evidenced in the growing number of Wellness Programmes, Employee Assistance Departments and the like, commonly housed in an organisation's Human Resources function. It is also seen in the increasing number of professionals, psychologists, life coaches, etc, brought in from outside the organisation for this purpose.

This myth is predicated on a notion that leadership is about achieving a result through people. The human problem can therefore be safely relegated to some third party, allowing those in the line of command to get on with their real work of producing results – be that production, sales, or maximising profits.

This notion is a fallacy. It denies the reality that a manager's right to demand delivery, to exercise power, is not granted on the basis of rank or because an employee is paid to deliver. Rather, a manager earns the right to ask someone to do something, to deliver, only if he cares about him sincerely.

To ignore this reality, to make Care someone's job other than the manager's, is not only wrong but dangerous.

In a manufacturing organisation, supervisors understandably saw their job as production since this is what they were measured on and reward-ed for. As a result, employees took their concerns to their shop steward. When their concerns were addressed, by the shop steward liaising with a manager up the line who had the authority to do something about them, the message to the employees from the shop steward was this: 'I have resolved your problem. See how much I care!' Guess who was trusted? Guess who workers were loyal to? Guess who ran the site?

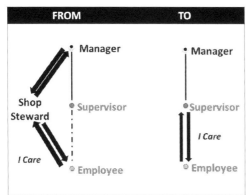

USEFUL SOURCES OF INFORMATION FOR EMPLOYEES

FROM	TO
1. Shop Steward	1. Posters and Signs
2. Co-Workers	2. Department Meetings
3. Department Meetings	3. Immediate Manager
4. Posters and Signs	4. Management Leaflets
5. Management Videos	5. Co-Workers
6. Immediate Supervisor	6. SHE Management
7. Notice Boards	7. Management Videos
8. Management Leaflets	8. Union Official
9. Union Meetings	9. Shop Steward
10. Public TV	10. Departmental Manager

An initial survey of em-ployee opinion in this company showed that the most useful sourc-es of information for employees were their shop steward and their co-workers (the grape-vine). Two years later there was much more emphasis on informa-tion sources emanating from management. The immediate manager in particular had moved from sixth position to third position.

The leadership had regained legitimacy in the eyes of their employees, not through an attack on the union, but through engaging with their people and doing what they should for them – caring and helping them to grow.

Referring the people issues to the People or Human Resources department is equally problematic. Again the research in the South African gold mines showed that, only when those in line roles were regarded as sympathetic to employee problems, was there positive trust in management.

Even the best Human Resources function cannot perform a surrogate role for managers in this regard. Employees are not fooled. They may make use of the department's services and programmes on offer, but they know that they are an abrogation of a manager's duty and they behave accordingly.

Human resources functions, psychologists and coaches have a role to play, but it is not to do the job of Care on the line manager's behalf.

THE PRECONDITIONS TO CARE

There is a precondition to Care and it is not a budget! For any manager to Care, firstly, she has to get to know and like those who work for her, as people, as human beings, not as human resources. Secondly, she has to have genuine regard for them.

I once asked a manager to tell me about any one of the seventeen people who reported to him. Victor (not his real name), he told me, was 'a hard worker who was generally reliable and good at his job'. Regarding Victor, the person, however, his knowledge was scant at best. This was despite the fact that Victor had been in his employ for over seven years.

In a Care and Growth workshop we sometimes ask managers to complete a Care Test for each of their direct reports.

What is interesting in doing this exercise is the range of scores. Some managers score well, even on the subordinate they know least. Others are shocked by how little they know about their people, even as employees.

How much managers know about their employees' personal circumstances is, more than anything else, a function of how much their people are of interest to them. Managers who care about their people, talk, as opposed to gossip, a lot about them. When these managers talk about their people they become animated. The inverse is true of those who don't really care. These managers, from observation, only really come alive when they talk about the business.

The degree to which a manager knows her people is both noticed and valued by them. Ross Duffy, a plant manager at AEL Mining Services, who knew, without being reminded, the favourite soccer teams of all 300 operators on his plant, was held in high regard. Similarly a CEO of First National Bank was legendary for enquiring, after a brief conversation eighteen months prior, whether a child was still struggling with his engineering degree.

To Care, however, requires leaders to not only know but also respect those in their charge. From experience this is not always the case.

> The majority of managers I spoke to at one organisation were very negative, bordering on hostile, towards their staff. Employees were consistently classified as 'lazy', 'arrogant', 'overly aware of their rights', 'unwilling to accept authority', 'having unrealistic expectations' and 'with an entitlement mentality'.

How valid their perceptions were is not the issue. The point is that relationships of mutual trust and respect are highly unlikely to develop as long as these views are the pervasive ones of those in authority. Simply put, it is hard to care for people, as their manager, if one neither respects nor has genuine regard for them.

The above may be an extreme case. Nevertheless the answers to two questions by subordinates in a Schuitema Leadership Assessment are very telling in this regard.

Both Leader B's and C's results are problematic, but Leader B's are more so. A manager who does not treat his people with respect does not respect them, and his people will intuitively know that.

	Score: Max: +10 Min: -10
Leader A	
My manager treats me with respect	5.3
I respect my manager	5.6
Leader B	
My manager treats me with respect	-0.9
I respect my manager	3.5
Leader C	
My manager treats me with respect	6.8
I respect my manager	2.7

For managers to love those in their charge may not be feasible, but without genuine regard for them as human beings, Care is simply not possible.

THE ESSENCE OF CARE IS INTENT

From the above, it is clear that Care is what one person does for another. In the context of legitimate relationships of power at work, it is what the leader does for those in his charge. For a manager to Care requires that he knows and respects the people who report to him as *human beings*, not as *human resources*.

The essence of Care, however, is intent, not behaviour. To Care for someone essentially means to have the best interests of the other at heart. It is, at the end of the day, an issue of the heart not the head.

This insight was first realised in the 'trust' research conducted in the South African gold mining industry in the 1980s. Managers, at every level in the hierarchy, were accepted or rejected on the basis of a single and very simple criterion: whether the manager had a genuine interest in the welfare of the employee. Trust was granted or withheld on this basis only.

That the core criterion is Intent is confirmed in a Care and Growth workshop when participants reflect on both the 'best' and the 'worst' boss they have ever worked for.

What distinguishes the 'boss from heaven' from the 'boss from hell' is not his biographical features, personality type, intellect, level of interpersonal skill, managerial style or behaviour. It is what is on the inside, not what is on the outside, which counts.

BOSS FROM HEAVEN AND HELL – WHEN/HOW DO YOU KNOW?

Boss from Heaven	Boss from Hell
"Things fell apart at work due to problems at home. Throughout that awful time she was always there for me."	"I really needed her support. But she wasn't going to stick her neck out for me if it meant putting her career on the line."
"In the last year before he retired he taught me all he knew. I was 22 years younger but they gave me his job when he retired."	"It was always about him. He was the hero, the person who did it all. He made me feel small."
"When the results were good he did not hog all the glory. He always gave me and others credit for our role in the success."	"He never listened. Our one-on-ones were very one sided. Even if I had an agenda, the focus was on what was important to him."

The Intent test is simply this – whose interests are being served? To what degree is the person prepared to suspend her own agenda for mine? The boss faces this test in every interaction she has with a subordinate. The more the subordinate's interests are cultivated, the more the boss grows in stature in the eyes of the subordinate, the more the boss is trusted and the more inclined a subordinate is to go the extra mile for the boss. A person's self-interest is indeed best served by serving the best interests of the other.

Clearly there is a continuum from malevolent/self-serving through to benevolent/serving the other. Good parents instinctively put the child's interests first, because they care unconditionally. Good managers put their employees' interests first. For most managers, however, this is not an involuntary or instinctive act. It is a deliberate choice they make which is fostered over time.

INTENTION AND ATTENTION

The prime indicator of what a person cares about is what she gives attention to and therefore where she spends her time. Those South Africans who were not in Paris spent the night of 20 October 2007 glued to a television screen to watch the Springboks defeat England in the Rugby World Cup Final. A person who works a 70-hour week and de-stresses on the golf course on the weekend is unlikely to convince loved ones that they are really a priority in his life.

By implication, therefore, a leader who Cares ensures that sufficient time and attention is spent on his people. When this is not the case, his people can only arrive at one conclusion: other matters are more important to the leader than them.

There are typically two reasons why a leader spends insufficient time on the Care and Growth of subordinates. The first reason is a means issue.

A manager's number of direct reports is the critical variable here, since there is a natural limit to the number of people a manager can meaningfully care for and grow. Nevertheless, in some organisations, team leaders are assigned between 60 and 70 direct reports. Even when work is routine and repetitive, and the leader is located in the same work area, Care and Growth for this number of subordinates is simply not realistic. The same is true of a senior manager with a dozen or so direct reports. In either case the only remedy is to change the structure so as to give those in command positions a manageable span of control.

Care and Growth AND Contribution to Results

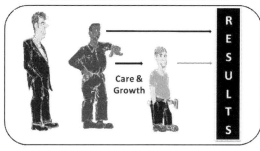

Care and Growth is also often compromised when a person is required to both make a direct contribution to the results and, simultaneously, to enable others to do so. A classic example of this is a sales manager, tasked with leading a sales team, while retaining responsibility for key accounts. Inevitability the Care and Growth aspect of the role takes second place, if it gets attention at all. Releasing the manager from personal delivery is the only lasting solution to this problem.

There are in fact a number of practical ways to provide managers with the means to spend sufficient time and attention on their people. Some examples include:

- **Specify a standard in terms of time spent.** At Continental Tyres in Port Elizabeth, factory shift managers were required to spend X% of any shift on the factory floor. The effect on scrap levels was dramatic. At Dulux South Africa, a sales director came up with a formula of 2x2x1 for his regional sales managers, where every one unit of time spent on administrative tasks was matched with two units of time on one-on-one/team discussions and two units of time on coaching sales people in the field. How the sales managers arranged their lives to do this was up to them.

- **Ensure geographic proximity.** Most obviously locate the manager as close as possible to her people. One company moved its plant managers out of the management office block into offices on the plant. At MBD Credit Solutions, only one work station was provided per four team leaders in the call centre. This meant that 75% of a team leader's time had to be spent on the floor rather than behind a computer screen.

- **Do whatever is necessary to reduce the amount of time that managers are holed up in meetings away from their people.** As the saying goes, most managers spend 16 hours a week in meetings, 8 hours preparing for meetings and an untold number of hours recovering from meetings! Schedule meetings for half the time normally allocated, allow people to attend only those aspects of the agenda that apply to them, be selective about who attends, and even (as was the case at a lysine plant in Durban) hold meetings standing up if that helps. One manager insisted that meetings with subordinates always took place in the subordinate's work area. A direct report of his told me that he had no idea what his boss's office looked like, because he had never been there.

- **Give managers total freedom/authority to decide when and where to work**. Both Ricardo Semler's concept of the 'seven day weekend' and Charles Handy's idea of 'a portfolio life' are instructive in this regard. A simple start may be for a manager to deal with the email tyranny while others fight the traffic – so that, when he gets to work, his full and undivided attention can be given to his people.

- **Provide crystal clear, and only a few, priorities.** One of the reasons managers don't have enough time is that those above them demand that they do too much all at once. The result of this is what Etsko Schuitema appropriately calls 'collective frenzy'. Facilitating a focus on what is critical (see the chapter *Clarifying Contribution*) is genuinely enabling of a person's time and attention.

Covey's Time Matrix

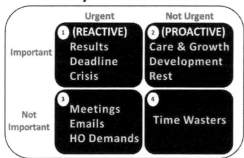

The primary reason for managers not giving sufficient time and attention to their people, however, is not because they lack the means to do so but rather the *will* to deliberately spend time with their people.

In terms of Stephen Covey's *Time Matrix*, all the Care and Growth activities (communicating, dealing with personal concerns, coaching, disciplining, etc) are Quadrant 2 activities. They are not about results or outcomes, they are about cultivating the capacity to achieve outcomes. They will only happen, therefore, when the boss's attention moves, from the results she wants to get from her people, to what she needs to do or contribute to enable exceptional people.

Covey's Time Matrix also highlights the fact that while Care and Growth are important activities, they are only rarely urgent. Clearly, if the entire workforce is toyi-toying (striking and provocatively dancing) outside the window, this is both an important and urgent matter! Generally, however, the Care and Growth of people is something that can be put off for another day and therefore typically is.

Things which are urgent (Covey's quadrants 1 and 3) are reacted to and therefore happen, be they dealing with a crisis (Quadrant 1) and/or responding to emails and telephone calls (Quadrant 3). Care and Growth activities, because they are not urgent, only happen if a leader is proactive – that is, she deliberately schedules for them to happen and then honours the schedule made.

This is as true of a team manager working on shift with a team of 20 operators as it is of the marketing director of a global business. The nature of the plan will differ from one context to another. A team manager knows realistically that Care and Growth will never happen during the frenetic start and end of a shift. The time to schedule Care and Growth activities is in the relatively quiet periods before and after lunch. These times, incidentally, tend to be empty times where nothing happens unless there is a crisis, like a machine breakdown to attend to. As a plant manager commented, these quiet times were times when team managers 'handed themselves over to God'.

Covey's insights are again useful here. As an exercise he takes a big glass jar with a number of fist-sized rocks next to it, each rock representing something important like a spouse, child, key customer, etc. Participants guess, and usually underestimate, the number of rocks that can be fitted into the jar. The now 'full' jar is not however really full. The many spaces between the rocks can be filled first with gravel chips, then with sand and finally with water.

The point that he is making is NOT that there are always gaps in the day and that, with enough stress and effort, you can keep putting more and more into a day. Care and Growth activities are like Covey's big rocks. If you put less important activities into your diary first (gravel, sand and water) then there is no room left for what is really important – Care and Growth. The correct thing is to schedule the Care and Growth activities first. That way it is amazing how many of them can be fitted in, leaving whatever time is left over for the less important stuff. As Covey says 'the main thing is to keep the main thing the main thing'.

THE LEADERSHIP DIARY

Before constructing a Leadership Diary it is useful for a leader to first review, from actual diary entries, where his time is actually spent. We recommend that leaders use the following filters to do this:

- Percentage of time spent in each of Covey's Quadrants 1, 2 and 3. Obviously no one diaries to spend time in Quadrant 4.

- Number of diary entries which are 'service down the line' (issues directly related to the Care and Growth of immediate subordinates) as opposed to 'service up the line' (events concerned with the boss's agenda or events focused on directly achieving an organisational result).

- Amount of time spent with each subordinate and how this aligns with his/her performance. If unequal time is being spent, is the focus of attention on the superstars or the squeaky wheels?

- For each of the eight Care and Growth activities (communicating, dealing with personal problems, coaching, team relationships, disciplining, rewarding, empowering and consulting), on which of those is sufficient time being spent, and conversely which are receiving limited attention?

In doing an analysis of where time is actually spent, a number of themes will emerge which need to be kept in mind when setting up a Leadership Diary.

OBSERVATIONS FROM ANALYSIS OF TIME SPENT

- ❖ 25% of time Q1. Too operationally involved.
- ❖ Spending too much time in meetings.
- ❖ Much email (1hr per day) is Q4.
- ❖ Currently spending <20% on Care and Growth. Should be at least 40%.

It is obvious that Care and Growth is a face-to-face activity and is therefore not something which can meaningfully be done by email! Moreover, Care and Growth essentially takes place in one or more of three contexts – one-on-one discussions, team meetings, or out in the 'field' where the subordinate is 'playing the game' or doing his job.

It follows logically that the starting point in setting up a Leadership Diary is for the leader to determine the appropriate frequency of individual meetings, team meetings and time spent in the field. Then to diarise accordingly.

Allied to this, the leader should consider each of his subordinates and ask the question: What are the 1-2 priority things that I need to give this person which will set him up for success in his role?

Note that there are only seven possibilities here in terms of what the leader can give: Care, Means, Ability, Discipline, Censure, Praise and Reward. Whatever should be given to each subordinate, should be translated into specific entries in the leader's diary in the near future – that is, within the next 90 days.

CHOOSE 2 PRIORITY AREAS PER SUBORDINATE

	Mpho	Rajesh	Sonja	Zola
Care	Concern for personal problem			
Means		Clarify standard and confirm authority in new role		
Ability				Coach her on new sales system
Praise/ Recognition				Publicly thank her for last job
Reward				
Censure	Warn attention is not on job			
Discipline			Fire her	

What the leader needs to give each direct report will obviously change as circumstances change and people grow. What is important is that what each subordinate needs to be given should be reflected, on an on-going basis, as an entry in the manager's diary.

In conclusion, Care is literally a license to Grow; it is the foundation block upon which Growth happens. For subordinates to grow, for the best in them to be realised, requires leaders to be intolerant of mediocrity and prepared to do whatever is necessary to enable the subordinate.

Even the toughest behaviour by the boss will be accepted by the subordinate, but only if he believes that what is being done is being done with his best interests at heart – if he believes that the boss really Cares.

Where genuine Care is missing, a leader may produce results and even be respected. But she will never engender the trust, loyalty and commitment of people that eventuate only when a boss genuinely Cares.

Growth by Handing Over Control

In its essence, the Growth 'role' of the leader is analogous to that of the gardener. The gardener does not grow the oak; he creates an environment conducive to the acorn breaking free of its shell and reaching to the sky.

Similarly, a leader does not grow those in his charge. It is not possible for one person to grow another. The best a leader can do is to provide a context which is helpful to her people in terms of advancing, rather than stunting, their maturity.

EMPOWERMENT/GROWTH

The gardener does not grow the oak

Indication of Growth

An increase in productivity, performance, ability, willingness, promotions, morale or results.

The primary behavioural measure of Care is time and attention since what a leader cares about is what he gives attention to, where he spends his time.

The measure of growth is different. Given that growth is a process which takes place over time, growth is evidenced in what has changed when people have grown.

When people are asked to come up with a single indicator – what they would point to as evidence that growth is happening – the suggested changes include 'higher productivity', 'better performance', 'enhanced ability', 'greater willingness', 'improved morale', 'career advancement', etc.

None of these changes, advantageous as they may be, are, we believe, the prime indicators of growth.

Improved results are not always synonymous with growth in people. Results can improve for

EMPOWERMENT

"Improvement in results is not always synonymous with growth in people."

"Growth does not mean 'accelerate my progress up the hierarchy'."

all sorts of reasons extraneous to the maturation of people. Similarly people can feel more positive, motivated or get a promotion sans development or growth.

EM/POWER

(AUTHORITY/CONTROL)

The critical change which evidences real growth is a change in scope of discretionary activity, in decision-making authority, in accountability. If people cannot make decisions which they were not previously making independently of their boss, if what they are accountable for does not change, then the leader is failing in the growth of her people.

Growth, or empowerment, requires the leader to go beyond asking people for their opinion, listening to them and only then deciding. It means giving up authority, handing it over and letting them decide. Ultimately it means living with their decision even when it is contrary to the decision that the leader would have made.

This in fact happened at Dulux South Africa, the paint manufacturer, a while ago. The recently-appointed marketing director came up with a new and different advertising campaign with the tagline *Any colour you can think of*. The managing director was dead against it. From time Immemorial the Dulux brand had only been associated with one thing, a big, sweet, shaggy sheepdog. Nevertheless he said, 'You are the marketing director, you decide.'

> Assume I am very knowledgeable in a job that both Fred and Joe have to do because I did that job in 1980.
> - "Joe, in 1980 I did what you have to do and what I did worked, don't argue with me. Do what I did."
> - "Fred, in 1980 I did what you have to do and what I did worked. It may be helpful to you. Take a look."

When authority is handed over so is control. Once control is suspended it is no longer possible to predict or to manage the outcome. As the Joe and Fred example illustrates, the outcome, in Joe's case, is both predictable and assured. The result will be the same as it was in 1980. In Fred's case however the outcome can no longer be foretold. The result could be better *or worse* than in 1980.

In the Dulux South Africa case the advertising campaign was ultimately a stunning success culminating in an increase in sales and a string of awards. Equally the campaign could have seriously undermined the Dulux brand!

DEMOCRATISATION OF THE WORKPLACE?

A leader has only empowered, therefore, when he has given up power. To enfranchise employees is only possible with its corollary – the disenfranchisement of management.

Democratisation of the Workplace

PROS √
- **Reduced bureaucracy**
- **Resilience**
- **Adaptability**
- **Initiative**
- **Innovation**
- **Engaged employees**
- **Tapping the collective wisdom**

Managers can typically argue with equal fluency both 'for' and 'against' a handover of decision-making authority.

The argument 'for' a democratisation of the workplace includes a reduction in overheads in the form of supervisory layers and auditing functions; less time wasted waiting for approval from on high; better decisions by those closer to the action; a more resilient and adaptable organisation less reliant on a few at the top; more engaged employees who are no longer resentful from being over-managed and controlled; increases in creativity, innovation and initiative at all levels, and so on ...

Democratisation of the Workplace

CONS X

- **Time Consuming**
- **Inefficient**
- **Loss of focus**
- **Dissipated energy**
- **Lack of alignment**
- **Pursuit of self interest**
- **Undue risk**
- **No predictable outcome**

Conversely, it is argued that democratisation is painfully slow and cumbersome; it undermines both productivity and efficiency; it leads to a loss of focus with effort being dissipated rather than aligned; letting employees, who may lack the skill or are not trustworthy, make their own decisions is simply too risky; experience shows that many employees don't want to take responsibility but want management to make the decisions for them, and so on ...

Needless to say, both sides of the argument, in the hands of eloquent presenters, can be compelling. In reality, the more critical question is: which of the two actually holds sway?

CURRENT REALITY

If people were in actuality being empowered this would be evidenced not only in a devolution of decision-making authority but also in reduced bureaucracy, flattened hierarchies, enabling support functions, and actions guided by policy, rather than prescription.

Although there is no internationally accepted empowerment standard or format for measuring a company's performance in this area (see the Empowerment Scorecard below), the majority of organisations that Schuitema has worked with over the past 20 years would not score well. In truth, a minimum number of our clients have fully empowered their

144

EMPOWERMENT SCORECARD

CATEGORY	SCORE 1-20
1. Vertical empowerment	7
2. Reduced bureaucracy	9
3. Flattened hierarchy	12
4. Enabling support functions	8
5. Action guided by policy not procedure	8
Total (Max 100)	44%

people. In our consulting capacity we have not always been successful in helping them really crack the issue of control.

While management may have become increasingly efficient, there is definitely more, not less, control. Despite some efforts to reduce layers, trim corporate staff groups and eliminate paperwork in the interests of saving costs, most employees have not gained more control of their lives.

This is evidenced in the following:

- Most decisions are made too high up in the hierarchy. The example, in a mining context shown here, is not untypical. The scope for empowerment is enormous.

VERTICAL EMPOWERMENT

Decision	Who makes it now?	Who should?
Approval of leave	HOD	Immediate manager – ultimately employee
Appointment decision	GM	Production Manager
Release of materials from stores	Mine Overseer	Originator
Discipline (dismissal)	GM	Presiding Officer (immediate manager / one up in the line)
Control of Budget	Section Manager	Mine Overseer
Approval of overtime	Senior Engineer	Engineering Foreman

- New, additional procedures are issued on a continuous basis while the number of cost centres and budget lines continue to multiply. Getting sign-off on even small expenditures is more and more arduous. It recently took us five months to get approval on a piece of work. Despite being a supplier to the organisation for over eight years we had to provide what felt like mountains of information. About the only thing they didn't require of us was a DNA sample! When managers use Schuitema's 'Snake-killing' methodology to determine which controls in their horizontal business processes can be removed, they are staggered by the possibilities. As a rule of thumb, whatever the process – from procurement to budgeting – it can be effected in half the current number of steps.

- People who have been in their jobs for five years generally report that they make fewer decisions now than five years ago. The frustration is not only felt by those at the bottom of the hierarchy. A CEO threw in the towel recently, no longer able to stomach the fact that he had to refer so many decisions to Chicago.

- In big corporates particularly, staff functions continue to grow. Generally staff functions are viewed as unresponsive and disenabling, rather than adding value to those in the line.

Failure to truly empower is an international phenomenon. According to an Employee Engagement Survey covering 86 000 employees in sixteen countries, a mere 14% of people were found to be highly engaged in their work. Reportedly 86% of those at work around the world are giving less of themselves than they could.

Similarly, Gary Hamel in his book *The Future of Management* (2007) could cite only a handful of companies globally which really empower their people. Notably his examples – Whole Foods, WL Gore & Associates, Google, Semco, a cement factory in Mexico and a software developer in India – are in different industries and locations.

This is not depressing. On the contrary, it is proof of the fact that real empowerment is not only possible but undoubtedly what will ultimately account for sustainable competitive advantage into the future. The challenge is to make what is currently an exception the norm.

ENGAGING THE WILL

A change in the status quo will only happen if, in the first instance, there is a will to do so. This is because energy for change is a necessary prerequisite for the change itself. This energy generally comes from a felt dissatisfaction with the status quo and/or a vision of a preferred future. The two forces of 'pain' and 'gain' are not necessarily mutually exclusive.

A crisis sometimes precipitates change in terms of authority and control. I have come across a few managers who have said they let go when the toll on their health and home life had finally become too great. The Brazilian businessman Ricardo Semler describes his defining moment most graphically in his book *Maverick* (1999). On a business trip to the US he collapsed and ended up in a clinic in Boston diagnosed as suffering from an advanced case of stress. He was told that he had two choices – 'continue your life, in which case you will be back with us, in a body bag, or change'. He was 25 at the time!

At an organisational level, turnarounds are typically initiated only once the organisation is in a state of crisis. Faced with the proverbial burning platform, real change, if it is not by then too late, is made.

The difficulty with the control problem is that it is experienced not as an acute illness but as a chronic infection.

The difficulty with the control problem, however, is that it is experienced not as an acute illness but more as a chronic infection. As such there is a tendency to live with and to tolerate the feelings of frustration, rancour, lethargy and impotence which too much control engenders – both in those being controlled and those doing the controlling.

People at all levels complain about the bureaucracy and do their best to circumvent or undermine the system. They opt for passive resistance rather than open revolt against the shackles which bind them.

A vision of a preferred future on the other hand, mobilises change through the promise of gains to come. The best visions are clear, concrete, shared and alluring.

The real risks of letting go loom large and just around the corner.

The advantages on the other hand are distant.

By definition, however, visions refer to what the world could be like at some future date other than now. Just as lifestyle changes spurred by desires to be thin, healthy and wealthy are snookered by the immediate possibility of a jam doughnut, nicotine fix or a shopping spree, so too are actions aimed at a future which is based on freedom rather than control.

The real risks which letting go and handing over control entail loom large and just around the corner. The advantages of doing so, on the other hand, are distant.

While increasing the positive or negative tension can go some way towards encouraging a handover of authority, a real determination to do so will only come once those in authority are truly convinced that they should do so.

This conviction can only be founded on a genuine belief that the pursuit of excellence in those in the leader's charge is the real purpose of leadership, not the achievement of a goal, vision or outcome through others; a belief that enables a conscious choice, by anyone in authority, to make his job nothing other than Care and Growth.

This conviction is a direct measure of the personal maturity of the person in charge. It is only from a place of personal maturity that a leader can evidence the requisite generosity and courage to relentlessly rise above the counter forces of fear and greed, which ensures a continuation and propagation of organisational controls.

The true spirit of the Third Axiom, the incremental suspension of control, can and will be realised, but only once those in charge finally grow up!

PRINCIPLES FOR DEALING WITH THE CONTROL PROBLEM

Managers' reluctance to practically tackle authority and control may be due to both the perceived enormity of the task and the risks inherent in doing so. When one considers all the 'things' put in place in pursuit of producing a predictable outcome (see a typical list of control mechanisms) one can forgive managers for viewing an onslaught on the control problem as tantamount to a deconstruction of the very organisation itself.

Control Mechanisms

THE INTENT TO PRODUCE PREDICTABLE OUTCOMES

Codes of conduct, access cards, targets, procedures, budgets, reporting lines, working hours, processes, operating instructions, job descriptions, limits of authority, policies, rules, meeting agendas, reports, contracts, organograms, deliverables, systems, auditing functions, etc.

Gripping the control problem, however, absolutely does not mean a wholesale obliteration of the systems and structures which make up an organisation while turning a blind eye to all the hazards in the process.

Controls have a vital role to play in any enterprise, but as a means not an end. The need for controls is fully recognised, but only when the aim of control is subordinate to the intention to empower, to produce people who are accountable for the contribution they make.

Dealing with the control problem is a continuous process, not a once-off project which will deliver a final solution in terms of either an organisation's structures or systems. For any empowerment process to succeed, however, there has to be a slavish adherence not to a rigid formula, but to the following three principles:

- Principle 1 – Do it incrementally.

- Principle 2 – Replace control with accountability.

- Principle 3 – Appropriate control.

Principle One: Do it incrementally

In practical terms, dealing with the control problem incrementally suggests that it is done slowly and with considerable patience. Even a leading icon of democratisation, Ricardo Semler, stated that after 12 years (of persistent effort) his business was only about 30% there.

Specifically the first principle suggests the following:

- One begins with the small things rather than the big things. One starts with allowing people to make decisions regarding what to wear, when and where to work, which meetings to attend, what title if any to put on their business cards, what to work on and how to execute their responsibilities. It progresses to giving people the reins in terms of operational decisions which have an impact on people and money. Ultimately it leads to inclusion in strategic decisions such as product changes, new markets, the location of assets, etc.

- It cautions against dramatic organisation-wide restructurings, favouring instead a series of finite adjustments to the organisational design. Similarly it does not mean that people should not be moved around, just not all of them all at once.

- It advocates stretching people continuously through new responsibilities and increased challenges, but not constantly tossing them in the deep end and waiting to see if they sink or swim. Certainly not promoting people when they are clearly far from ready and into positions way outside their abilities.

- It requires a gradual relaxing of rules and procedures, replacing them with broader policies and guidelines, not jettisoning all the rule books or burning all the paper in one glorious bonfire.

- It does not mean the closure of head office and a total disbanding of support functions. But it does suggest that these functions be trimmed down, with expertise built up in the field rather than stockpiled at home base miles from the action. Moreover, it suggests that support functions be weaned off their auditing and compliance function to rechannel their time and effort into enabling the line.

- It probably means opting for lots of small ideas made often rather than betting everything on an occasional big throw. It surely means encouraging experimentation by allowing the space and time for testing and learning; without having to get approval every step of the way.

Principle Two: Replace control with accountability

The real price paid for control is not in time and money. Strangely enough increased control, in the fullness of time, actually leads to an absence of control. A small example pertaining to compassionate leave makes the point.

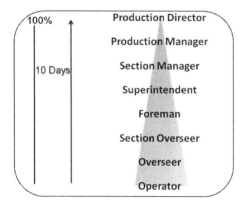

According to company rules, five rather than three days' compassionate leave was due if travelling time to and from the funeral necessitated it. It was not the overseer who authorised this however, but the production director, many levels and several kilometres removed from the bereaved employee. The average time taken to get approval was ten days which practically meant that the individual had been back at work almost a week before permission to go was granted. Further to this the production director had signed approval to every request made in the past year. The net effect of all this control was no control.

The way to get control is not to impose more control but to replace control with accountability. The stated purpose of the National Credit Act, instituted in South Africa in June 2007, was to restrain money lenders from giving credit to those who cannot afford it. To be a debt-free nation, however, requires those who overspend to be held accountable for their overspending.

The even bigger price to be paid for control is the absence of accountability. Whenever a control, in the form of a checker, is introduced into the system, accountability shifts from the person doing the task to the person controlling it.

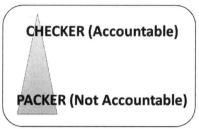

My husband and I go out at weekends to our cottage an hour from the city. The initial squabble over whose turn it is to pack the food box can become a full scale fight when it is discovered that the packer has left vital items at home. Endeavouring to get the weekend off to a good start, my husband volunteered to pack on condition I did a check of the contents. I rejected the proposal on the grounds that, as the checker, I would be liable for all omissions. His response: 'Can't we leave this Care and Growth stuff for the weekdays!'

Those doing the task will only take accountability for it when no one checks afterwards that they have done it. Only when this is the case, does it become possible to hold them accountable for doing the task well.

In practical terms, replacing control with accountability means the following:

- When there is a deviation from standard, the right action is not to impose a control on everyone but to find out who is responsible for the deviation and hold them appropriately accountable.

Three months before year-end the alarm bell rang in a banking environment when it was discovered that there was a significant variance from budget on the people line. An immediate freeze on recruitment was instituted rather than ascertaining which of the nine provinces were guilty of the transgression and punishing those guilty for their misdemeanour.

On average, 2-5% of any workforce will take advantage of an employer's trust. This is not a valid reason to subject the majority (the other 95%) to a system based on mistrust.

- Whenever authority is given, so too is accountability. Before people are granted the freedom to operate without control, a tight link must be forged between autonomy and accountability (both positive and negative).

Historically, when brokers sent through their client's application form to Old Mutual Group, two separate groups of people (Quality Controller and Verifiers) were engaged in ensuring that the policy document which went to the client was correct. Despite the phalanx of checkers in the process, the error rate was 20%. When a single job

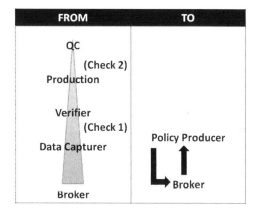

(Policy Producer) was created, and the name of the Policy Producer inserted in the policy document, the error rate reduced dramatically.

> At Whole Foods, the supermarket chain in the USA, decisions which are normally made at the centre – pricing, choice of supplier, store staff levels, product selection, in-store promotions – are made by those who work in and run each store.
>
> While employees at Whole Foods are highly empowered they are also highly accountable. Each store's performance relative to similar stores across the chain is known to all. Every four weeks those teams which have performed are rewarded with a bonus. They have the freedom to do the right thing. They are also rewarded for doing so.

In short, the incremental suspension of control which is implicit in the empowerment process is not possible without the concomitant growth in the accountability of the person.

 ### Principle Three: Appropriate control

Control is a tool in the growth process. It is a 'means' not an 'end'. As such, the level of control which is exercised must be commensurate with the maturity of the subordinate in the relationship. The starting point is the current level of maturity of the person being empowered. Over time, as a person matures, the degree of control should become less stringent.

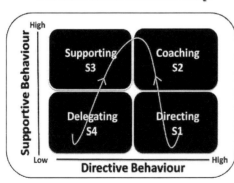

In this sense, Blanchard's Situational Leadership Model, which requires the leader to match the amount of direction and support that she provides to the needs of the follower, is useful. The leader's style changes from S1 (Directing), where decisions are made by the leader and announced, through S2 (Coaching)

and S3 (Supporting) to S4 (Delegating), where control is now with the follower. Which style the leader adopts with a particular individual at a point in time is dependent on the development level of the follower.

In practice it is possible to both over-control and under-control. If the leader is committing either error (over-control or under-control) this evidences itself in the follower's reaction. From an ability point of view, when people are able and the leader is over-directing, this induces resistance. Conversely, when the leader under-controls, by giving people something which they can't yet handle on their own, this leads to demotivation and to a loss of confidence.

From an intent perspective, when people who are trustworthy are not entrusted with something they become resentful and retaliate. Ironically in some instances, retaliation takes the form of them becoming untrustworthy, which then justifies the leader's lack of trust in the first place.

Conversely, trust which is misguided, in that control is handed over to those who can't be trusted, leads to disappointment and reluctance by the leader to trust again in the future. Those who are untrustworthy take advantage, while those on the side-lines may conclude that they can get away with it, too.

FINALLY DOING IT

Given everything that has been said so far, it is clear that an advance on the control problem should not be in the context of some grand plan. All that is required before finally 'doing it' is to make two decisions:

- Firstly, decide where to start. Whether to commence with a particular aspect – be it vertical empowerment, flattening the hierarchy, reducing bureaucracy, enabling support functions or shifting from policy to procedure or a combination of these.

- Secondly, decide how to ensure that the process is continuous and never ends.

Both decisions need to be appropriate to the individual organisation and its culture. Throughout the process, the three core principles – Incremental Suspension of Control, Replacing Control with Accountability, and Appropriate Control – need to be top of mind.

In addition, there are two tools or methodologies to assist line managers. *The Five Steps to Empowerment* is a method for incrementally suspending control in order to enable individual contribution. *Snake Killing* is a tool for reducing and removing controls in horizontal business processes in order to free up those who serve the customer (internal or external) to do so.

FIVE STEPS TO EMPOWERMENT

The Five Steps to Empowerment provides a structured sequence to follow where control is being suspended and people are being entrusted with authority.

These five steps would translate into the following in the instance of a project director entrusting each project manager with the authority to expedite purchases related to execution of the project plan.

5 Steps to Empowerment

1. Identify the next step
2. Teach people to take the step (why and how)
3. Test ability (why and how)
4. Hand over means
5. Hold people accountable

Step 1: Identify the next step – decide to entrust each project manager with his/her own credit card.

Step 2: Train (how and why) – teach the project managers how to reconcile the credit card statements to the company's accounts. Explain to them why they are being given the card and what the consequences for the project are if the cards are misused.

Step 3: Test Ability (how and why) – test the 'how' by giving each person a dummy set of accounts to see if he/she can reconcile them. Test the 'why' by getting each person to explain the importance of what he/she is being entrusted with.

Step 4:   Hand over Means – issue each project manager with his/her own card.

Step 5:   Hold people Accountable – dismiss X, who misuses the card, and hand over the case to the police for a criminal investigation.

The Five Steps to Empowerment tool can be used both to plan for enablement and as a diagnostic instrument.

Whenever an entrustment has been less than successful there is an opportunity created to review the reason(s) why this was the case. Was it because one or more of the five steps have either not been done or not done properly?

Was the next step not incremental enough? Was the training process poor or the importance of what was being entrusted, or the consequence of not doing it right, not understood? Was it assumed that the person was ready to assume responsibility when in fact this was not the case? Was the authority never actually transferred?   Once entrusted, did neither positive nor negative accountability transpire?

In Schuitema, consultants were entrusted with the submission of billing information on a monthly basis, a task which was not done to the required standard. On reflection it seems that the root of the problem lay with Steps Two and Five. The consequences to the business in terms of cash flow had not been understood. All negative consequences of non-compliance were borne by the business rather than the consultants.

All five steps are necessary but one step is more important than all the rest. It is Step Five. Unless there is a preparedness to do Step Five, there is no point in starting with Step One. This is because Steps 1–4 are the means to an end (Step 5). The end is not a delegated piece of work, it is the delivery of a person who accepts accountability and who is accountable for what he does.

SNAKE-KILLING

Snake-killing

Snake-killing as a process has similarities with the now well-known methodology called business process re-engineering. Both methods require documentation of the current (as it exists in reality, not in a procedures manual) and a specification of the ideal.

1. Identify the snake.
2. Identify the ideal.
3. Identify and remove superfluous controls.
4. Rank remaining controls from biggest to smallest risk.
5. Identify means and ability issues associated with each control.

The two methods however are used for very different reasons. Business process re-engineering is motivated by a desire to increase efficiency and reduce costs. The intent of the Snake-killing method is to empower or grow people.

Snake-killing as a method is also very deliberate about how to move from 'current' to 'ideal'. Applying the method requires an incremental approach. Controls are removed one control at a time. The removal of controls is, moreover, sequenced according to the risk involved, moving from smallest to biggest risk. Finally, to minimise the risk involved, the requisite means and ability must be in place before control is shifted from one person or place to another.

When organisations list their Snakes we find that the same 'puff adders' and 'pythons' come up irrespective of what the company does or what industry it is in. The top ten always include procurement, recruitment, the disciplinary process, the customer complaints process, repairs, budgeting and capex approval.

The controls that are in place in organisations are typically set up for the lowest common denominator and to cover any eventuality, both from the past and those which may happen in the future. What effective Snake-killing enables is initiative and creativity. It is about putting pressure on the system in such a way that pressure is put onto people to grow.

The sum effect of continuously working at and on the control problem is that neither the organisation nor its members are static. Both are fluid and ceaselessly changing.

As Charles Darwin said: 'It is not the strongest of the species that survives, nor the most intelligent. It is the one that is the most adaptable to change.'

SECTION THREE

Enabling Ability

The second precondition for employee contribution is that employees have the ABILITY to contribute. Ability means that people both know 'how' and 'why' to make the contribution required of them. Without the requisite Ability, employees cannot contribute optimally, even if they have the means and are willing to do so.

The leadership task associated with ensuring that people know 'how' to do what is required of them is coaching. *Coaching for Excellence* (Chapter One) deals with the role that leaders fulfil in continuously polishing and refining their subordinates' ability, as an end in itself.

The core argument in this chapter is that the potential exists for on-going learning in the tasks that a person executes anyway in order to perform his job. That is, a person can continuously grow without having to change his job or even take on new accountabilities. How leaders, as coaches, can use the job as the gymnasium, and the tasks to be done as the apparatus for developing the person, is the focus of this chapter.

There are two issues relating to Ability: the issue of the 'how' and the issue of the 'why'. The 'how' is subordinate to the 'why'. If someone has a good enough 'why', he will probably work out the 'how'.

The chapter *The Motivating Why* (Chapter Two) defines what those in authority can practically do to motivate those that they exercise authority over, within the broad ambit of caring for and growing them.

The 'Work Values Model' is used as a framework for understanding what motivates people at work. It explains what leaders can do to enable a shift in motive from 'taking' to 'giving' at work. In particular, it shows how they can unlock people's infinite capacity to act for reasons higher than self-interest in their working lives.

Coaching for Excellence in Ability

The Care and Growth model argues that the crux of the difference between management and leadership is an inversion of means and ends. Managers use people as the means to get the job done and produce results. Leaders use tasks and results as the means to enable people.

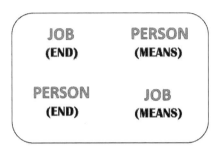

JOB	PERSON
(END)	**(MEANS)**
PERSON	**JOB**
(END)	**(MEANS)**

When there is a job to be done, a manager assigns the job to the person she perceives to be most willing and able to do it.

What concerns a manager is that the required output, in terms of both quantity and quality, is delivered. Whether the person who does the job is excellent or mediocre is in fact immaterial. Excellence in the person is not the manager's job.

A leader, unlike a manager, is concerned with the excellence of her people. A leader is relentless in the pursuit of excellence in people not as a means to an end, but as an end in itself. The tasks to be done, and the results to be achieved, provide the leader with an opportunity to achieve just that.

The coaching process enables those in positions of authority to make a fundamental shift in means and ends. This is because coaching requires a leader to deliberately use the task as the means to enable a person – more specifically, to bring about the highest levels of excellence in a person's ability.

THE EIGHT REALITIES OF COACHING

Eight commonly-made statements about the realities of the coaching process provide a useful vehicle to convey what the Care and Growth model believes about this critical aspect of leading others.

	TRUE	FALSE
STATEMENT ONE: Coaching is a useful process for improving employee contribution.		√

This statement is only partially correct. Coaching is an exceptionally useful process for enabling or improving employee contribution but ONLY when the issue affecting contribution is ability. Coaching is not useful when either means or accountability issues are at stake. This is because means issues are remediated through the provision of means, while accountability issues are addressed by holding people accountable.

To Grow Someone means to Empower Him:

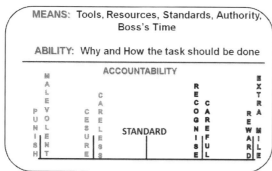

Neither means nor accountability issues suggest coaching. In fact, using coaching on an accountability issue, which by definition is a matter of the will, is detrimental because doing so entrenches the 'soft' mistake. Accountability issues, be they of carelessness or malevolence, require some form of *sanction*.

Failure to sanction, when sanction is appropriate, not only leads to those who are careless or malevolent escaping accountability, but convinces others that they can get away with it, too. Coaching for accountability issues, in the fullness of time, cultivates the conditions whereby no one in the organisation is accountable for anything.

	TRUE	FALSE
STATEMENT TWO: People can be coached to do anything if the coach is good enough.		√

In the Care and Growth model a distinction is made between capability and ability. Capability is akin to talent: it is the foundation block upon which ability can be built. The absence of a capability or a talent which is essential for performance in a particular role must inevitably impede success in the role.

This does not mean that sheer willpower won't assist someone to get a little better at something, especially if it is critically important to him to do so. It also does not suggest that dedication to the acquisition of specific knowledge and skills cannot go some way to counter an absence of talent.

What it does indicate, however, is that even the best coach cannot fabricate talent which is not there. The most a coach can do is work with what is there in the first place.

When there is a significant disconnect between a person's actual capability and the capability required to perform well in a particular role, then coaching is not the best route to follow. The better solution is to fit the person to a role that matches his capability – as Jim Collins says in his book *Good to Great*, to 'put the person on the right seat on the bus'.

Even a small change in fit can have a dramatic effect both on a person's performance and his motivation. Conversely, failure to recast the person into a role for which he has the requisite capability can only result in poor performance and an on-going sense of failure. The right thing to do, the caring thing to do, is to remove the person from the role.

	TRUE	FALSE
STATEMENT THREE: Superior ability is inborn.	√	√

There is a widely held belief that superior ability is inborn – that talent is innate. Moreover, that superhuman performers are those who are truly 'gifted' in a particular area and fortunate enough to discover their extraordinary talents early in life.

The counter view is that superior ability, in any area, is not determined at birth. In fact the only clearly innate limit to the development of ability is a physical one. General abilities like IQ and memory, which have a genetic component, may predict performance on an unfamiliar task but are not predictive of success thereafter. Even personality traits, although they may have an effect on the specific field in which an individual is likely to excel, do not limit a person's achievement in general.

The Care and Growth model is not wed to either side of the talent debate. Both the view that people either have talent or they don't, and the thesis that people can be good at anything, are too extreme.

In any event talent, whether it is innate or developed, is not necessarily the critical factor, and certainly not the only variable, which accounts for excellent performance. There are clearly numerous factors, including upbringing, dedication and luck, among others, which account for superior performance.

While the talent debate rages on, the Care and Growth model continues to subscribe to a firm belief that good leaders significantly affect the continuous growth in ability of their people by, among other things, coaching them effectively.

	TRUE	FALSE
STATEMENT FOUR: Developing excellence in anything takes time.	√	

While the will can change in an instant, an increase in ability does not happen immediately. The development of any ability or talent takes time.

Prodigious ability in a specific domain apparently takes many years to come to fruition. According to the neurologist Daniel Levitan (cited by Malcolm Gladwell in his book *Outliers* (2009)), roughly ten thousand

165

hours of practice is required to achieve real mastery. He says no one has yet found a case in which true world-class expertise was accomplished in less time.

An extraordinary investment of hours, however, is not on its own enough. People can work at something for most of their lives, being good at what they do, but never exceptional. Apparently it is necessary, but not sufficient, to work hard and put in the hours.

THE 10 000 HOUR RULE

Ten thousand hours of practice is required to achieve the level of mastery associated with being a world class expert. No one has yet found a case in which true world class expertise was accomplished in less time.

Daniel Levitan (neurologist)

In addition, according to Anders Ericsson (also cited by Malcolm Gladwell), who coined the term *deliberate practice*, what is required is concerted, repeated and focused engagement with the intention to improve what is being done. Deliberate practice is in fact the key to excellence. Moreover, deliberate practice is most effective under the guidance of a coach.

	TRUE	FALSE
STATEMENT FIVE: Excellent performers also need coaching.	√	

Every great athlete has a coach. In most fields of endeavour, not only in sport, those who have become exceptionally good at what they do have received help along the way and continued to do so even in their prime. The person who provided help in achieving excellence acted as a coach or mentor, whether or not she was formally designated as such.

There are of course exceptions to this rule. Roger Federer, for example, spent most of his career without a coach, analysing his own game and making changes himself.

In a world of ever-rising standards, however, getting really good at something without a coach is rare.

	TRUE	FALSE
STATEMENT SIX: Coaching should focus on improving areas of weakness; strengths take care of themselves.		√

Marcus Buckingham (2004) puts forward the argument for focusing on strengths rather than weaknesses. He maintains that excellence, be it of an individual or a group, comes from maximising strengths, not from minimising weaknesses. Improving on weaknesses at best leads to mediocrity, making someone average but never outstanding.

It is difficult to think of any aspect of Tiger Woods' game, until recent times, as being less than perfect. Allegedly, however, he isn't totally amazing at getting out of bunkers. This of course may be because he rarely gets into them! The undisputed strength in his game, however, has been his drive. Hearsay has it that this is what his coach spent most of his time on. As a result, something which was already an exceptional strength for Tiger Woods became at a time unequalled in the world.

From a Care and Growth perspective, coaching should be for both strengths and weaknesses. Coaching can both make a weakness less of a weakness and a strength more of a strength.

	TRUE	FALSE
STATEMENT SEVEN: Coaching is the same as on-the-job training.		√

On-the-job training and coaching are distinctly different. Training, be it on- or off-the-job, aims to increase a person's knowledge or skill in a particular area. Coaching has a higher goal. Its purpose is to enable the person being coached to realise the very best in himself from an ability point of view.

Training is, or should be, an integral part of the empowerment process. Before handing over a specific task or new accountability to someone, the person should be given the means and ability he needs to take on the

167

accountability. Both Step 2 (teaching) and Step 3 (testing) for competency are vital for the success of the empowerment process.

Unlike training or teaching, however, coaching is not about the transfer of skill or knowledge from one person to another. Coaching is about being able to see the potential ability that is in the other person and helping to bring it out.

5 Steps to Empowerment

1. Identify the next step
2. Teach people to take the step (why and how)
3. Test ability (why and how)
4. Hand over means
5. Hold people accountable

Two different artists put it best. Michelangelo said 'my work is to release the hand from the marble that holds it prisoner'. In a similar vein, the sculptor Henry Moore said of his famous sculpture of a horse: 'I call the horse out of the rock. I take away all the rock which is not the horse.'

	TRUE	FALSE
STATEMENT EIGHT: A person will only respond to coaching once his will has been engaged.	√	

A precondition for coaching is that the person's will to learn has been engaged; that the person has accepted accountability for his growth. If a person is unwilling to learn and has not accepted accountability, then it is premature to coach the person.

There is a process for enabling accountability in a person but it is not coaching. It is a counselling or mentoring process called the Gripe to Goal process (see the chapter *Making Masters*, Section Five).

The Gripe to Goal process addresses matters of the will. It therefore pertains to issues of intent, not ability. As a process, it enables the maturation of a person's intent from being here to *get* to being here to *give*. It puts the person in a state to hone his ability to the highest level of excellence.

CRITICAL REQUIREMENTS OF A COACH

There are some fairly obvious requirements to be a successful coach – characteristics which all good coaches have in common.

A GOOD COACH

- ✓ **Is knowledgeable**
- ✓ **Exercises patience**
- ✓ **Avoids teaching**
- ✓ **Is a tough taskmaster**
- ✓ **Shares the limelight**

In the first instance, a good coach needs to be knowledgeable, but not necessarily more skilful or expert than the person being coached. To be a good tennis coach, for example, requires an understanding of the game, but not a level of play equal to, or better, than the person being coached.

Secondly, a coach needs to exercise patience. The person will not learn if the coach becomes impatient and intervenes too early or, worse still, takes over and does the task for the person being coached.

Thirdly, the good coach enables learning, not by teaching, but by helping the other person to learn. The primary skills of coaching therefore are listening, observing and giving feedback, not the transfer of information. The good coach is able to see what the person herself cannot see and then conveys what he has seen. He is able to convince the person what she should be working on next in order to improve her ability.

Fourthly, a coach must be a tough taskmaster. Most people under-perform because they don't push themselves to their limits. The good coach performs a critical role by taking the person beyond her comfort zone. In order to do so the good coach is likely to be exceedingly tough, even hard, on the person. While the person being coached is unlikely to enjoy the experience, she will accept what the coach is doing because she knows that it is being done in her best interest.

Finally, the good coach puts his significance second to that of the person being coached. He recognises that ultimately it is the player, not the coach, who gets up on the podium. He is, therefore, not only prepared to share the limelight, but deliberately puts his own need for recognition to one side, making it possible for the person he is coaching to shine.

The single most important requirement for successful coaching, however, is the intention of the coach. This becomes obvious only when the true transformation that is the purpose of coaching is understood.

What Coaching Effects

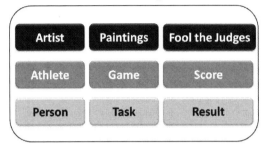

An episode from the BBC series *Faking It* illustrates the point. In one of the episodes, a painter of houses is plucked out of his small business in Liverpool and taken to London. Once there, three coaches work on him around the clock for a month, after which he exhibits his paintings at an art exhibition along with four commercial artists. Of the three leading art critics brought in for the task, only one is able to identify him as the fake.

In one month the coaches are able to transform a decorator from Liverpool into a 'Rembrandt'. What the three coaches produced was an artist, who then produced a set of paintings which fooled the judges.

Similarly, in sport, what the coach delivers is an athlete who is able to play the kind of game which puts the winning score on the scoreboard. In the workplace, also, the measure of the leader/coach's success is the degree to which the person being coached has changed. It is the transformed employee who then excels at the task(s), which leads to positive organisational results.

What this suggests, quite simply, is that coaching is a 3rd Attention engagement. The conventional manager operates in the 1st Attention (is here to get/achieve the *result* with the person as a *means* to that end).

Progress to the 2nd Attention is made when the manager's attention shifts from the result to the task. In practical terms this happens when the person in authority makes it her business to provide the required means, ability and accountability which will enable excellence in the task. This is evidence of giving but is nevertheless still a *giving to get*.

Only when the superordinate is finally focused exclusively on polishing and refining the person, as an end in itself, is the leader/coach in the 3rd Attention. This is because, for the first time, the leader is truly *giving unconditionally.*

WHAT IS COACHING?

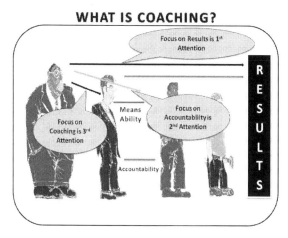

This is hugely significant for two reasons. Firstly, it is only when the relationship between boss and subordinate is a coaching relationship that both parties are being empowered. This is because the boss and the subordinate are now focused on what they can do something about, namely effect a change in the person being coached.

Secondly, whenever leaders put themselves in the role of coach they automatically make the task and the result the concern of the person being coached. Ironically, the degree to which the coach puts attention on the person, and is therefore prepared to take a risk with the task and the result, is the degree to which the person owns both the task and the result.

SHIFTING FROM A REPORTING TO A COACHING RELATIONSHIP

For a person to continuously hone and improve her ability it is not necessary for her to change jobs or even to take on new accountabilities within her current role. The potential for on-going learning exists in the tasks that the person has to execute anyway in order to perform in her present job.

The change that has to happen is not a change in job content, but a change in how the tasks which make up the job are viewed. Whenever a task is performed, an opportunity exists to address a learning requirement or development need in the person. The task becomes the means to strengthen a specific ability in the person, rather than an end in itself.

Etsko Schuitema (2004) in his book *Leadership: The Care and Growth Model* suggests that the job that the person is doing be seen as a gymnasium and the tasks to be done as the apparatus for developing the person. A good gym instructor matches the athlete's learning need (for instance, stamina) to the appropriate apparatus (for instance, treadmill). Similarly, a good coach in the workplace matches a chosen learning need to those task(s) in the job that put pressure on the learning need.

The example given shows the key tasks performed by a management consultant.

LEARNING OPPORTUNITY	TASK
Listening	1. Identifying potential clients
	2. Making sales calls / presentations
	3. Writing proposals
	4. Facilitating workshops
	5. Designing new products / services
	6. Designing an intervention
Conceptual thinking	7. Conducting onsite diagnosis
	8. Coaching individuals
	9. Consulting on implementation
	10. Building client relationships
	11. Managing implementation projects / coordinating delivery
	12. Reading relevant texts

Every time the consultant makes a sales call or presentation, facilitates a workshop, coaches a client, consults on an aspect of implementation, builds a relationship or coordinates delivery on a client project, the opportunity exists to improve the consultant's listening ability.

The task(s) which put pressure on the consultant's conceptual ability, on the other hand, include the design of new products, a diagnostic exercise, design of an intervention, and again consultation on implementation within the organisation.

The critical insight here is that all jobs have within them a possibility for learning and growth. This is true even of a call centre agent tasked with contacting clients and verifying their personal details for eight hours of the day. Each call made by the agent provides the means, if it is used as such, to enhance the agent's diplomacy or influencing ability. Whenever a leader deals with a subordinate from hell likewise offers the possibility of developing what is a key leadership competency – that of confronting.

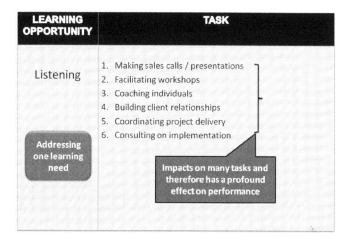

Training typically enables the performance of a single task. Coaching, however, has a much more profound effect. In the example of the management consultant above it is clear that addressing the one learning requirement (in this case listening) impacts on many tasks and can have a dramatic effect on the consultant's overall performance.

Practically, therefore, using the task and the result as a means to enable the person means the following:

Firstly, the coach needs to ascertain the competencies which differentiate the average from the superb performer in a particular role. Secondly, based on an assessment of a specific individual's learning requirements, the coach should select a competency as the focal point of the coaching interactions that she has with the person.

The chosen competency should remain the key element in the interactions between the boss and the subordinate until such time that both parties are convinced that real progress has been made. At that point, attention shifts to strengthening another ability in the person.

A coaching relationship is clearly very different from a conventional reporting relationship. In a conventional reporting relationship the person is there to produce a result, not to spend time improving her abilities. The routine interactions between boss and subordinate are therefore typically centred on progress against agreed tasks/deliverables.

In a coaching relationship the conversations between boss and subordinate are very different. Most importantly they include content which is not there in a conventional reporting relationship. In a coaching relationship what is discussed is the subordinate's progress against a learning requirement, what constitutes the next learning opportunity for the subordinate, and what tasks will enable the person to strengthen the ability which is the current focus of the coaching.

THE COACHING CYCLE

Coaching is not a single event. Rather it is a series of activities which re-peat themselves over and over in an on-going cycle. Coaching activities which make up the cycle are *reviewing*, *monitoring* and *designing*.

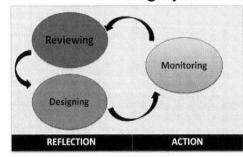

The purpose of the Review is diagnostic. It requires the coach to reflect on what the person needs to learn and what then will become the focus of the coaching. The product of the Review is the identification of a learning need and the specification of a learning opportunity.

174

The remedial activity in the coaching cycle is concerned with Designing and setting the task(s) which will enable the person to strengthen whichever ability is the current focus of the coaching.

The Monitoring activity requires the coach to observe the person while he is doing the job and give the person feedback on what she has observed. The aim of the observation is for the person being coached to both gain insight into his mastery of the current learning requirement and to identify what the next learning opportunity is for him.

The Review and Design activities take place off the job, in a one-on-one conversation between the leader and the person being coached. The Monitoring task, on the other hand, takes place while the person is actively doing his job.

Within the coaching cycle, moments of action and reflection repeat themselves over and over again. In due course, what changes is the specific learning opportunity and, hence, those aspects of the person's job which are the points of focus in the coaching relationship.

▷ Identifying the learning need and the learning opportunity

A good sports coach would never work on all aspects of an athlete's game simultaneously. Similarly, in the work context, it is appropriate for the coach to focus on and work to improve only one aspect of the person at a time.

What the coach does in this phase of the coaching cycle is help the person to identify very specifically what he should be working on and to phrase this as a learning opportunity.

Some examples of learning needs and learning opportunities for individual managers are given below.

By definition, a learning opportunity is a defined ability or competency which can be enhanced through coaching. A learning opportunity is not a particular skill (for instance, reading a profit and loss statement) or a piece of knowledge (for example, how to draw up a business plan), both of which are best addressed through training.

A learning opportunity is also not a value such as respect or honesty. A value is what a person is prepared to put his self-interest second to. As such it has nothing to do with ability. It is a matter of the will.

	LEARNING NEED	LEARNING OPPORTUNITY
A	Talks too much and does not get to the point. Is unstructured and not direct.	Communicating clearly and succinctly.
B	Does the work of his subordinates. Interferes when things go wrong.	Handing over accountability/letting go.
C	Keeps referring back to boss for clarity. Requires a level of structure and detail inappropriate to the job.	Being independent/self confident.
D	Is too nice/too empathetic. Does not challenge. Effect is to feed/cultivate victim mentality.	Confronting/challenging victim behaviour.

The role of the coach in the Review phase is to elicit the diagnostic information which leads to the specification of the learning opportunity. When the person being coached has a high degree of self-awareness, the information can be elicited from him directly. Alternatively, the coach needs to source the diagnostic material either through direct observation, or by getting input from those who can bear witness about how the person performs in real time.

Watching the person doing the task and determining what he needs to learn next to improve his ability

The purpose of *watching the game* is to identify what it is *specifically* that the person needs to learn which will further improve his ability. The problem with a learning opportunity, stated as a competency, is that it is still too global.

What does the person need to improve/change in order to enhance his listening ability for example? Does he need to learn not to interrupt? Is it that he is not fully present? Is he analytical, and therefore able to ascertain the crux of the issue, but insensitive to the feelings behind the facts?

Only by watching the game, while it is being played, can the coach put her finger on the next step forward for the person in terms of the ability which is the current focus of the coaching.

The insight gained by the coach is of course only useful if it is conveyed to the person in a manner that convinces the person of what he needs to work on next to improve his ability. There are a number of obvious dos and don'ts when it comes to giving feedback. The crux of good feedback, however, is that it looks to the future. It tells the person how to do better going forward, not what he did wrong.

Setting the task(s) which put pressure on the learning need

Practice task(s) are, or should be, deliberate. The coach does not simply implore the person to go out there and work on his listening, delegating or whatever. Rather the coach determines the specific task(s) which, when performed, will put pressure on the current learning need.

Practice tasks can be designed well or badly. The best practice activities stretch the person beyond his current abilities. They require the person to stretch just out of reach of his current level of ability. They place the person in a learning zone.

Task(s) which are in the person's comfort zone, on the other hand, fail to extend ability since by definition they are already activities which can be done easily. Activities which are too hard engender panic rather than learning.

Specific task(s) which can be used to pursue particular learning opportunities are as shown in the following table.

Person	Learning Opportunity	Task(s) used to pursue Learning Opportunity
A	Communicating clearly and succinctly	Project and team meeting agenda. Specific items to be presented in given timeframe.
B	Handing over accountability	Daily review of work categorised into task(s) which should have been done by self versus should have been delegated / report back on negative exceptions in own area and how dealt with.
C	Independence / self confidence	Responsibility for project implementation on specific site. Agree upfront limit of support to be provided.
D	Confronting / challenging victim behaviour.	Feedback to client on diagnostic findings / particularly client's role in the perpetuation of organisational dysfunction.

Part of setting the task(s) is for the coach to agree the level of support/ monitoring she will provide while the task is being performed. The amount of support provided by the coach must of course be directly proportional to the level of ability of the person being coached.

Superficially, coaching can appear to be a relatively easy, if not mechanistic, aspect of a leader's Care and Growth role. Nothing could be further from the truth. Engaging in the coaching cycle, unconditionally, with no motive other than to realise the very best in the other person tests the very essence of a leader's generosity and courage.

It clarifies, like nothing else does, how far the leader is really prepared to go or to what extent the leader is prepared to sacrifice her own interests to realise the very best in the other.

The Motivating Why?

A core belief that underpins the Care and Growth leadership model is that the key determinant of an individual's motivation at work is the nature of the relationship which exists between the individual and his immediate manager.

Only when those in command positions make, as their primary purpose, the care and growth of those that report to them directly, will employees be truly motivated to do what is asked of them and more.

The question which arises most obviously from the above is *what can those in authority practically DO to motivate those that they exercise authority over* within the broad ambit of caring for and growing them?

This is an important question because, as Gary Hamel points out in his article *The Hole in the Soul of Business* (2010), only 20% of employees are truly engaged in their work, heart and soul.

Before we can answer the question of how leaders can motivate their employees, however, we must first ask another question: *what does in fact motivate people at work?*

THE WORK VALUES MODEL

The focus of the 'Work Values Model' was initially on what motivates those in leadership positions in organisations. The model has subsequently been extended to include the motivation of anyone at work.

The basic premise of the Work Values Model is that what differentiates people at work is their motive. More explicitly, is their motive primarily a *giving* or a *taking* motive? On the basis of this first distinction, people's reasons for going to work can be placed on either the left side or the right side of the model.

Superimposed on the *taking* versus *giving* distinction is another distinction: the difference between focusing on *people* or *things*. Giving, in other words, can be to other people or to things. Equally, taking can be from things or from other people.

Work Values Model

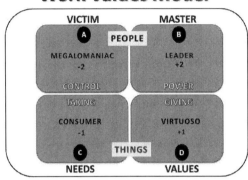

This further distinction *people* versus *things* results in four different types of motives or reasons for going to work. They are depicted in the Work Values Model as four quadrants, A through to D.

All the reasons for going to work on the left side of the model are about the satisfaction of one's needs, about getting for oneself what one wants at work. They are in essence about the pursuit of one's own agenda.

What differentiates the A from the C quadrant, however, is the source of the satisfaction. In Quadrant A what the person wants can only be given or come from other people. In Quadrant C, on the other hand, the source of the satisfaction is the job itself or things associated with the job.

In contrast to the left side of the model, all the reasons for going to work on the right hand side are *giving* reasons. People with these reasons for going to work do so for reasons that are bigger than their immediate self-interest. These reasons we refer to as *values*.

The reasons for going to work in Quadrant B are reasons which have a positive impact on other people, be they individuals, groups, society or the world at large. Quadrant D reasons, on the other hand, impact positively on the work itself and on the environment in which the work takes place.

In short, people's behaviour at work, at any given time, can be driven by their *needs* or their *values*. Which of the two takes precedence is a matter of choice.

A person's reasons for going to work, in other words, are not predetermined or set in stone. Accordingly, a person can on two different occasions have the same or different reasons for going to work. Irrespective of their circumstances, why people go to work sits in their hands only. They decide.

The Four Quadrants

Quadrant A

Quadrant A can be summarised as the need for power over others and/or harmony with others.

All the reasons for going to work in this category arise from a need for recognition, a need for significance, for acceptance by others.

The Quadrant A needs are expressed behaviourally in one of two ways: there is a 'hard' outer

> **QUADRANT A – TAKING / PEOPLE (MEGALOMANIAC)**
>
> I come to work ...
> - To pursue my brilliant career
> - To be the top performer
> - To be in a position to influence others
> - To control the output of others
> - To be recognised for my contribution
> - For companionship
> - For the status which comes with my position
> - For a sense of belonging

shell associated with the need for power over others and a 'soft' underbelly, which relates more to the need for harmony with other people.

An extreme example of the need to be on top (excuse the pun) took place on Mt Everest one year when two parties of climbers were making their bid for the summit. The Indian party got into trouble, ran out of oxygen and collapsed in the snow. When the Japanese climbers caught up with them they elected not to share their oxygen but to continue on their quest to stand on the top of the world. On their way down they stepped over the Indians, all of whom had died in the interim. Amazingly, when the Japanese got back to base camp they were brazenly open about what they had done. In their minds being one of a handful of people to bag the highest peak in the world took precedence over attempting to save the lives of fellow mountaineers.

What underpins the hard outer shell is a drive to succeed as reflected by one's position, level or status relative to other people at work. The label 'megalomaniac', derived from the condition megalomania, meaning the delusion that one is great or powerful, is apt here.

Like the Japanese climbers there are people at work for whom winning is all-important. They will do whatever it takes to achieve their goals, to be successful. Their extreme competitiveness is experienced by others as ambition, sometimes even as ruthless ambition. Woe betide anyone who gets in the way of these people on their path to the top.

Similar to a need to win is a need to dominate or to control other people. This need is expressed as a desire to be in a position of authority, to be able to control other people and get them to do what one wants them to do. Ultimately, to have the destiny of other people at work in one's hand.

Slightly more subtle is the need to influence others and to have them aligned to one's point of view. At an extreme, this need to influence others is experienced as the person always having to be right or insisting on having the last word.

The soft underbelly of a need for significance, on the other hand, is evidenced as the person acting to secure and maintain harmony in his relationships with other people at work. A need for affiliation, acceptance, popularity or friendship, are all examples here. Common to all of these needs is a basic need, which we all have as human beings, to be liked.

The need for harmony is expressed differently by those who are in positions of authority and those who are not. Those in authority, who are strongly affiliative, have a need to fraternise with their subordinates. Their need to be closely connected, to be friends with their people, can make it difficult for them to establish an appropriate distance from those in their charge or to take disciplinary action when it is required. Taken further, a strong need by a leader to always put the relationship first can result in nepotism or undue patronage of people with whom the leader has a special relationship.

Non-managers within an organisation who have a strong need for acceptance are susceptible to peer pressure. Fear of being rejected by the group can lead to them going along with something, even if they don't agree with it or believe it is right. Similarly, this need can result in them keeping quiet about injustices that are occurring within their organisation. One of the reasons why whistleblowers, for example, are so rare is because they know that in speaking up they face almost certain exclusion and isolation by other members of their group.

Quadrant C

The reasons for going to work which sit in Quadrant C are those of the Consumer. They are about the acquisition and retention of things which are perceived to be important to a person at work such as money, job security, expertise and job satisfaction. The reasons for going to work in Quadrant C can be summarised as a need for security and fulfilment at work.

A person's security needs translate into a requirement that something tangible

QUADRANT C – TAKING / THINGS (CONSUMER)
I come to work ...
• To earn a living
• Because I would be bored at home
• To become financially independent
• To feed my family
• To achieve certain goals
• To increase my knowledge and skills in my chosen field
• Because I like the variety in my work
• Because it provides me with a good income

comes his way on a predetermined date in the month. This need for a pay cheque is ubiquitous in the modern world. Testimony to this is the fact that, in our workshops, the number of people in the last 20 years whose reasons for going to work did not include matters financial, can be counted on one hand.

All other Quadrant C reasons for going to work relate to certain conditions or requirements which people have of their job or work context which, when met, give them a sense of satisfaction or fulfilment at work.

People with C Quadrant reasons for going to work are doing what they are doing for the satisfaction that they derive from it. A metaphor for this would be running. The person is not running for the sake of running; he is running for the sense of satisfaction he gets at the end of the run.

What one person wants from her work can of course be very different from that of another person. Some people require routine and stability at work while others require novelty and variety. For some people it is very important to work in a high-tech environment, while for others what matters are flexible working hours. Only when these people's Quadrant C requirements are met, and not before, can they *give* at work.

Quadrant D

The reasons for going to work that are typical in Quadrant D are about giving to things – to the job itself, to one's discipline or chosen field of work. People with these reasons for going to work tend to be responsible, to have a strong sense of duty and to work hard at what they do. Coupled with this strong work ethic is an inner sense of gratitude for having a job. Being meaningfully employed, for some people, is a motivation in and of itself.

QUADRANT D – GIVING/ THINGS (VIRTUOSO)

I come to work ...
- To do a quality job
- Because I am fascinated by my discipline
- Because I am grateful to have a job
- To be the best that I can be at what I do
- To discover new ways to do things/to create something
- To learn
- To be engaged in something that really challenges me
- Because it is my duty to do so

The first type of Quadrant D giving is that of subscribing to task-related standards of excellence. Irrespective of the task being done, the person will do it without compromising on whatever excellence in relation to the task means. The old fashioned way of describing this would be to say that the person has pride in her work, or that the person has high standards which she lives up to on a consistent basis. She comes to work, every day, motivated by the desire to do a quality job.

Beyond a concern for standards is a passion for the work itself. There are people, with Quadrant D-type reasons for going to work, who are driven by a fascination for what they do. These people are not doing what they are doing for money, for fame, to advance their career or even for the benefit of society. They are doing the work for the sake of doing the work. Their attention is therefore on the task rather than on what doing the task will do for them.

These reasons for going to work are those of a Virtuoso. Although one automatically thinks of musicians and artists, or even master craftsmen, who fit this bill, other examples abound. There are scientists driven to carry out experiments by scientific curiosity; mathematicians immersed in discovering new ways of solving a problem; computer geeks who just love code; plant operators at one with the chemical process; game rangers in awe of nature; and accountants who come alive when they pore over a set of figures.

The last type of giving in Quadrant D is about learning or growth. The people for whom this is a reason for going to work are driven by an urge to get increasingly better at what they do, to relentlessly hone their abilities, to develop self-mastery or to be the best that they can be at what they do.

These individuals come to work to be challenged, to step outside their comfort zones, to go to places, be it physically, emotionally or mentally, where they have never been before. This drive to learn, to actualise one's full potential, requires a propensity for risk-taking and for courage.

Quadrant B

The reasons for going to work in Quadrant B are all *giving* reasons which have a positive impact on people. They are those of a Leader.

Most obviously, there is in Quadrant B the giving which is done by many in the helping professions: teachers who see their jobs as preparing the next generation to fulfil a useful role in society; social workers who dedicate themselves to helping those less fortunate; doctors who care for the sick and the dying; and so on.

There are also some people in government service like policemen, firemen or even refuse collectors, who see what they do as being of useful service to society.

Then there are those in authority in organisations who choose to conceive of their function as being the cultivation of others; who see themselves as being there to make their people successful rather than themselves or even the business successful.

> **QUADRANT B – TAKING/ PEOPLE (SERVANT)**
>
> I come to work ...
> - To serve my customers
> - To help my team members
> - To make a contribution to something eminently worthwhile
> - To help the economy grow
> - To make a difference / to add value to other people
> - Because I am committed to the mission of the organisation that I work for
> - For the company
> - To care and grow those in my charge

Some business owners can also elect to see what they do as contributing to making the world a better place. Google for example states as its purpose, 'helping to raise the world's IQ, democratise knowledge and empower people with information'. Singita Game Reserves, closer to home, is dedicated to wildlife conservation. The staff in its various lodges, moreover, go to extraordinary lengths to deliver an exceptional bush experience for their clients. This drive to serve the client comes from the collective leadership of the company. It is a value, driven uncompromisingly from those at the top, and embedded in the very fabric of the organisation.

All the reasons for going to work in Quadrant B are about service or about making a contribution to others, however small. In many instances they are about a dedication to a cause or a noble purpose which is greater than oneself. They are about making a difference to humankind.

Consequences of the Four Quadrants

Work Values Model

	VICTIM	MASTER	
A	PEOPLE		**B**
	Power Harmony	Service Contribution Noble purpose	
	CONTROL	POWER	
	TAKING	GIVING	
	Security Fulfilment	Task Excellence Passion Learning / Personal Mastery	
C	THINGS		**D**
	NEEDS	VALUES	

The consequence of having needs-based reasons for going to work (Quadrant A and C) is that they can lead to opportunistic and expedient behaviour in the workplace. We all have needs for security, fulfilment, power, significance and harmony. We wouldn't be human if we didn't. When satisfaction of a need becomes all important, however, it can override what is the right thing to do in a particular work context.

The following scenario illustrates this point:

The employee concerned is a family man with considerable legitimate commitments. He has twin daughters, who he is putting through medical school, a dependent mother-in-law and great danes which eat him out of house and home. He is two years short of retirement and, as a 58-year-old in an economy in recession, is highly unlikely to get alternative employment. In short, this man needs to hold on to his job.

His boss issues him an instruction to get rid of a handsome young man who is part of his team. The boss is in her 50s and finds it excessively depressing to have good looking, youthful people in her vicinity. The implication is clear – get rid of this young man or I will get rid of you!

Faced with the choice of holding onto his job and standing up for what is right, most people believe that the man will do the former. This is despite participants also agreeing that the person who has lost the least in the situation is the young man himself. He has only lost a job, and can get another one, perhaps even in a modelling agency now that he knows how handsome he is.

> *This, however, is not the end of the story. A few months later the boss confronts the man with complaints by his subordinates that he has favourites and that this is making it intolerable to work for him. At this point the 58-year-old not only could, but should, say to his boss the following: 'This is rich coming from you. When we kissed goodbye to Mr Handsome, we also kissed goodbye to fairness. You made it clear back then that whatever mattered around here was not fairness. You can't come back now and pull the fairness card out of your pocket.'*

What the story illustrates is what we all know from experience: that acting for reasons of self-interest very often results in getting what one wants, short term. Acts of expediency, however, in the fullness of time, come back to bite one.

More specifically, the implications of the reasons for going to work in each of the Four Quadrants are outlined below.

Quadrant A – The first consequence of having strong needs related to people is that they render those who have them manipulable. This is because the satisfaction of ego needs, by definition, sits in the hands of others. As pop-stars know well, it is their fans that grant them pop-star status in the first instance, and can as easily take it away again.

At work, those that need to win, to occupy a certain box in the organogram, to influence or control others, to be popular or accepted, are weak, not strong. Other people, not them, decide to give them what they desire, or withhold it from them. The greater the Quadrant A person's need for significance or harmony, the weaker he becomes.

The second problem with ego needs is that they are difficult to ever fully satiate. A person can, for example, elect to stop eating once he is full. A need to be stroked, however, can be like a bottomless bucket. The more praise that is given, the more it is hungered after.

Similarly, no matter which 'sticks' are wielded or 'carrots' are dangled, people on the receiving end of these things can, with the will to do so, choose not to be totally subjugated or bribed. The person being controlled determines the degree to which she will be coerced or persuaded, not the person doing the controlling.

Quadrant C – Consumers at work, because they are driven by a desire to get more and/or by a fear that what they have acquired or gained will be taken away from them, tend to be insecure and discontented. People with C Quadrant needs, in the first instance, become entrapped by them. They don't have a job, the job has them.

There are many people in the modern workplace, for example, who are unhappy in their jobs but who 'can't' leave them – because of the perks, the pension, the secure income or even the short commute between home and work.

Further to this, the relationship that Consumers have with their employer tends to be conditional and characterised by an on-going haggle of 'if you …, then I …' People with very strong Quadrant C needs, in other words, stay in a job or in an employment relationship only for as long as it suits them. They will leave, either figuratively or literally, if the going gets rough or if they are presented with a more attractive offer. Once a person has been bought, he can be bought again, and again, and again …

Quadrant D – The effect of Virtuosity – of pitching oneself against criteria of excellence, of being passionate about the task at hand, of being in pursuit of mastery or learning as an end in itself – is not enjoyment. All these things are hard, demanding and taxing. If a sense of satisfaction comes, it comes later.

What giving absolutely to the work does produce, however, is something which Mihaly Csikszentmihalyl in his book *Flow: The Psychology of the*

Optimal Experience (1990) refers to as 'the flow experience'. Flow arises when a person is totally focused or absolutely concentrated on the task that she is doing; when she concerns herself entirely with process without regard for outcome.

In the flow state a person operates in the present and does not worry about the past or the future. Similarly, she is not concerned about where she stands relative to other people or even what they may think about her. While she is totally engaged in this way her sense of time is often transformed, with hours sometimes being condensed into minutes or a few seconds seeming like minutes. She is so deeply involved in what she is doing that she loses herself in it. In certain instances, she may even find herself transformed by what she does.

Virtuosos, because they do not rely on external sources of satisfaction like Consumers or Megalomaniacs, are neither manipulable nor conditional. They are in fact truly free.

Quadrant B – Those who view their work as something which is really worthwhile, as having a higher purpose, as making a contribution to society or the world, are prepared to invest of themselves, their hearts, minds and soul, in that work.

People who see purpose in their work can, moreover, maintain interest and enthusiasm even if they don't receive a pay raise or promotion. The contributory nature of what they do inspires them to make sacrifices and to show perseverance even in the face of setbacks and hardships. They are devoid of cynicism, of feeling that 'it's good enough' or 'what does it matter?'

People with Quadrant B reasons for going to work have a strong sense of meaning. They do not pursue meaning. Meaning is something that ensues as an unintended consequence of their personal dedication to a cause greater than themselves. The primary beneficiary of this sense of meaning is, of course, themselves.

In summary then:

QUADRANT	CONSEQUENCES
A (Megalomaniac)	• Manipulable • Weak • Never satiated • Controlled • In conflict with others
C (Consumer)	• Insecurity • Discontent • Entrapment • Conditionality
D (Virtuoso)	• Focus / absorption / engagement • Being in the now • Personal transformation • Freedom
B (Leader)	• Personal investment • Sacrifice / perseverance • Devoid of cynicism • Sense of meaning / higher purpose

RESEARCH AND EXPERIENCE

Work Values Model

As a result of asking thousands of people over the last 20 years the question 'Why do you go to work currently?', we have amassed a rich data base from which to draw a number of conclusions about people's motivation at work. Our findings, and how they relate to recent research in the field of work motivation, are outlined below.

 ## Motives are not a function of what people do

Yale psychologist Amy Wrzesniewski, quoted in *The Happiness Advantage* (2010), has found after years of research that employees have one of three 'work orientations'. Irrespective of the job that a person does, she claims, an individual views his work as either a *Job*, a *Career*, or a *Calling*.

People with a job see work as something that they have to do for a pay cheque at the end of the month. Their primary focus is on the financial rewards that the work brings. They fall into Quadrant C in the Work Values Model.

Those who view work as a career, on the other hand, are primarily focused on advancement at work (Quadrant A in the Work Values Model). They are motivated by prestige, status and the power that comes from the position. People in this category are not as likely to move for money as those who have a job, but rather for a promotion.

Finally, there are those who view their work as a calling. They find their work fulfilling, not because of external rewards, but because they love the work itself or because they view their work as making a contribution to society or the world – Quadrants B or D in the Work Values Model.

Furthermore, according to Wrzesniewski, in any occupation, from nursing to investment banking, about one third of people see their work as a job, one third as a career and one third as a calling. As a friend of mine who was in hospital recently said 'are you sure that it is only a third?'

Our experience accords with these findings. Certainly we have found that people's motivation at work bears no relationship to their actual occupations. People's reasons for going to work, in other words, are not a function of nationality, gender, age, academic qualifications, seniority or choice of occupation.

That this is true is validated by my personal experience.

> *When I was 16 I was convinced that I wanted to be a lawyer. Prior to enrolling for a law degree my dad organised for me to have tea with a judge. Bubbling over with enthusiasm I told him he must have the most fascinating job in the world!*
>
> *On the contrary, my dear, the esteemed judge told me, there wasn't anything that came into his courtroom that he hadn't seen a million times before. The esteemed judge was bored with his job. Needless to say that put an end to my desire to pursue a legal career.*

At the other end of the spectrum I remember the mailman at the explosives factory that I worked at for many years.

> This man was a treasure. You could set your clock for when your post would arrive. I never saw him not cheerful and smiling. Then, one day I was attending a graduation for employees who had successfully completed their literacy training and was amazed to see the postman go up on stage for his certificate. How on earth had he done this job when he was functionally illiterate?
>
> He told me, with a grin, that he hadn't been asked in his job interview whether he could read and write. In the handover period he memorised a great number of the names and locations on the brown envelopes used for internal mail purposes. Thereafter, he had a standing arrangement with a friend at work, who would enlighten him on any inscriptions that he was not familiar with. How easy it would have been for him to lob these envelopes into a bush on his way around the site.

From experience, a CEO, an engineer and a tea lady have much in common with each other when it comes to what motivates them at work.

▷ People at work have mixed motives

We have not found that people fit neatly into categories – or for that matter into any of the four quadrants in the Work Values Model.

For example, we have found it to be exceedingly rare for someone to come to work for the sole purpose of earning a living. Equally, we have found very few people who work exclusively for either B or D quadrant reasons.

What we have found is that a typical list of reasons for going to work includes reasons in more than one quadrant and, very often, in all four quadrants in the Work Values Model. This is not surprising since we are, as human beings, of mixed motive. Our behaviour is not driven exclusively by needs or values, but rather by a combination of the two.

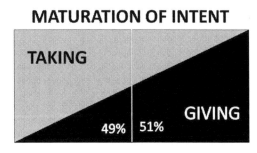

This finding supports our understanding of personal maturation – namely, that as we mature as human beings, the mix in our motives also changes. A point is reached, in terms of the maturation of our intent, at which our motives are less about taking and more about giving.

▷ There are currently more Takers than Givers at work

In Schuitema workshops participants apply a scoring mechanism to their lists of reasons for going to work. Those with negative scores sit on the *taking* side of the Work Values Model while those on the *giving* side reflect overall positive scores. Our finding, over many years, has been that when people score themselves honestly, 15-30% of participants in any group end up with a positive score.

In other words, we have found that there are currently more *takers* than *givers* at work. Gary Hamel's thesis that only 20% of employees are truly engaged in their work does appear to be the case.

Consistent with this finding is our regretful observation that in organisational life needs-driven behaviour/acts of expediency tend to outweigh behaviour which is values-driven. What, unfortunately, permeates the modern workplace is greed and fear rather than generosity and courage.

Similarly, our observation is that the consequences of Quadrants A and C reasons for coming to work – namely, insecurity, discontent, weakness and conflict with others – are far more prevalent in organisations than the sense of meaning and engagement which are associated with reasons in the B and D Quadrants.

Focus on addressing 'needs' versus promoting 'values'

It is our experience, moreover, that the primary focus of most organisations is on addressing employees' needs rather than values at work. The energies of the collective leadership of organisations, their human resources functions, and those who consult to them on the human side of their enterprises, are taken up largely with satisfying employees' Quadrants A and C reasons for going to work.

This is reflected in the time and money which big corporations, at least, invest in reward and incentive schemes, career and succession planning, talent management programmes and the like. All have to do with extrinsic rather than intrinsic motivators.

Implicit in this focus is an unconscious assumption that most people at work are enslaved by what Gary Hamel refers to as their 'ignoble appetites' and by the immediate gratification which comes from the pursuit of self-interest. It ignores completely the possibility that what is most satisfying at work is being in the service of something eminently worthwhile. Moreover, that it is feasible to cultivate more people in the workplace who see what they do as a calling, rather than as a means to an end.

Dan Pink, in a talk entitled *The Surprising Truth About What Motivates Us* (2010), refers to a mismatch between what science knows and business does. He points to countless studies over the past 40 years, in different parts of the globe, which show that contingent rewards most often do not work and very often have unpredictable and harmful consequences.

What he advocates is not greater endeavours to find the perfect formulae for extrinsic motivation. Rather, he pleads for an entirely new operating system for work motivation based on three intrinsic drivers. The first is a drive for *autonomy* or a desire to be *self-directed* at work. The second is *self-mastery,* or a motivation to get better and better at something. Finally, there is *purpose*, defined by Pink as a yearning to do what we do in the service of other people.

In essence Dan Pink is appealing for a shift away from Quadrant A and C type motivators to those of Quadrants B and D in the Work Values Model. The question, of course, is whether or not it is possible to effect that shift, and how.

We believe that it is possible, although certainly not overnight and not to the extent that every *taker* at work becomes a *giver*.

We believe this shift is feasible because we have experienced workplaces where the average employee does come to work with the intent to make a contribution – where most employees are concerned more with *what they can put in* than with *what they can take out*.

Currently the number of organisations where the above is the case is small. The challenge, of course, is to make what is currently the exception the norm.

SO WHAT CAN LEADERS DO TO MOTIVATE THEIR PEOPLE AT WORK?

SHIFTING THE FOCUS FROM THE LEFT HAND SIDE TO THE RIGHT HAND SIDE OF THE WORK VALUE MODEL

- Re-examine one's own motives at work
- Acknowledging, not fuelling, Quadrant A and C reasons for going to work
- Inculcating values-driven behaviour
- Cultivating a sense of purpose

Enabling the shift in attention from *needs* to *values* requires the following. Firstly, leaders must re-examine their own reasons for going to work and ensure that their reasons are predominantly *giving* rather than *taking* reasons. Secondly, they must adopt leadership practices which deal positively with the needs that employees have in the workplace. Finally, they should institute leadership practices which both inculcate values-driven behaviour and cultivate a sense of purpose in the members of their organisations.

 It all starts with me!

First and foremost, leaders must re-examine their own motives at work since the ratio of 15-30% *givers* to 70-85% *takers* applies as much to leaders as to those not in authority at work.

As mentioned previously, no person's reasons for going to work currently are set in concrete. A person's intent or motives are the one thing about them which can change, and moreover can change instantaneously.

There is nothing to stop someone in authority at work from taking a fresh piece of paper and writ-

The person that I would work for willingly is someone who CARES and GROWS me	The reason I come to work currently is to CARE for and GROW my people
EXPECTATIONS OF THOSE IN AUTHORITY	THE REASONS FOR GOING TO WORK OF THOSE IN AUTHORITY

ing down an entirely different set of reasons for going to work today.

Leaders have in fact truly cracked the leadership problem when their reasons for going to work are the same as their subordinates' expectations of them. That is when the answer to the questions 'Who would I work for willingly?' and 'Why do I come to work currently?' are the same. The person who I would work for willingly is 'someone who cares about me and grows me'. The reason that I come to work as a leader currently is to 'care for and grow my people'.

LEADERSHIP DERAILERS

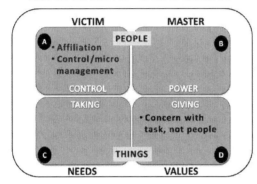

It has become apparent, after 20 years of experience working with those in positions of authority at work, that there are three reasons for going to work that seriously undermine a person's capacity to lead. One of those reasons sits in Quadrant D and the other two in the A Quadrant of the Work Values Model.

A Virtuoso, in a position of authority is typically less than successful at the job of caring for and growing others. The Virtuoso wants to make a contribution, but to things, not people. Classic examples are the master craftsman who is made an engineering foreman or the software engineer who is put in charge of a team of developers. This was graphically brought home to me when I was working with Dulux in South Africa.

> *A sales manager who had been with the company for 17 years resigned. In his exit interview, he gave as a reason for his leaving the company's Care and Growth intervention. As you can imagine, the CEO had me in his office within minutes wanting to know 'what are you SAYING to my people?'*
>
> *It turned out that this man had loved working for the company for the 12 years that he was in a sales position. He was fascinated, he said, by the sales process – by the virtuosity of eliciting needs and then matching the features and benefits of the company's products to these. Then they promoted him!*
>
> *The penny dropped for him when he wrote down his reasons for going to work. What 'turned him on' was the nuances of the selling process, not the cultivation of a team of salespeople.*
>
> *He duly resigned, took an estate agents' exam, and to this day is as happy as Larry selling houses.*

Virtuosos who are offered the opportunity to exercise authority over others should not be tempted. If they are already in positions of leadership they should probably get out of them. They would be doing themselves a favour. They would certainly be doing a favour for those who are counting on them for care and growth. More importantly, they should recognise and appreciate the very important contribution they can make through their virtuosity.

The first Quadrant A need which is seriously deleterious to those in positions of authority is a strong need for affiliation. For strongly-affiliative first-line managers in particular, the shift from colleague to boss can be impossible to make. This is particularly so if the people that they exercise authority over at work reside in the same home community.

For these people, the wise option is to go back to the shop floor, or return to their previous staff status. In one organisation, 15% of its supervisors, when confronted with the choice of being a leader or a member of the team, elected to relinquish their positions of authority over others in favour of their need for collegiality.

Finally, there is the Quadrant A need to produce predictable outcomes. This need for control over others is typically experienced by the others as micro-management. From experience those in authority with this need may be good managers, but they will never be good leaders.

The growth/empowerment piece of the Care and Growth model is not possible without the capacity for trust and entrustment, which is not within these people's reach. Micro-managers are best put in charge of systems and processes, rather than human beings.

Dealing with the left side of the Work Values Model (Quadrant A and C reasons for coming to work)

We are not suggesting for one moment that those in authority at work ignore the needs that their employees have at work for security, fulfilment, power, significance and harmony.

What we are proposing, however, is that leaders do not make addressing the needs side of the Work Values Model either their exclusive or their primary concern. Rather, that they invest their energies in cultivating the values on the right hand side of the model – specifically those of task excellence, passion, learning, service, contribution and purpose.

DEALING WITH THE LEFT HAND SIDE OF THE WORK VALUES MODEL

- Do not make presumptions about people's needs
- Acknowledge the importance of Quadrant A and C needs
- Don't fuel the fires of greed and fear in the workplace

In terms of the needs which employees have at work, however, the following is required. Firstly, that leaders do not make presumptions about what needs are important to either categories of employees (those on the shop-floor, people in sales, young people, teachers or South Africans) or specific individuals who report to them.

Secondly, that they continue to do, and do more of, those things which acknowledge the importance which employees ascribe to Quadrant A- and C-type reasons for going to work. Finally, that they stop doing, or at least minimise, the kinds of leadership practices which fuel the fires of fear and greed in the workplace.

I read somewhere that we are all inclined to attribute the significance of external motivators, in particular money, more to other people than we do to ourselves. Makes you think, doesn't it?

I certainly recall running a workshop for shop stewards in a factory who were totally convinced that the only thing that mattered to senior management was money. 'Just look at the cars they drive!' Needless to say, management were equally resolute in their view that money was everything to the operators on the shop floor, whose earnings were a fraction of theirs.

What this means is that anyone in a leadership position should make it his business to find out what makes each of the people reporting to him really 'tick' and tailor the nature of his engagement with each accordingly.

The management of a call centre wisely decided to ask its call centre agents, most of whom were in their early 20s, what they wanted most at work. The answer was the acquisition of skills and knowledge which would increase their employment options, a sense of progress, and shift patterns which would allow them to live a reasonable life.

Rather than spending money on higher salaries and incentive schemes the management chose to invest in a learning centre which employees could access out of working hours. They replaced the once-off salary hike given to agents on completion of their basic training with a series of mini-increments based on the achievement of set goals. Finally, they gave the best performers in the call centre first choice of the shifts they wanted to work. Retention and productivity improved remarkably.

Those things that organisations should be doing, and doing more of, are learning and development, teambuilding, job design and empowerment.

The phrase 'a learning organisation' has become a cliché. Nevertheless, one of the best investments a company can make in its people is in their learning and development. In addition to the functional skills necessary for job competence, the leadership of the enterprise should provide opportunities for their people to grow and develop as human beings. This type of training does not realise the immediate return on

CONTINUE/DO MORE OF

- Learning and Development
- Team Building
- Job Design
- Empowerment

investment that job-specific training does, and is therefore not as easy to justify, but in due course it pays back in spades.

At BankserveAfrica the annual training budget was historically not spent in full. This all changed with the appointment of a senior person into the position of Head: Organisational Development. The effect on the culture of the organisation was dramatic. The company is now on track to invest 3% of its payroll in people development on an on-going basis.

One way of encouraging cooperation/teamwork (a value) rather than competitiveness (a need) in an organisation is to foster teamwork within natural work teams. This is particularly true of the senior management team. When members of the top team make it their business to set their peers up for success, and to confirm their significance rather than their own, they set the example for the rest of the organisation to follow.

Strong teams do not arise spontaneously. Building a team is hard work. It necessitates 'time out' in order for the team to examine its modus operandi and commit to a manner of working together which will facilitate, rather than frustrate, the achievement of the group's goals.

Earlier in the book we dealt with the importance of designing organisational structures which create head room for individual growth and development. In addition, within the overall structure, individual jobs need to be crafted which make work challenging and interesting for people.

The American psychologist, Frederick Hertzberg, first developed the concept of 'job enrichment' in the 1950s. While no longer in vogue, there is much to be said for investing time in making people's work more 'whole', more varied and more interesting. A company's organisational development function can play an important role in this regard. Developing innovative ways of using the work to be done as a means to grow people is probably a far better use of their time than implementing job evaluation systems, industrial relations procedures and the like.

Finally, the empowerment of people talks to the need that people have to be self-directed; the need, in other words, to get on with the job without undue interference by those that they report to.

This requires those in authority to do less *managing* and more *leading*. Instead of constantly checking up on people and requiring them to report back on what they have done, they should give their people the means and ability to do what is required of them, stand back, let them get on with it, and thereafter hold them accountable for the contribution made.

What this implies is that managers need to be taught to let go and to stop trying to manage predictable outcomes. They also need to be held accountable for the incremental suspension of control – that is, for ensuring that, over time, decisions which were previously taken by them are now in the hands of their subordinates.

Reducing the pervasiveness of greed and fear in the workplace is no simple task. Nevertheless, the following changes in leadership practices can help to dampen down, or at least not fuel, the anxiety and longing for ever more, which is currently so characteristic of organisational life.

Fear among employees can be ameliorated by reducing the number of restructurings and associated retrenchments which take place in organisations. There is nothing more likely to induce acute apprehensiveness in people than the possibility, however small, that they will lose their jobs. Likewise, the use of threats, perceived by employees as intimidation, should be curtailed. They cultivate a deep sense of unease in staff and make them wary, not motivated.

Avarice, by unions, staff, and some would say in particular top management, cannot be overcome simply by, as Dan Pink suggests, 'paying people enough to take the issue of money off the table'. Avarice can be reduced, however, by the leadership of the organisation demonstrating a combination of generosity and courage when rewarding their staff. By that we mean inter alia:

- Not capitulating to improper or excessive demands simply for reasons of expediency or because of a lack of fortitude to simply say 'no'.

- Resisting the temptation to put ever more complex and sophisticated incentive schemes on the table.

- Having the courage, in the first place, to differentiate the solid citizen from those who have really gone the extra mile. Thereafter, evidencing the generosity to reward those who have made an extraordinary contribution significantly more than those who have not.

Inculcating values-driven behaviour

The leaders of many organisations have gone to considerable lengths to elucidate values for their companies and to pledge themselves to running their companies in accordance with stated values. Having done this work, often through an inclusive and participative process, they unfortunately stop there. The 'Company Values', along with their behavioural indicators, are put on the wall and everyone gets back to doing 'the business of the business'.

For a set of values and their behavioural indicators to be truly inculcated into the fabric of an organisation requires much more than that. It is a process that takes years, not weeks or months. From experience the following three managerial activities are required:

- Firstly, people need to be helped to make a very clear connection between the company's documented values and their day-to-day experience in the business. They need to see very clearly what acting consistently with the values, in the process of performing their job functions, actually means.

- Secondly, the company's values need to be fully integrated into the organisation's on-going management practices and processes.

- Finally, people need to be held accountable for living the values. That is, there needs to be positive consequences for those who act consistently with the values and negative consequences for those who do not.

COMPANY VALUE AND ITS BEHAVIOURAL INDICATORS

Respect

- Accept and value other people who are not like me.
- Discipline people in private.
- Treat people with dignity. Don't swear at them, humiliate them or put them down.
- Put the issue on the table – don't gossip.
- Keep calm, even when it is difficult.

Schuitema has worked with two client organisations recently to co-design a very powerful 'Living the Company Values' workshop.

At Cargo Motors, participants were taught the difference between values- and needs-driven behaviour, and how values are put to the test on a daily basis in the workplace. They then developed an understanding of the specific behaviours which accord with each of the company's values.

The core of the workshop, however, is a 'Values Calibration' exercise. Participants review a series of real examples of incidents which typically occur at Cargo. For each example, the following is considered:

- 'Which of the company's values are most operative in the situation?'
- 'What is the correct, as opposed to expedient, thing to do in the situation?'
- 'If the exact/similar situation arose now in the company, how would we act?'
- 'So what do we need to do differently going forward?'

MBD Credit Solutions has come up with a very innovative way of integrating its values into its managerial practices. It has made 'Living the Values' a standard agenda item at all operational review meetings. Each person in the meeting reports back on incidents which have happened in his area since the last meeting and whether or not they were handled consistently with the value which is operative in the situation. The best examples are sent through to the senior management team for review. As the leadership of the organisation, they are in a position to track, on an on-going basis, the degree to which the values are being lived in the business.

The process that MBD Credit Solutions has designed is, in fact, a formalisation of the Care and Growth practice of 'watching the game'.

Many organisations have incorporated their values into their annual performance appraisal process. A percentage of an individual's rating, and hence increment, is a function of the degree to which she is living the company's values. Although well intentioned, I am not sure of the impact that this has. Firstly, the percentage tends to be small – typically 5% of the total rating. Secondly, without having really 'watched the game,' it is difficult to make a valid call on the degree to which a person is values- as opposed to needs-driven. This may be the reason that, in one company I know of, everyone gets the statutory 5%.

I would like to see more examples of people in organisations not only being censured, but actually being fired for deliberately contravening the company's values. By this I mean not only dispensing with the services of those who have been blatantly corrupt or stolen the company's money, but removing those who have delivered the results, but destroyed the company's values in the process.

That is, executives are fired for their moral failing long *before* this inevitably catches up with them and the company's performance takes a dive. Then, and only then, will values-driven behaviour take precedence over expediency in organisations.

Cultivating a sense of purpose

On occasion we take the opportunity to put to the test the assumption that people in organisations always act for reasons of self-interest. We select a participant, preferably one for whom money is a key driver, and make the following proposal.

> Whatever you are currently earning, I will treble your salary. Your new job is to sit in an air-conditioned office without outside windows. There is a desk and a chair but no computer, writing materials or telephone. You have to leave your cell phone outside. You may not sleep or walk about unless during a normal lunch break. Your job is simply to sit, watch and remain totally alert all day. Will you take this job?

Most people reject the offer. Those who do take the job say that they probably wouldn't last more than a few days. The reason is that they have nothing to do to keep them busy.

> Let's offer you an active job then. One that has clear measures and targets, since these are good motivators. Your new job is to dig holes to specification – 2m deep, 2m long and 1m wide. You will receive feedback on time taken to dig the hole, spades per minute, muscle growth and so on. The bonus you will be paid will be in line with your performance against these key performance indicators. Before you go home you must fill in all the holes which you have dug. Will you take this job?

Needless to say most people find the second job hardly more palatable than the first one. What's missing this time is a sense of purpose. Nothing has been achieved at the end of the day.

> Functionally the first job is that of a night watchman sitting and watching. The second job's activities of digging and filling up a hole are those of a gravedigger. Why does this make a difference? Because, only when a job is perceived by the person doing it to make a value-added contribution, does it have meaning.

What the exercise simply illustrates is that what really motivates people is not the 'get' of a job but the 'give' of a job. What truly motivates people at work is the sense that they are making a contribution. The ultimate motivation, therefore, is finding meaning in the work that we do, not the reward.

CULTIVATING A SENSE OF PURPOSE

• Defining the benevolent intent of the enterprise.

• Finding meaning in individual jobs and connecting the job with the benevolent intent of the enterprise.

Leaders of enterprises can help, both themselves and their employees, find meaning in their work in three ways.

Firstly, the executive team can define the purpose of the organisation in benevolent, as opposed to malevolent or self-serving, terms. Secondly, they can provide their employees with tools to phrase what they do in such a way that they find greater meaning in their work. And, they can help everyone in the business to create a line of sight between the specific job that they do and the overall benevolent intent of the enterprise.

The aim of an organisation is normally encapsulated in its mission or vision statement. Here are two examples:

> To be a world-class academic hospital, leading the way in quality service, training and patient care.
>
> To concentrate platinum group metals and produce base metals to derive maximum value in a safe and sustainable manner, through a committed, disciplined and engaged team.

The problem with both of these two statements, and those like them, is twofold. Firstly they talk more to the organisation's aspirations than to its contribution. Unconsciously, they are more about US than they are about those for whom the company is here to serve.

Secondly, they specify what the company does, and the good manner in which it does it, but not how the customer's life is better as a result, or even how the world has been made a better place as a function of what the company does.

There is a process which Schuitema uses with its client organisations to help them to clarify their noble purpose. It revolves around the answering of four questions in the following sequence:

1. Who are our customers?

2. What are their needs and wants?

3. What is the transformation we are trying to make or effect?

4. What is the benevolent intent of our organisation?

Schuitema
The Human Excellence Group
Our Client
21st century human beings
Their Needs and Values
Security, Fulfilment, Harmony and Power
Transformation we seek to bring
The shift in attention from Taking to Giving
Our Benevolent Intent
To enable people to triumph as human beings

The answers that emerge from these questions, with a bit of word-smithing, clarify the organisation's worthwhile contribution. A few examples from different companies are given overleaf.

> 'We keep the brave men and women who live and work at sea safe' (an engineering marine business which refurbishes oil rigs and ocean-going vessels).
>
> 'We enable peace keeping and the security of nations' (designer and manufacturer of military aircraft).
>
> 'We connect people, which makes it possible for them to transcend boundaries and realise their dreams' (a mobile phone operator in Pakistan).

Every time we have worked with people to define the benevolent intent of their enterprise we have found them to be immensely enthused, even moved, by the process. The reason for this is obvious.

At the end of the day leaders can choose to phrase the role of their enterprise as being here to get something in the interests of the owner, or as fundamentally to make a contribution to the market.

Only the second phrasing is benevolent and noble enough to ask everyone in the organisation to act for reasons other than their self-interest. Only the second phrasing will unite those who work there and mobilise them to sustainably go the extra mile.

Finding meaning in a job and creating a line of sight between a specific job and the benevolent intent of the enterprise

There is no such thing as an important or a menial job. There is only a job that either has or does not have meaning. What this suggests is that people do not have to chuck their jobs and join the Peace Corps in order to see what they do as meaningful. Nor do they have to, in any way, make changes to the job that they are in. With some attention and effort, they can find a greater meaning in the job that they are doing right now.

They can do this by answering the same four questions which uncover the benevolent intent of an enterprise, but this time with respect to their individual job. In this context the questions are:

1. Who pays me for what I do?

2. What do they pay me for?

3. What is the product of what I do? What is the before and after state?

4. If I consistently do this well, how does this enable others or make the world a better place?

There are other ways of helping people discover the positive effect of the work that they do. They can be asked to answer the question 'What is my sentence?' In other words, what would I like other people to say about my life's work? They can be asked to rewrite their job descriptions in a way that would entice others to apply for their jobs. They could be asked to think about what their customers would call their job, what title they would give them, if they described them by the impact that the jobs had on their lives? And so on.

In a Care and Growth workshop, after people have established the benevolent intent of their job, we ask them to revisit the reasons they gave for going to work. In response to the question, 'What is more motivating: the reasons you gave for going to work or your statement of the benevolent intent of your job?' we have always found that the statement of the benevolent intent wins hands down.

All that remains is to help employees to connect the job that they are doing to the benevolent intent of the enterprise. In most instances people do not find this difficult to do. Establishing a clear line of sight between an individual job and the overall purpose of the enterprise sustains a person's motivation at work.

There will always be times in anyone's work life when the work is boring, too overwhelming, or simply difficult. When people remember the value that they add, by virtue of the work that they do, they can sustain their motivation even at times when it is not easy for them to do so.

In conclusion I am convinced, based on nearly 20 years of working with the Care and Growth and 'Intent' frameworks, that people have an infinite capacity to act for reasons higher than their self-interest at work and in life.

It is the core purpose of those in positions of authority to enable those who work for them to act with generosity and courage, to be values-driven, rather than needs-driven at work.

SECTION FOUR

Cultivating Accountability

One of the organisational outcomes that Care and Growth seeks to achieve is an organisation in which people take accountability for, and are held accountable for, their contributions.

This is not easy to achieve for two reasons. Firstly, organisations are good at cultivating people who feel that they do not have control over their lives and are at the mercy of forces beyond their control. Under these circumstances people feel and behave like victims. Secondly, people in organisations are held accountable inappropriately. They are held accountable for what they *get* rather than for their contribution or for what they *give*. They are disabled by the fact that they are held accountable for results, which by definition, are outside of their control, rather than for what sits in their hands.

To cultivate ACCOUNTABILITY in an organisation therefore means, in the first instance, dealing with victim behaviour whenever and wherever it arises. That is, enabling people who are weak to become strong and to reclaim their power.

In the second instance it means instituting a contribution-based, rather than a result-based, individual performance management process.

Finally, it means holding people appropriately accountable for exceptions in the business, rather than applying a 'quick fix' or implementing another control.

In *Making Masters* (Chapter One), victim behaviour is defined with its consequences for the individual and the organisation. The rest of this chapter provides a simple but powerful process, the Gripe to Goal process, for making Masters out of Victims. The process should be a critical part of any leader's toolkit.

A Performance Management Process which is aligned to the Care and Growth model is based on the following assumptions:

- Individuals should be held accountable for contribution made/ for their unique value add to others.
- Individuals should be held accountable for their own actions, for what sits in their own hands.
- What individuals are held accountable for should be clarified and agreed upon on a regular basis.
- Rewards and sanctions should be matched to the intent which drives individual contribution.

In *Re-inventing the Individual Performance Management Process* (Chapter Two) the application of these assumptions to each element of a performance management process is explained. How each element contributes to the enablement of employee contribution, as well as the criteria for the successful implementation of each element, is outlined. Finally, the successful implementation of an Individual Performance Management Process, both in terms of the *why* and the *how,* are dealt with.

The basic premise underpinning *Dealing with Exceptions* (Chapter Three) is that the results which show up in the scoreboard are a *symptom,* not a *cause*. Dealing appropriately with both positive and negative exceptions in a business means identifying the command issues which sit behind, and are the cause of, all exceptions, and then taking the appropriate leadership action based on this diagnosis. The methodology for establishing the command issues behind exceptions, and dealing with them appropriately, are outlined in the final chapter in this section.

Making Masters

It is not easy for employees to contribute in an environment which is disenabling; when the organisation's structures are dysfunctional and its systems are suffocating.

What really disempowers people in organisations, however, is not their surroundings but themselves. As a general manager on one of South Africa's platinum mines commented: 'The real shackles which bind people on this mine are not external, but internal.'

This implies that the leader's empowerment job comprises two tasks, not one:

- 'Barrier busting' – instituting a freedom-based rather than a control-based environment.
- 'Making masters' – confronting and addressing victim behaviour whenever and wherever it occurs.

The former empowers through cultivating an empowering context. The latter does so by nurturing powerful people, irrespective of the setting that they are in.

Of the two tasks, it is the making of masters which is most important. This is because strong people not only withstand, but often overcome, their circumstances. Weak people, on the other hand, can wane in even the most benign environments. When making masters, weak people are enabled to become strong, to reclaim their power.

THE ANATOMY OF A VICTIM

Spotting a victim is not difficult. This is not because the biographics of victims are the same. On the contrary, being a victim bears no relationship to age, gender, nationality, culture, or life circumstances. Any person, regardless of his station in life, can be a victim.

VICTIMS

Gripe

Blame others

Behave inappropriately

Across the world what distinguishes a victim from a non-victim is, first and foremost, that he is unhappy, miserable and aggrieved by the situation in which he finds himself.

Some victims suffer in silence but more often than not they give voice to their concerns. They complain or gripe about whatever is causing them pain and dissatisfaction.

Behaviourally, victims do very little, if anything, to relieve their own suffering. The primary action of victims is no action. Rather than take ownership of their plight, they spend their time blaming others, or the world in general, for their unhappiness.

Victims very often behave in ways which are inappropriate. In their view, others or life itself have been nasty and unfair to them. As a consequence, they feel entitled to act in a similar vein. They do whatever they like in retaliation; their misbehaviour, if they acknowledge it at all, is seen by them to be not only acceptable but absolutely justified.

A victim's misery, anger and bad behaviour are notably not a function of what has happened to him in his life. It is his response to the negative events which have impacted on him which makes him a victim. The source of any victim's gripe(s) are, by definition, events in the past or the

VICTIMS

Stuck in/defined by the past

External locus of control

Sense of entitlement

present; what has happened, or is still happening to him, is making him so disaffected. Consequently, a victim is literally stuck in, or trapped by, his history.

> *A classic case is a woman I met whose husband walked out on what she believed was 25 years of happy marriage to move in with his 20-year-old blonde secretary. Understandably she was devastated. Her level of anger and bitterness led me to assume that this was a recent tragedy. In fact he had left her seven years ago!*

Similarly there are people at work who cannot get over things which happened to them much earlier in their working lives. They cling to the past disappointment and hurt and in effect allow what has happened to define them now.

Whatever the specifics of the case, victims' gripes boil down to one of two things. Victims are unhappy in essence because they did not get what they wanted to get (a promotion) or they got what they didn't want to get (the end of a marriage).

Since what a person gets or does not get is never entirely within her control, a victim feels herself to be at the mercy of forces beyond her control. She has what psychologists refer to as 'an external locus of control'.

Stephen Covey puts it slightly differently when he makes a distinction between what he calls a person's 'circle of concern' and a person's 'circle of influence'. Victims typically focus on what concerns them rather than on what they can influence. They are overwhelmed by their concerns, quite simply because they have no power over them. They fail to focus their attention on what they can influence, on the power that they do have.

Finally, victims believe that they have a right to get what they want from other people and the world at large. They, therefore, have a deeply-rooted sense of entitlement. If they do not receive what is owed to them, someone or something other than themselves is accountable. Consequently they neither feel accountable nor take accountability for their lives.

WHY VICTIMS ARE A PROBLEM

Victims are a problem both to themselves and others. In the first instance, victims' concern with what they are getting/not getting in any situation leads them to try and control the outcome. This is a futile exercise, because outcomes, no matter how well engineered, are never guaranteed.

Consequences

Insecurity

Discontent

Weakness

Conflict

The world is not set up to provide everything that people want just because they want it. The world is certainly not designed to deliver what is wanted exactly the way and the instant it is desired. Consequently, victims end up anxious and insecure.

Allied to this, because it is not possible for a person's expectations always to be met, victims consistently experience what they get as falling short of, or not exactly in line with, their expectations. There is always something for a victim to complain about, something which has disappointed or let the person down. As a result the victim is generally left feeling unfulfilled and discontented.

Victims' need to have their desires met by sources outside of themselves, moreover, makes them manipulable. Both the situation that they are in, and the other people in the situation have control over them in the sense that they can withhold from the victim what the victim wants. As a result, victims find themselves in a position of weakness, not strength.

Finally, victims are in conflict with other people and with the world in general. Their fear that what they want will be withheld from them makes them feel under threat. The people they want to get something from equally feel under threat because they experience the victim as predatory. This being the case, there is conflict, not harmony, in the relationships that victims have with others.

Victims as members of a group constitute a problem for the immediate group and the enterprise at large. This is because victim behaviour is contagious. Victims infect others with their victimhood such that the victim virus ultimately takes over and brings down the organisation as a whole.

The degree to which victim behaviour prevails in any group is easy to ascertain by simply asking members of the group the question 'What stops or constrains you from making a contribution?'

The answer to this question clearly differentiates victims from non-victims. As shown below, victims' constraints are about *other/getting* while a non-victims' concerns are about *self/giving*.

Victim Constraints		Non-Victim Constraints
• Changing of the goalposts/ inconsistent behaviour from management. • Production makes unreasonable demands on us (engineering). • Uncertainty due to sale of the business. • Have to get too many signatures to get things done.		• I don't trust others. • How will I grow people to be the best they can be? • I am too soft on my people. • We haven't put the right structure in place. • I cannot say no to requests.

In any leadership group, when the percentage of *other/get* constraints outweighs those of *self/give*, the prognosis is poor. This is because victims in leadership roles beget victims. If there are victims aplenty at the top of the organisation, you can bet that there are victims to the power of ten lower down.

Victims to Masters

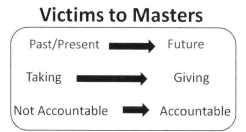

For a *victim* to transform into a *master* requires the victim to make three changes.

The first change is in attention. This amounts to a fundamental shift in attention from the gripe, which is in the past/present, to the goal, which by definition, is positioned in the future. The victim becomes a master by looking forward, by focusing on the future, not the past.

The second change on the way to becoming a master has to do with a change in intent, with what a person chooses to make significant to herself. Masters give priority or importance to what they want to *give* or to their *contribution*, rather than to what they want to *get*. In doing so, they become givers, not takers.

The third change is from the *known* and *secure* to the *unknown* and *insecure*. What makes the victim state so attractive is that it is devoid of risk. As the saying goes 'better the devil you know than the devil you don't'. To become a master necessitates taking a risk, and then accepting accountability for having done so. Masters, in contrast to victims, take full accountability for the situation that they are in.

These three shifts in attention, intention and accountability can be made in four steps.

The first step is to get to the heart of the matter, to determine the problem which sits underneath the gripe. This is because the gripe is the symptom, not the cause. The next step is to restate the problem as a

Gripe to Goal

Determine root cause / Problem

Restate problem as a goal

Establish action plan to achieve goal

Establish accountability

goal, to change the problem causing the complaint into a goal that the victim can pursue.

With a goal in place it becomes possible to brainstorm ways in which the goal can be achieved; to generate a list of possible actions which, if taken, would achieve the goal. Then, from all the possibilities, distil out those actions most likely to deliver the goal and sequence them into an action plan. The final step is to commit to the action plan; to turn the plan into reality by taking full accountability for making the plan happen.

These four steps, taken together, constitute a process, called the Gripe to Goal process. The Gripe to Goal process is not complex. It can be and is applied to both minor gripes, like the weather, and to major concerns such as the global economic meltdown. Individuals can and do apply the process to their own gripes, just as group(s) can and do to theirs.

The problem, however, is that neither individuals nor groups use the process all the time. Most people get stuck in victim mode on occasion. The person for whom this has never been true is exceedingly rare. Others, the chronic victims, seemingly get stuck and stay stuck most of the time.

This is when another person can be of assistance, by helping the griper negotiate his way through the process and reclaim his power. In the work situation, that other person should ideally be the boss. In a Care and Growth leadership environment, bosses confront and address victim behaviour whenever it arises. They consistently help weak and powerless individuals and groups to become strong and powerful.

There are many examples of disaffected employees, seemingly intractable victims, who have been helped by bosses who cared about them to regain their motivation and will to contribute. An operations manager once used the Gripe to Goal process with a seasoned quality professional on a Friday afternoon. Having 'retired on the job' for most of the past decade the employee came back a changed man on Monday and went on to win a coveted service award within a year. Similarly, a plant manager (and later CEO of AEL Mining Services) was able to make willing and productive employees out of a militant and destructive workforce in a matter of months by essentially following the four steps in the process.

Barriers to Making Masters

- Tolerating Victims
- Don't Listen
- "Take the monkey"
- "Ag Shame" Syndrome

Unfortunately, the above examples are not commonplace. Many managers avoid using the process altogether and tacitly accept the victims in their midst. Ironically, those managers eventually end up victims themselves, endlessly griping about the failings of their people.

Other managers attempt the process but are frankly not very good at it. They feign interest in the concerns of the griper but the real message is 'voetsek' ('go away') implying that, as managers, they have more important matters to attend to.

Some managers 'take the monkey' and make the griper's problem theirs or, alternatively, provide the solution for the griper, thereby ensuring a lack of commitment by the griper to the proposed action plan. Worst of all, however, managers fall foul of something called the 'ag shame' syndrome. This is shorthand for 'you think you have a problem, let me tell you about mine'. Now there are two gripers in the room, not one.

With some training, followed by deliberate practice, managers can however become very skilful at the process. It is imperative that they do. A leader will ultimately fail at the job of leading if she doesn't have the ability to cultivate accountability in her people and enable them to accept responsibility for their present situation.

GETTING THE STEPS IN THE PROCESS RIGHT

Step One: Listen

The first step in the process has been successful when the griper has uncovered the real problem behind the gripe. If the listener has blinding clarity on the problem, but the griper has not, then Step One is not complete.

Only when the griper responds 'yes' to the question 'so is ... what really concerns you?', is it time to move on to the second step in the process.

AIM

To identify the root cause

RULE

Seek to understand
not to be understood

A patient rarely walks into a doctor's room and announces an illness. Instead the patient describes the symptoms, such as 'I have a headache and my tummy hurts'. The doctor's task is to make a diagnosis starting with the patient's presenting symptoms. Similarly, the griper's initial gripe is an expression of concern, not a determination of the problem. The role of the boss, as helper, is not to pronounce the problem but to help the griper to work out the problem, get to the root cause, himself.

After listening, the initial gripe statement and the actual problem statement are rarely the same. Two recent examples make the point. In a banking environment, the gripe as first presented was that 'decision-making authority levels are unclear and slow me down'. The problem finally acknowledged by the griper was that '(some) branch managers are not empowering their account managers'. In another case, the employee's concern was 'an office relocation and concomitant unaffordable increase in transport costs'. The real problem pertaining to the change however was her 'child's safety, now that I arrive home later than before'.

The role of the helper at this stage is to seek to understand, not to be understood. This requires the helper to exercise patience, to really listen and listen some more.

In the first instance, the listener has to give full and undivided attention to what the griper is saying. This only happens when the listener is able to silence his inner dialogue. Only then does the listener become truly and unconditionally present in the moment and available to the person with the concern. In doing so, the listener is genuinely suspending his own agenda for the agenda of the other.

Listening, however, does not imply total silence. Nor does it suggest a reflecting back verbatim what the person has said. Listening means asking the right questions of the griper. This is necessary because the griper very often does not present the full story at the outset. The information given is frequently incomplete ('I was promised a promotion and not given it'), exaggerated ('every time he says he will do something he doesn't'), or based on assumptions ('I am being underpaid').

Skilful listeners do not refute or argue against what is being said. Rather they ask the griper the kind of questions which enable the griper to become more specific and to check the validity of what is being said by her. The questions useful to the griper may include: 'Who/how specifically?'; 'Never?'; 'Compared to what/to whom?'; 'What stops or constrains you?' It can also be helpful to simply ask 'Why?', and to keep doing so until the griper has got to the root cause, to what is really the stone in her shoe.

Most important of all for Step One, however, is not to rush through this first phase. The purpose of Step One is for the griper to get to grips with what is really bothering her. This insight takes time.

The listening phase is the step in the process which takes by far the most time. In a good Gripe to Goal process, Step One can account for up to 70% of the conversation. When the Gripe to Goal process is not very effective, most often it is because not enough time was given to the first step in the process.

Step Two: Phrase the Goal

AIM

Focus Attention Forward

RULE

No new content

Unlike Step One, Step Two is very quick. It literally consists of getting the griper to restate what she now understands to be the problem as a goal. The problem statement and the goal statement are in fact the same. All that has changed is that the situation is no longer phrased as a problem but as a goal.

The problem that '(some) branch managers are not empowering their account managers' becomes the goal of 'getting branch managers who are not empowering their account managers to do so'. The problem that 'my child is not safe when I come home later than before' translates into a goal of 'ensuring my child's safety until I get home at a later time'.

The golden rule in Step Two is simple but critical. The rule is: *no new content*. All that is required is to flip the problem statement over to a goal statement, without introducing new content by, for example, offering a solution to the problem. The problem 'I am lonely' should become a goal 'not to be lonely'. When the goal is given as a solution – 'get a pet', 'join a dating club', 'make friends' – new content has been introduced.

In rephrasing the problem as a goal the person is being empowered in two ways. Firstly, the nature of the problem itself has changed in the sense that it has become an ability problem or a matter of skill. What the person is facing has been translated into a 'How do I?' issue – 'How do I persuade branch managers to empower their account managers?' or 'How do I ensure my child's safety?'

Secondly, the person is empowered by the fact that her attention is now focused forward. Rephrasing the problem as a goal has taken the person from past to future. In a brief moment it has also released all the negative energy which has been tied up in the problem and re-channelled it into something useful – namely, the pursuit of a goal.

Step Three: Brainstorm

AIM

Establish an action plan to achieve the goal

RULE

Cook a rich stew
Get your ducks in a row

The purpose of Step Three is to enable the griper to embrace some new possibilities, which hitherto have not been considered or, if they have, have been dismissed by the griper. Sometimes a victim knows what the real problem is and has a goal in mind to achieve it. The reason that she has become stuck, however, is that she has tried something and it hasn't worked, or she has not achieved her desired goal.

Her lack of success has immobilised her, in that she has literally sat down on the white line and become inert.

Step Three of the process is designed to do the following:

- Generate new ideas or ways of progressing towards the goal which have not been tried or thought of before.

- Discard those ideas which are immoral, illegal and impractical in that order.

- Sequence the ideas which remain into an action plan which stipulates what actions will be taken by the victim, in what sequence, and by when.

Let's say that I have unresolved difficulties in my relationship with my mother-in-law. My goal is to resolve those difficulties. The possibilities for doing so are endless. They may include hiring someone to take care of my problem (it has been done), getting a divorce, being a 'nicer' daughter-in-law, or changing my attitude towards my mother-in-law. Editing the list is not difficult. It is clear what I should do and in what order.

Notably, as long as a person has breath and is not brain-damaged, there is always something she can do; change her attitude towards, or perceptions of, the situation that she finds herself in. There are countless stories of people who having suffered horrors, have avoided being victims by exercising control over their thoughts and feelings – sometimes the only thing they still have power over.

Step Three seems very easy – It Is after all about facilitating a classic brainstorm. Yet, the Gripe to Goal process can be *derailed* at this stage by a number of things.

Firstly, the boss, as helper, can try too hard to proffer solutions on the premise that, if the victim knew what to do to solve the problem, she would have already done so. Unfortunately, by being overly helpful, the boss makes the griper passive, if not resistant. The griper is now in a position to shoot down the ideas put forward by the helper. There are always reasons why X, Y or Z won't work. The griper typically has a fine time delineating the reasons 'why not' while the helper tries desperately to find a solution which will satisfy the griper.

The rule 'cook a rich stew' applies here. The helper can provide some ideas but, at the same time, make the victim work at options also. From experience with the Gripe to Goal process, most people actually know what they need to do. They have the answers already and just need to be prompted to voice them.

The process can also be derailed at this point by what can best be described as the 'soap in the bath' problem. Just when the victim seems to have got to grips with what she could do, she deviates from the task of determining what could be done. Worse than that, she dives back across the dividing line between Victim and Master and goes back to Step One. In a single backwards leap, the almost-Master has regressed to a griping Victim. The reason for this is obvious. The person has gone back to her comfort zone, back to the known. From this place of safety there is no risk to her. Everyone else is accountable.

The helper, if this happens, needs to be firm. He needs to bring the griper back out of her place of safety to confront the unknown. The way to do this is to remind the victim of the goal and to insist that she at least gives countenance to ways of achieving it.

Finally, Step Three can literally fizzle out because the victim resists nailing down the workable ideas into a concrete and time-bound action plan. Now the helper needs to be persistent: 'So if this action is the most viable option, when can you do it?'

It must be emphasised that the Gripe to Goal process is about restoring a person's sense of accountability for the situation in which she finds herself – in her best interests. What is required by the helper is tough love, that is, benevolence in the heart but steel in the hand.

Step Three effects the second shift in the transformation from Victim to Master. It enables the shift in intention from being 'here to get' to being 'here to give'. It does this by focusing the person on what can be done, what sits in her hands. It is simply not possible for anyone to simultaneously be occupied by what she is getting and what she is giving. The shift in focus to giving thus effectively nullifies the focus on getting.

Step Four: Seek Commitment

AIM

Establish Accountability

RULE

Get a clear decision and make its consequences clear

Just as Step Two is quick, so is Step Four, the final step in the Gripe to Goal process. This step consists of a single question for the griper: 'Are you committed to this action plan or not?' In response to this question, the person can only really say 'yes' or 'no'.

If the person says 'yes', then clearly she has ownership of the action plan and is accountable for executing it. If her answer is 'no', the person is still accountable. She has simply declined to pay the price that has to be paid to achieve the goal. The person has weighed things up and decided not to take the risk(s) inherent in the action plan.

Clearly this is her choice and she is entitled to make it. If this is her decision, however, the helper needs to indicate that this decision implies accountability by the person for the situation she is in.

This is tough for both the griper and the helper to do, but it is ultimately what is empowering for the griper.

It is so much easier, and more politically correct, to collude with people in their victimhood rather than confront them with it. As David Cameron (now prime minister of Britain) was quoted as saying, in response to the high levels of obesity in Britain: 'It is time that we stopped referring to people as being vulnerable to excess body mass and started to say madam/sir you are fat and the reason that you are fat is that you eat too much and take too little exercise!'

SUCCEEDING WITH THE PROCESS OVERALL

From experience with using and assisting leaders to use the process, the following has become evident about succeeding with it:

- It is critical, throughout the process, to keep the end in mind. The end is a person who is accountable, who is strong and has reclaimed her power. The end is not the resolution of a problem. Nor is it to make a person feel better, although this is often a by-product of the process. Individual(s) can, and often do, emerge from the process walking ten feet tall.

- The helper does not have to have any knowledge of the content to be helpful. Too much content knowledge may in fact be a hindrance rather than a help. This is because the helper is then tempted to be pulled into, and get involved in, the content. The Gripe to Goal process is, in fact, an opportunity for the boss to be most useful when she is being useless.

- The Gripe to Goal process does not have to be done all in one sitting. It can be very effective to do steps One and Two and then, at another date, steps Three and Four. Sometimes it is appropriate to meet several times to just listen (Step One) before progressing with the rest of the process.

- The process itself is rarely a once-off event, done and then over. It is critical for the leader/helper to follow up in any case after Step Four. This not only convinces the griper that the leader's Care is genuine but will make the griper realise that the leader is holding him accountable for what he undertook to do.

- Before embarking on the Gripe to Goal process, the leader needs to take self-interest out of the discussion. If the way out for the griper (and there always is a way out if the person is prepared to pay the price) is to get another job, it is entirely appropriate for the boss to support the person to do so. If the helper lets his own interests intervene, then he stands the danger of being viewed, quite correctly, as manipulative by the griper. If the leader feels that it is too difficult for him not to have a vested interest in the process, then he should recuse himself from it.

Finally, it becomes apparent from doing the Gripe to Goal process that the problem/goal statements that are derived from the listening phase can be of two types. They can pertain either to 'other' or to 'self'.

The problem that 'my husband is not treating me nicely', and hence the goal 'to get my husband to be nicer to me' is about 'other'. The problem that 'I am unhappy in my marriage', and, therefore, my goal is to 'regain my happiness in the marriage' is about 'self'.

Of the two, the problems/goals which relate to 'self' are the ones which the person has more control over. It is feasible to act in ways which may influence the 'other', but ultimately it is not possible to change the 'other', only the 'self'.

The Gripe to Goal process is designed to enable a person to make the shift from outcome to process. It is most successful, however, when the person stops seeking to change *others* but rather pursues a change in the *self*.

The Gripe to Goal process does not take the person to full maturity, because the very pursuit of a goal is, by definition, a 'giving to get'. Nevertheless, the more the goal being pursued has to do with a change in the self, the further the person has progressed in terms of her maturation. The closer she is, in other words, to finally escaping all goals and giving unconditionally.

Re-inventing the Individual Performance Management Process

Care and Growth is about people and relationships – it is NOT about systems, processes and structures. Implementing Care and Growth, nevertheless, necessitates, at some point in time, a modification (more often a re-invention) of the performance management process in any organisation. This is because, in most organisations, the performance management process is seriously at odds with the Accountability aspect of the Care and Growth framework.

The analogy which springs to mind is of the pig farmer who returns his freshly cleaned pigs to a dirty sty and wonders why they are soon back to the colour they were before he removed them. Convincing leaders of the principles of Accountability (through Care and Growth workshops) when their day-to-day context is blatantly in contravention of these principles, is at best an exercise in futility.

Alignment of a company's performance management process to the 'Principles of Accountability' is therefore a key enabler in translating Care and Growth into day-to-day leadership practices.

PRINCIPLES OF ACCOUNTABILITY

1. People should be held accountable for what they give (their contribution) not for what they get (the results).

When people are being held accountable, one of four things is happening to them: they are being punished, censured, praised or rewarded. At a very fundamental level, therefore, the question arises as to what people should be paid for: *what they give (contribute)* or *what they get (results)*? To pay people for the results not only sabotages the cultivation of accountability in an organisation, it is fundamentally wrong for the following reasons.

- Firstly, paying for results is ultimately like playing a game in a casino. Results are always, at least in part, due to factors outside of people's control. When people are paid for results, they are paid for what they have little control over. A retail manager in a small town

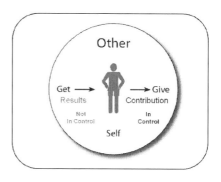

in the Karoo in South Africa earned an obscene bonus for one reason only – he got lucky. Without him doing anything, his only competitor moved out of town, store revenue almost doubled instantaneously and he was rewarded for the result 'achieved'. Luck was also a decisive factor in determining which CEOs in South Africa earned the most in 2005. According to A. Crotty and R. Bonorchis in their book *Executive Pay in South Africa: Who gets what and why?* (2006), the highest earners were those in the 'right' sector (retail/banking) compared with their less well placed counterparts in media, technology and construction.

- Secondly, there is a time lag between contribution and the result, which can lead to a person riding on the back of a predecessor's past excellent contribution, or conversely, paying the price for the previous incumbent's poor performance. A talented manager in Old Mutual Group, known for his ability to turn around underperforming regions, learnt this the hard way. Just as his herculean efforts were paying off and beginning to come through on the scoreboard, the company moved him on to the next trouble spot. Eventually, after three years of mediocre remuneration, he refused to move, preferring to stay and reap the rewards of his turnaround efforts.

- Thirdly, since most organisational results are collectively produced, it is not easy to ensure that the right people are rewarded or punished. The 'passengers' in the group share in the fruits when the results are positive. Conversely, when the overall result is bad, the individual 'high contributors' have to suffer along with the rest. A good overall CSI (Customer Service Index) at First National Bank Branch Banking can put money in the pockets of individuals who couldn't care less for the customers, while a poor CSI ensures that those dedicated to their clients are punished for being so.

- Finally, paying for results leads to short-term thinking and expedient action, sometimes with disastrous medium and long-term consequences. The business press abounds with stories of executives who have stripped out costs and been paid handsomely for the subsequent knee-jerk improvement in the bottom line, only to leave behind a disabled organisation, sometimes beyond recovery.

In practice, though, what do corporations actually pay their employees for? Despite all the hype around 'pay for performance', it is highly debatable whether it is the results which actually determine the reward handed out.

Employees, almost by definition, are protected from the vicissitudes of life in a way that business owners, who genuinely share in the good and bad fortunes of their companies, are not. Despite the plethora of variable pay schemes, the primary determinant of what an employee gets to take home at the end of the month is a function of which box he occupies in the hierarchy and possibly also length of service, not the results in his area. People are paid for their presence, which is a necessary precondition for making a contribution, but not a contribution per se.

In many companies the performance management process is not even set up to reward for results, but for personal 'attributes' like skills/competencies or how a person is perceived by others (the 360° feedback

WHAT SHOULD EMPLOYEES BE REWARDED FOR?

Their Position / Length of Service	Personal Attributes – Competencies / Perceptions	Contribution / Value Add	Results
✗	✗	✓	✗

currently in vogue). Whatever companies actually reward for, it is certainly not for contribution – for what a person has actually delivered or added value to someone else.

To be consistent with the first principle of accountability, the base building block of the performance management process must be individual contribution. Reward should follow on from, and be a direct consequence of, contribution made.

Not only is this fair, it is truly empowering because it enables people to focus on that which they can do something about.

2. People can only ever be accountable for their own actions. There should only ever be one person accountable.

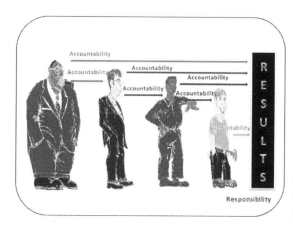

Responsibility and Accountability are different. People in organisations are assigned areas of responsibility from the top down. Plant manager X, for example, may be assigned responsibility for one of four plants on a manufacturing site. The plant manager, along with everyone else in the plant, is then collectively responsible for the plant's performance – that is, for the results achieved in terms of safety, quality and output.

Accountability, however, is different. Accountability is unique to the person – it relates to what an individual personally does. The human resources manager may have overall responsibility for the HR function but can hardly be accountable for an error made by the pay clerk at month end.

In Care and Growth workshops we often, tongue in cheek, use the following example. A trainer is standing innocently next to the flipchart when a stranger enters the room, whips a rolled-up newspaper out from behind his back, whacks the trainer around the ear and departs. The trainer then proceeds to smack the smallest trainee in the room with the newspaper left behind by the stranger. Workshop participants are unanimously in agreement that the trainer is accountable, and should be punished, for laying into the poor trainee. Who is accountable for what befell the trainer, however, generates more debate. Maybe the trainer deserved to be smacked? Maybe the person who is accountable is the guard at the gate for letting the stranger in with the rolled-up newspaper?

This is absurd! People, at least adults who are sane, should be accountable for their own actions. There is no such thing as 'they made me do it' (Adam is not off the hook for eating the forbidden fruit just because Eve told him to) or 'they should have stopped me' ('I cheated, but it's not my fault – you didn't put a monitor in the room to watch me').

Accountability, unlike responsibility, is also not something which should be shared. Once more than one person is accountable, no one is accountable. When accountability is shared, everyone takes the credit for what is well done, but no one owns up for what was done badly.

Nowadays, most organisations are very good at specifying the results that need to be achieved. The use of balanced scoreboards, with their lead and lag measures adhering to the needs of all stakeholders, and sophisticated goal alignment processes, have meant that most employees – from the call centre agent to the managing director – know exactly what the company desires to *get* out of them.

Sadly, the same is not true of what people need to *give* as their unique contribution to the desired result(s). Assumptions as to what is *my job* as opposed to *your job* are made. Consequently, accountabilities are duplicated, overlap and are not balanced, with some employees being overwhelmed by what they have to do while others are woefully underutilised.

Who is accountable for what, moreover, becomes increasingly opaque as one moves up the hierarchy. Any one level in the management structure is not differentiated, in terms of its unique value-add, from either the level above or below it.

Worse still is the tendency to make managers accountable for what is done by those who report to them. Since the results to be achieved at each level subsume the results of a level down, managers take both the glory and the flack for what does not sit in their hands. In so doing, they inadvertently take away the accountability from those who should be accountable.

To be consistent with the second principle of accountability, each individual's unique contribution in the context of the results to be achieved needs to be clarified and agreed on a regular basis.

3. Those performing a task should be accountable for doing so. Leaders should be held primarily accountable for the Care and Growth of their subordinates.

People cannot be held accountable if what they are accountable for is not clear. Once contribution has been clarified, that is what people should be held accountable for.

Principles of Accountability

237

There are, in essence, two types of contribution. The first type is the doing of tasks which impact directly on the results to be achieved. This is the contribution made by the salesperson, the business analyst, the forklift driver. Then there is the type of contribution made by those who are leading others wherever they sit in the line of command.

The two types of contribution are fundamentally different. The direct contributor gives to the task. There is a direct line of sight between what is done by the contributor and the results to be achieved. A leader's primary contribution is not to a task but to the people who report to her directly. The players are there to play the game. The coach is there to enable the players.

In a very real sense, therefore, a leader has as many pieces of work/tasks as she has people reporting to her. For each direct report the leader's job is that of caring for and growing the subordinate. As such, the leadership role presents itself at any point in time as one of only seven possibilities or things that the leader needs to give – care, means, ability, discipline, censure, praise or reward – to each one of her direct reports.

In most organisations, leaders are measured and rewarded not for what they *give* to their people, but for what they *get* out of them. They are held accountable for getting work done through people, not for getting people done through the work.

To be consistent with the third principle of accountability, the success criteria for anyone in a leadership role has to change. Success has to be not about making the self successful, nor even making the business successful, but making one's people successful.

The primary criterion against which leaders should be judged is the calibre of their people.

> **4. People can only be held accountable once they have been given the means and ability to contribute. If they have the means and ability, they should be appropriately punished or rewarded for their performance.**

To make the unique contribution required of them, people need to be provided with the requisite means and ability. Without adequate means (tools, resources, standards, and authority) people are not allowed to contribute. When they lack ability (in terms of how and/or why) they can't do so. This is not enough, however. People must want to make the contribution required of them. What engages people's will to contribute is accountability. A person's contribution can either be above standard or below standard. When a person's contribution is above standard either the person is going the ex-tra mile (in which case it is appropriate to reward the person), or the person is careful to meet the stan-dard (in which case the person should be recog-nised). Similarly, if the per-son has the means and ability, but is below stan-dard, it is for two kinds of reasons: either the person is careless and should be

TO GROW SOMEONE MEANS TO EMPOWER HIM:

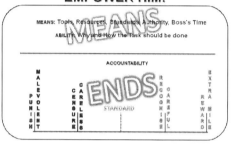

censured, or the person is malevolent and should be punished. In the business context, punishment means discipline up to and including dis-missal, while censure implies a verbal reprimand or warning. This also suggests that there is an incremental process between censure and pun-ishment.

There are, in essence, two ways of getting empowerment wrong. The 'hard' mistake happens when the person either does not have the means and/or ability to contribute to standard, but is nevertheless held accountable (censured/disciplined) for below-standard performance. The 'hard' mistake happens because means and ability issues are treated as accountability issues.

The 'soft' mistake is the inverse of the 'hard' mistake. It happens when accountability issues are treated as means or ability issues. For example, when a person's performance is below standard due to carelessness or malevolence, and he should therefore be held accountable, the 'soft' mistake is sending him for retraining or giving him additional means.

Of the two mistakes, the 'soft' mistake is the more dangerous for an

239

organisation, because it cultivates malevolence. The problem with the 'soft' mistake is that eventually no one is held accountable.

In most organisations, the 'soft' mistake rather than the 'hard' mistake is most prevalent. If the 'hard' mistake happens at all, it is at the bottom, not at the top, of the organisation. In the last decade I have only come across one organisation, both in South Africa and internationally, guilty of the 'hard' mistake. The leadership failure is not one of a lack of generosity but rather a lack of courage.

More specifically, failure to hold people appropriately accountable in an organisation evidences itself in the following:

- Carelessness and deliberate malevolence are tolerated. Disciplinary action is not taken even in cases of serious misconduct (sleeping on duty), while 'retirement on the job' is accepted. If sanctions are imposed, they are generally too lenient. Disciplinary action is taken mainly for misconduct, not poor performance.

- There is a hesitancy to move beyond censure to discipline, with people being verbally reprimanded over and over for the same issue. Just as children learn that mum is not really serious about them picking up the dirty clothes and putting them in the wash basket, employees realise that management is not serious about the standards they impose.

- Irrespective of the level of reward, people feel unappreciated for their contribution. In the words of a mine overseer 'thank you is very much expensive around here'. The focus is on finding out what is wrong rather than deliberately catching people doing things right and recognising them for it. Holding people accountable is then misconceived as being only about discipline and not reward. If we assume that most organisations work, then by implication more things go right than go wrong. Therefore more recognition and reward should be handed out than anything else.

- People are compared with each other rather than against a standard. Competitive reward schemes both elicit unhealthy internal competition and severely demotivate, if not terrorise, the losers.

The sum effect of these leadership practices, over time, is mediocrity.

To be consistent with the fourth principle of accountability, the consequences (rewards/sanctions) for people in an organisation must match the intent behind their contribution.

People who are careless must be cautioned, while those who are deliberately malevolent must be disciplined. Equally deliberate benevolence/going the extra mile must be rewarded, while those who show good concern for their jobs should be recognised.

In summary then, when a performance management system is aligned to the Care and Growth principles of accountability, the following applies:

ALIGNMENT TO THE PRINCIPLES OF ACCOUNTABILITY

- Accountability is for contribution made or for unique value add to others.

- Individuals are held accountable for their own actions/for what sits in their hands.

- What individuals are accountable for is clarified and agreed on a regular basis.

- Rewards and Sanctions are matched to the intent driving individual contribution.

Total alignment of an organisation's performance management process with all four principles of accountability is clearly not a trivial exercise and should not be underestimated. Alignment does not happen overnight – it takes time to effect.

ELEMENTS
OF A PERFORMANCE
MANAGEMENT SYSTEM

1. Clarification of contribution in the context of results to be achieved.

2. Assessment of contribution by 'watching the game'.

3. Regular review of contribution with the purpose of enabling enhanced contribution going forward.

4. Discipline and reward consistent with holding people accountable for their contribution.

A number of organisations have embraced the challenge of aligning their performance management process to the Care and Growth framework. What is generically referred to as the 90 Day Accountability Process has been given various labels – The Deliverables Process, The Accountability Review Cycle, Contribution Contracting, etc. Every organisation rightfully has its own forms and methodologies tailored to its context and culture. Those processes which have delivered, by cultivating accountability and unleashing a spirit of generosity and courage in the work environment, have all comprised of the above four elements or steps.

Clearly each element does not happen in isolation of the other, but rather takes place in an on-going accountability cycle. Element One and Element Three happen in one-on-one discussions between the boss and the subordinate, while Element Two and Element Four take place outside these regular, diarised conversations.

THE ACCOUNTABILITY CYCLE

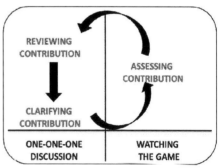

REVIEWING
CONTRIBUTION

ASSESSING
CONTRIBUTION

CLARIFYING
CONTRIBUTION

ONE-ONE-ONE
DISCUSSION

WATCHING
THE GAME

Most performance management processes emphasise elements One and Three. While the one-on-one discussions are vital to the process, they are not where the primary emphasis should be placed. The emphasis in the performance management process needs to be on the action part (assessing contribution and holding people accountable) rather than on the reflection piece (reviewing the contribution of the last reporting cycle and clarifying contribution for the next).

The four elements, their critical success factors, and what each element delivers in the process of enabling accountability are outlined below.

1. Element One: Clarification of Contribution in the context of the Results to be achieved

Critical to the success of *Element One: Clarifying Contribution* is the following.

CRITICAL SUCCESS CRITERIA FOR CLARIFYING CONTRIBUTION IN THE CONTEXT OF THE RESULTS TO BE ACHIEVED

- ❖ Both Responsibility (for the Results) and Accountability (Contribution) need to be clarified.

- ❖ Clarification needs to be ongoing – Results (annually) and Accountability (every 90 days).

- ❖ Clarification of Responsibility should precede the definition of Accountability.

- ❖ Accountabilities need to meet the following criteria: line of sight, unique, specific and concrete, appropriate, manageable but stretching, time bound, forward, focused.

- ❖ A leader's accountability has to include the provision of care, means, ability and accountability required by immediate subordinates.

- Both Responsibility (Results) and Accountability (Contribution) need to be clarified. There is a misconception that the 90 Day Accountability process is something divorced from the results. On the contrary, the very fact that there is complexity in the relationship between contribution and results dictates that both are clarified and seen in relation to each other.

243

By Responsibility is meant the demarcation of result areas and the specification of the critical results to be achieved by the workgroup/function/team to which the results have been assigned. By Contribution is meant the definition of the unique value-added contribution of each role in the organisation as well as the key deliverables within a reporting cycle for the individual incumbents of each role (see Clarifying, Contribution, Section Two).

- The clarification of Responsibility must precede the definition of Accountability because contribution takes place in the context of a set of results. In the absence of a clear set of results, contribution takes place in a vacuum – people could feasibly do anything.

- The clarification of Responsibility and Accountability must be an on-going process, although the frequency at which they are revised should be different. Responsibility is reassigned whenever structural changes are made, while the results to be achieved are set annually. Contribution is more dynamic and should be clarified more frequently, ideally every 90 days.

- Agreed Accountabilities need to meet a number of criteria. They absolutely must be of added value and unique. Further to this, they should be appropriate to the role or level in the organisation, forward focused, and manageable but stretching. Finally, they must be specific and concrete, simply because it is not possible to hold someone accountable for a generalisation.

- For those in leadership roles, the specification of their Accountability has to include the provision of care, means, ability and accountability for direct reports.

When the first element of the performance management process (Clarifying Contribution) is done well, it is enabling both for employees and for those in leadership roles.

For employees it is truly liberating to be released from the tyranny of results to actually attend to what they should be doing. Clarity of Contribution typically also impacts positively on performance. As Marcus

Buckingham says in his book *The One Thing You Need to Know* (2006): 'I have never met a confused, productive employee.'

Courage, a rare quality in most organisations, is also cultivated. Specifying upfront the unique value-add for the next reporting period shifts employees from reactive to proac-

CLARIFYING CONTRIBUTION ENABLES

Employee	Leader
Clarity of Contribution	Yardstick against which to hold people accountable
Focus / remove the clutter	
	Indicate what the leader should
Stop the 'sticky beak syndrome'	be giving / leadership accountability
Shift from reactive to proactive	
Empower / attend to what is in my control	

tive mode, forces a deliberate choosing of what to focus on and puts a stop to what they call in Australia 'the sticky beak syndrome'. With a clear and challenging listing of Accountabilities, an employee cannot spend too much time looking over the neighbour's fence; she needs to get on with what needs to be done in her own back yard!

Most importantly, employees grow because what they are accountable for is reviewed every 90 days and it is accountability, not training programmes, which drive development. While training may increase ability, and hence the capability to contribute, people only really grow when what they are accountable for changes.

Leaders are also enabled because, at last, they have a decent yardstick against which to hold people accountable. Since accountability is defined bottom up, they get clarity on what they should be *giving*. Now, in the most positive sense, no one has anywhere to hide.

2. Element Two: Assessment of Contribution by 'Watching the Game'

A result is measurable. It can be quantified and is normally expressed as a number. A contribution is generally not measurable, but that does not mean that it can't be assessed as being below/on/above a standard. Also, while a result can be monitored and communicated from a distance, the assessment of contribution requires first-hand observation

In soccer, for example, a fan can source the score from the media, but for him to know what actually accounted for the result, he would have to have watched the game. Did the team lose because the goalie had butter fingers or was the striker off his game? He would only know the answer if he was at the game or, second prize, if he asked someone who was there, whose observations he trusted.

Critical to the success of *Element Two: Assessing Contribution* is the following:

CRITICAL SUCCESS CRITERIA FOR ASSESSING CONTRIBUTION – WATCHING THE GAME

> ❖ Contribution can only be assessed through first-hand observation.
>
> ❖ Watching the Game needs to be done with the right intent.
>
> ❖ Adherence to the rules of Watching the Game.

- Leaders need to dedicate the time required to assess the contribution of each of their direct reports. Unless they do so they can't be helpful to them. For the coach to add value he has to go to the match and watch the players in action. By doing so, he helps the player identify the nature of the game he is playing and how that affects the results. Similarly, the manager can only add value once she has gained first-hand experience of each subordinate's performance against standard and the effect this is having on the results. This is not something that happens by accident. Watching the game requires a deliberate focus on process over outcome and, for most managers, this feels totally counter-intuitive. It only happens, therefore, when those in leadership positions have the insight that in fact they are most useful to their people when they are being useless! It only happens when managers deliberately plan to spend time watching the game and then follow through on their plan.

- Watching the game needs to be done with the right intent. In other words, the reason for the manager spending time in the subordinate's area should be benevolent. The key difference between watching the game and auditing/checking-up in fact lies in the issue of intent. When a manager is doing the latter he is essentially concerned with identifying and eliminating non-conformances. He is concerned with the result. When a leader is watching the game her intent is to understand what is at issue for the subordinate in her area and what she can do to enable the subordinate. Watching the game is about the leader determining what the 'give' is that the leader needs to make for the particular individual whose game she is watching.

- When watching the game, the person doing the watching needs to stick to the rules of doing so. First and foremost, the manager needs to watch the game, not play it. When watching the game the leader's attention should be focused on the person playing the game and not the outcome. The subordinate needs to be informed that his game is being watched. Watching the game, in other words, should not be a clandestine activity done in secret to the subordinate. Finally, feedback needs to be given as soon as possible after observation. Imagine the coach waiting until the end of the season before giving feedback on the team's first few games. Yet, managers can surprise subordinates in the year-end appraisal with information from long ago that the employee hadn't been made aware of at the time.

ASSESSING CONTRIBUTION ENABLES

Employee	Leader
Unselfish boss's time	Seeing is believing
Feedback: What doing right and what needs to change.	Understanding how to help the subordinate grow.

When the second element of the performance management system (Assessing Contribution) is done well, it enables employees and leaders in several ways. Leaders develop their understanding of how they can help their subordinates grow. They get a real sense of the means, ability and accountability issues, which are either facilitating or constraining employee contribution. In fact, the acid-test for whether watching the game has been successful or not is whether leadership has gained this understanding.

In addition, employees get quality time with their boss. This time is unselfish time because watching the game with the right intent requires the boss to truly suspend his agenda for the agenda of his subordinate. Employees also get honest, between-the-eyes feedback on what they are doing well and what they need to change in order to improve. Importantly, this is feedback that they can do something about, because it is specific, behavioural and based on first-hand observation.

3. Element Three: Regular review of contribution with the purpose of enabling enhanced contribution going forward

The actual frequency of the formal review discussion will vary but should, as a minimum, be consistent with the annual 90-day accountability cycle – that is, three times per year. The purpose of the review is for the manager and the subordinate to have a quality discussion which will enable the subordinate's contribution, growth and accountability going forward into the next reporting cycle. It is not about identifying and communicating the size of the bonus.

Critical to the success of *Element Three: Reviewing Contribution* is the following:

- The discussion should not be about negotiating a performance rating. The moment that a score becomes

CRITICAL SUCCESS CRITERIA FOR REVIEWING CONTRIBUTION

- ❖ Not about negotiating a performance rating.
- ❖ Adequate preparation.
- ❖ Focused on the future, not the past.
- ❖ Include clarification of Accountability for next reporting cycle.

the issue, the benevolent intent of the discussion is undermined. The absence of a score does not, however, mean that the person should not be held accountable (censured/disciplined/praised/rewarded) in the review. Holding a person accountable should be an on-going activity, not something that just happens at year-end. If holding people accountable is on-going, in the words of the group human resources manager at AEL Mining Services, the rating discussion at the end of the year is 'no different really than any other discussion because it flows naturally from previous discussions during the year'.

- Adequate preparation for the discussion should have been made. Prior to the conversation the scoreboard should have been updated (the results achieved over the reporting period established) and contribution assessed (as above/below standard on each deliverable) by watching the game. If this is not the case the review meeting simply becomes a report-back on what has been done, serving the information/control needs of the manager rather than the Care and Growth needs of the subordinate.

- The meeting should be focused on the future, not on the past. What happened in the previous reporting cycle (results achieved/ contribution made) is only useful from a diagnostic perspective. 80% of the meeting should be on the 'why' (Means, Ability, Accountability issues) which sit behind the 'what' (Results/Contribution). The discussion will then deliver a set of actions for both parties going forward, which will address means deficiencies, enhance ability and/ or cultivate the subordinate's accountability.

- The meeting must include a revision of accountabilities/clarification of contribution for the next reporting cycle. Revision of accountabilities every 90 days ensures flexibility in that people are not locked into a set of actions which may be done well, but do not necessarily contribute positively to the results. More importantly, unless accountability is revised, accountabilities remain static, and employees do not grow.

As with the first two elements, the third element (Reviewing, Contribution) is an enabler in the process of cultivating accountability and unleashing people's generosity and courage.

When the review discussion is done well, the outcome for the employee is a clear set of actions which should lead to enhanced contribution in the next cycle.

ACCOUNTABILITY REVIEW FORMAT

ACCOUNTABILITY	ASSESS-MENT On[=], Above[+] or Below[-]	WHY? SKILL	WHY? ABILITY	WHY? ACCOUNT ABILITY	ACTION	WHO/WHEN
1	Above			Reward	Special award	SS
2	On			Praise		
3	Below			Censure		SS
4	Below	Lacks Authority		None	Provide Authority	SS
5	Below		Influencing Weak	None	Coach/develop skills	TP
6	below			Censure		

For the manager, the focus on the 'why' ensures that both the 'hard' and 'soft' mistakes are avoided in holding subordinates accountable. As the example Accountability Review Format shows, sanctions/rewards are only given after the preconditions for accountability have been met. Conversely, where either positive (praise/reward) or negative (censure/discipline) accountability is due, it is put into effect. Accountability does not have to wait for the year-end rating/increment/bonus process, but is on-going throughout the year. The review discussion enables this to happen.

For the manager also, the revision of accountabilities at the end of the conversation ensures that the growth of the subordinate happens as it should. That is, incrementally and commensurate with the growth of accountability in the subordinate.

4. Element Four: Discipline and Reward consistent with holding people appropriately accountable

When the Fourth Element of the performance management system (Discipline and Reward) is implemented successfully, people in the organisation agree that deliberate malevolence is punished, carelessness is censured, performance to standard is recognised and exceptional contribution is rewarded.

Critical to the success of *Element Four: Discipline and Reward* is the following:

- Line managers are given the means to hold their people appropriately accountable. For example, they have the authority to discipline those who report to them directly. At the same time, they are able to reward those who consistently and tangibly go the extra mile significantly more than those who deliver to the agreed standard.

- Managers have the skills and knowledge required to hold their people accountable. They understand both the disciplinary process and the recognition/reward system and are competent to apply them. They have been trained and coached to do so.

- Managers have the will to hold their people accountable. They evidence the requisite generosity and courage to do so. There are positive conse-

CRITICAL SUCCESS CRITERIA FOR REWARD AND DISCIPLINE

- ❖ Managers have the Means and Ability to hold people appropriately accountable.

- ❖ There are consequences for managers for holding people appropriately accountable.

quences for managers who hold their people accountable. Managers who fail to hold their people accountable, having been given the means and ability to do so, are sanctioned for their cowardice/ selfishness.

When the fourth element of the performance management system (Discipline and Reward) is done well, employees' will to contribute is engaged and the very best in people is realised. Because people are motivated to *give* their all, they become truly powerful.

Teamwork is also enhanced, because the resentment which exists when passengers are tolerated is eliminated. The endless round of restructuring and retrenchment is dramatically reduced because these mechanisms are no longer used as an alternative to dealing with poor performance. Ultimately, those in leadership roles are trusted and held in high regard.

Effective implementation of a performance management process aligned to the Care and Growth framework obviously requires that the success criteria for each element of the system, dealt with above, are met.

IMPLEMENTING AN ALIGNED PERFORMANCE MANAGEMENT PROCESS

Standing back from the detail of each of the four elements, experience shows that the successful implementation of a performance management process aligned to the Care and Growth framework nevertheless revolves around two key issues:

- Getting the intent or the 'why' behind the process right.

- Taking care of 'how' the system is implemented in the organisation.

The issue of intent – the 'Why'

When people report to an excellent leader they excel; they are more productive working for that leader than working for someone else.

The Care and Growth model argues that excellent leadership is first and foremost about leaders having the best interests of their people at heart. This is an issue of intent. It is a reflection more than anything else of an individual leader's personal maturity. It is not a human resources policy matter. No people system can do this intent thing for the leader.

It is because excellent leaders care about their people that they are deeply preoccupied with the challenge of making the best in them possible. This being the case, the performance management process then becomes a useful tool in a leader's hands to turn his people's talents into exceptional performance. The performance management process literally becomes the means to the end of growing people.

Organisations are successful in implementing a performance management process aligned to the Care and Growth criteria, therefore, only when their 'why' for doing so is benevolent. That is, when their primary purpose for implementing the process is to grow leaders in their Care and Growth role.

The criterion which is then used for assessing whether the performance management process 'works' is whether people in the organisation have grown. Is exemplary contribution being enabled? Are more and more people in the organisation *givers* not *takers*?

For this reason, time needs to be spent by the senior leadership upfront clarifying and confirming their purpose in re-inventing the company's performance management process. If, in implementing the process, it appears that there is a deviation from that purpose, then leadership needs to act quickly and decisively to address it.

The following are two examples Schuitema has experienced where malevolent intent undermined implementation of the process. In the first instance, managers used the process to micro-manage and control people. Overly specified and detailed accountabilities were presented to subordinates like tablets of stone from on high. Managers spent much of their time controlling and checking-up that what was on the tablet of stone had been done.

In the second case, a lack of maturity throughout the organisation was at issue. Employees worked hard at agreeing accountabilities with their immediate manager that they couldn't fail to deliver on because they were so undemanding. Their motive was clear – to get rated highly on easy deliverables and hence guarantee for themselves a good year-end bonus.

In both cases the process inevitably failed.

The process of implementation – 'the How'

Earlier it was said that implementing a performance management process aligned to all four principles of accountability is not a trivial exercise because of the enormity of the change required. Each of the four shifts implied in the system is significant in its own right.

- Focus on results to focus on contribution.

- No/limited accountability for own action to absolute accountability for what sits in own hands.

- Getting work done through people to getting people done through work.

- Committing the 'soft'/'hard' mistake to holding people appropriately accountable.

Each shift, therefore, needs to be made with full cognisance of the change-management issues which need to be addressed in making the shift. Re-inventing the organisation's performance management process is, in effect, a strategic change and needs to be managed accordingly.

More specifically, successful implementation requires the following:

- All four elements should be implemented over time. To do the reflection part of the process (clarifying and reviewing contribution) without the action part (watching the game and holding people accountable) or vice versa is sub-optimal. Doing only the reflection part leads in practice to one-on-one discussions which are experienced as boring and meaningless. No wonder in many organisations they stop happening even when they are commanded to take place. On the other hand, only focusing on action develops, over time, a 'sticks' and 'carrots' culture.

- The four elements must be introduced in the right order. One retail bank kicked off with a dramatic change to its reward system. From a situation where everyone was rewarded solely on results, the annual increment decision was instantly changed to being anything from 40% to 80% contribution based. The rationale behind the percentages was sound; the higher up the hierarchy and, therefore, the further removed from the results, the higher the contribution percentage. The sum effect, however, was to throw the company into turmoil. Increment time was around the corner and contribution had not been clarified. Quite correctly, the human resources manager was at a loss as to how he was going to explain this to the employee representative body.

- Implementation needs to be slow and incremental. Johnson Matthey Catalysts ring-fenced manufacturing as the pilot for the new process. Only once it had success there did it extend the system to other parts of the business. Business Solutions Group (Africa), a small IT solutions business of about 160 people, spent four months clarifying the value-added contribution of each role in the company. It found that getting its people's minds around contribution versus result was not easy and only took the next step in the implementation process once it had done so. Another company ran the 90 day Accountability process in tandem with its traditional annual objective setting and six-monthly review system. It finally pulled the plug on the traditional system 18 months later, when employees, not management, professed to prefer the 90 day process.

- Finally, an organisation waited almost three years to make changes to how people in the business were held accountable for their contribution as follows. Salaries were adjusted annually, in line with market forces and business affordability, for everyone except those not contributing to the level required for reasons of malevolence. The latter did not get a salary adjustment. In addition, lump sum bonuses were deliberately made twice during the year, but only for those deemed to be exemplary contributors.

Each company's 'how' or implementation process will and should be different. Success, however, dictates that implementation of a performance management system aligned to Care and Growth should include all four elements, should be implemented one step at a time and in the right order, and should be incremental. When this is the case, the generosity and courage which is unleashed in the organisation is amazing.

Dealing with Exceptions

An exception can pertain to either a specific incident or to a result. Both incidents which are negative (a disabling injury, a customer complaint, a protracted breakdown) and those which are positive (a project delivered significantly below budget, an exceptional product launch, a shutdown completed in record time) constitute an exception. Similarly a result, as reflected as a score on a scoreboard (profit, sales revenue, picking error rate, customer service index), can be defined as an exception when it is unusually better or worse than the norm.

Dealing appropriately with exceptions means seeing them as instructive, as golden opportunities to learn about and enhance the quality of leadership in an enterprise. This is because whenever an exception arises in an organisation there is an opportunity, created by the exception, for one or more managers to gain clarity regarding what they should be doing with their immediate subordinates.

In due course, as more and more exceptions are analysed, the real command issues in a business will emerge. Understanding the command issues, which are the real causes behind all exceptions, in turn lays the foundation for a strategy to raise the calibre of leadership at every level in the line of command.

THE RESULT IS A SYMPTOM NOT A CAUSE

There is a basic premise which underpins the Care and Growth perspective on exceptions. It is that the exception per se, the unusual event or result, is a symptom not a cause. Behind any exception there are, in fact, two types of causes. The first type is external factors or factors outside of people's control. An example would be a lightning strike on an electricity substation, which led to certain parts of Johannesburg experiencing a power outage for several days. By definition, nothing can be done about truly extraneous factors. The legal term for them is 'force majeure'.

DEALING WITH EXCEPTIONS

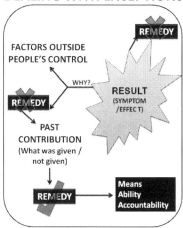

The second type of causes, on the other hand, are ones which something can be done about. These causes relate to past contribution – to what was done or not done, to what was given or not given – which caused the result. Past contribution, however, is itself a function of Means, Ability and Accountability factors which sit behind the contribution. People's actions, in other words, are determined by a combination of environmental conditions, by the skills and knowledge at their disposal and by their will or lack of it at the time. Dealing appropriately with an exception means that what is addressed is not the result itself, or even the human actions which led to it, but the Means, Ability and Accountability issues which determined the human actions in the first place.

In Pakistan this is expressed wonderfully: *'When the leaves on the tree turn yellow don't paint them green – rather water the roots.'*

What this means is that the effects of any remedial action which is taken at the level of a result, will at best be temporary. This is because when issues are not dealt with at source they come back again; either the exact same event repeats itself or the issue returns, but presents itself in a slightly different guise.

DIAGNOSING AND REMEDIATING MEANS, ABILITY AND ACCOUNTABILITY ISSUES

To deal appropriately with exceptions therefore requires, in the first instance, an ability to flush out and correctly identify the Means, Ability and Accountability issues which sit behind them. The type of remedial action required depends on whether it is a Means, Ability or Accountability issue. In other words, the medicine given must be right for the disease.

DIAGNOSIS	REMEDIATION
1. Means issues	Provide the means
2. Ability issues	Train / coach / redesign / redeploy
3. Accountability issues	Praise / reward censure / discipline

Means issues are those things in a person's environment that allow him to *give*. They include tools and resources, authority, time, enabling systems and processes, clarity of expectations and information or data. A lack of means is addressed by the provision of means; by taking whatever measures are required to ensure that environmental impediments to contribution are overcome.

Ability issues, on the other hand, have to do with the person and whether she can or cannot *give*. They relate to capacity, skills, knowledge, understanding and competence. Both the 'know-how' and the 'know-why' affect *Ability*. Unlike *Means* issues, *Ability* issues are best addressed by training or coaching, through job redesign or correct deployment of people to positions which match their capabilities.

Lastly, *Accountability* issues have to do with the will. That is, whether or not a person is willing or not to *give*, whether he takes accountability for making the contribution required of him or not. Accountability issues are addressed by holding people accountable both positively (by means of praise and reward) and negatively (through censure and discipline).

From experience, those in leadership positions do not find it altogether easy to define what they are actually dealing with, and hence what the appropriate leadership action(s) should be.

In a Care and Growth workshop, participants are given an exercise which requires them to diagnose a number of performance issues using the schematic outlined above.

Typically the exercise highlights two things.

PERFORMANCE ISSUE	DIAGNOSIS
1. I was not informed of the change in schedule.	Means
2. I keep forgetting to tell my manager to order more stock. Now we have run out.	Accountability
3. Sales figures have dropped by 10% this month.	Result / symptom
4. I do not know how to ensure a high quality of product or service.	Ability
5. I believe that the new targets we have been given are totally unrealistic.	Contribution
6. I am angry because I did not get the promotion. Now I am not interested anymore.	Accountability
7. I am not following the procedure in the manual.	Contribution
8. I am too busy to train new members of the team.	Means
9. I feel out of my depth when I have to deal with customer complaints on my own.	Ability
10. Quality has improved by 30% in the last month.	Result

Firstly, that there is a tendency to jump too prematurely to conclusions. For example, participants categorise items 3, 5, 7 and 10 as either *Means*, *Ability* or *Accountability* issues when they are not. They are results or actions, be they behavioural or cognitive. As such, the 'why' behind them still needs to be ascertained in order for the correct diagnosis to be made. Secondly, there is a tendency to make assumptions which are not necessarily valid. Item 7 is a classic in this regard. Participants typically assume that this is an *Accountability* issue. They make the supposition that the person is taking a shortcut, is doing what he wants to do rather than what the procedure requires of him.

The failure to follow the procedure could indeed be an *Accountability* issue. It is just as likely, however, to be a *Means* issue (the operating instruction was out of date and did not reflect best practice) or an *Ability* issue (the person has not been trained in what is the right thing to do and why).

A correct diagnosis can only be made on the ground. That is, by 'watching the game', literally observing first-hand what is actually happening and asking the sort of questions which will provide an understanding of what really is at issue.

I was party to an exercise which involved 'watching the game' of operators at AEL Mining Services Safety Fuse Plant over a 72-hour period. Our job was to witness any deviations from critical operating standards and to then ascertain the reasons for them. 70% of the reasons were *Means* issues, 20% were *Ability* issues and 10% were *Accountability* issues.

In all the diagnostic exercises that I have participated in since then *Means* issues have always been the most common, followed by *Ability*, and lastly *Accountability* issues. This makes sense to me. The majority of people come to work wanting to do the job right. The leader's task is to make it possible for them to do so.

HOLDING PEOPLE APPROPRIATELY ACCOUNTABLE

Taking action based on *Means*, *Ability* and *Accountability* issues, rather than in response to an action taken or a result, has far-reaching implications for how individuals are held accountable in a business. The following two exceptions in a sales environment illustrate the point.

Exception 1. (Specific Event) – a technical sales representative (TSR), in his mid-30s, with knowledge of the industry, has been with the company for nine months. During his first solo regional tour, he promised a customer a replacement catalyst, even though the current catalyst had only been in service for 80% of its expected life. Specifically, he committed to a delivery within a month at 45% off list price. His offer was in response to the customer's vociferous contention that the problems he was experiencing on his plant were primarily due to the under-performance of the supplier's catalyst. The effect of the TSR's decision was that the company not only lost considerable revenue, but it also set a dangerous precedent in replacing catalysts before the due date.

The action taken by the TSR was clearly wrong. He should have insisted that an independent investigation be carried out to establish the root cause of the client's poor plant performance. Moreover, by making the commitment to the customer that he did, he contravened company policy, which dictated that any discount of more than 15% off list price must be referred to a formal review.

The critical question in this incident, however, is why the TSR did what he did? What the TSR's manager, the regional sales manager (RSM), should give the TSR in this situation depends on the answers to the *Means*, *Ability* and *Accountability* questions shown below.

MEANS	Did the TSR have access to the conditions of sale? Did he have access to the RSM to ask for advice? Was the standard with respect to discounts clear? Did he know what the limits of his authority were?
ABILITY	Did the TSR lack the technical knowledge to counter the customer's claims? Did he lack assertiveness? Did he understand the implications of his actions?
ACCOUNTABILITY	Was his motive to serve the client? Did his desire to meet his sales targets for the quarter influence his actions?

The real value of this exception, in other words, lies in the opportunity it affords the RSM to understand what he should be doing with his subordinate. It enables him to act appropriately, as a leader, in the situation.

Exception 2. (Result) – a technical sales representative (TSR) has been in the job for four years and is a competent and conscientious person. He establishes multiple contacts in client organisations, stays up to date with his clients' operations and encourages local agents to maintain regular contact. As a result, he not only retains but wins new business with a strategically important client. In other areas of potential business, however, customer shutdown delays lead to business deferments. Recognising this, the TSR makes many customer calls and telephone contacts to try and make up the project shortfall in budgetary targets. He nevertheless misses his sales target by a substantial margin.

Under these circumstances it would be tempting for both the TSR and his manager, the regional sales manager (RSM), to write off the poor sales result to factors outside their control. In fact this exception provides the RSM with an opportunity to do two things.

Firstly, for him to review the TSR's sales target and possibly revise it for the next reporting period. Secondly, to assist the TSR to analyse his sales process and determine what changes he could make which would yield a better result in the future. Perhaps the RSM could increase the number of leads that he passes onto the TSR. Perhaps the TSR needs to keep closer contact with prospective customers so that he can react earlier to events in their business, etc.

ESTABLISHING THE COMMAND ISSUES BEHIND THE EXCEPTION

Very often, when exceptions arise there is a tendency to limit the investigation and resultant action taken to those who directly caused the exception. This is not appropriate, because whenever *Means*, *Ability* or *Accountability* factors are at issue for the person directly impacting on the result, there are command issues up the line which also need to be addressed. Ensuring that a person has the *Means*, *Ability* or *Accountability* to do what is required of him is the job of those in leadership positions. Being appropriate, therefore, means to not only determine 'why' whoever caused the exception did so but, in addition, to unpack the command issues which also had a bearing on the exception. Two actual incidents, a safety incident and a quality incident at a major chemical manufacturer in South Africa, are cases in point.

Safety Incident – third-degree burns suffered by an operator while trying to restart an extruder after it had tripped were directly caused by his failure to wear the required PVC raincoat at the time of the incident. Two other people also had an impact on the accident. The operator's colleague was aware that the operator was not complying with safety regulations but did not correct him. The shift manager, in contravention of company rules, left the plant during the shift, which delayed the time for the injured operator to get medical attention.

Management's response to the incident was to hold the relevant individuals accountable for their deliberate malevolence and to put in place additional means to prevent a reoccurrence of the problem. The operator, his colleague and the shift manager were all disciplined for wilfully doing what was wrong (*Accountability* actions). Clothes lockers were moved closer to the extruder area, the standard for the wearing of Personal Protective Equipment (PPE) was made more stringent and a system put in place to ensure that PPE was not removed from the plant (*Means* actions).

In fact what was most instructive about the safety incident was the command issues that it highlighted for those higher up in the line.

Firstly, the exception revealed that shift managers, across all four shifts, were generally not sufficiently in touch with what was taking place on their shifts. What was needed, therefore, was a clear standard regarding the amount of time shift managers should be out on their plant rather than in the control room. The process manager (whom the four shift managers reported to) needed to take accountability for ensuring that all his shift managers adhered to the new behavioural standard. Secondly, the exception pointed to a need for senior management to review the efficacy of the 'haz-ops' system on site. Despite a number of hazard studies having been conducted on the plant in the last 15 years, no recommendations had been made to redesign the system to remove a noted, hazardous condition in the first place.

Quality Incident – the operator did not take the corrective action that he should have taken in response to temperature changes on the reactor, such as dropping rates, reducing pressure or stopping cat-feeders. At 13h10 there was sufficient reason for him to institute a Type 1 Kill (shutdown the operation) but this was only done by him an hour later on the direct instruction of the production engineer. The direct cost to the company of his failure to act when he should have done so was estimated to be more than R1.6 million, excluding the company's loss of reputation amongst its customers.

The chairperson at the enquiry quite correctly recommended a two-week suspension without pay in lieu of dismissal for the gross negligence of the operator in this instance. More important than the specific action meted out to the operator, however, was the opportunity, created by the exception, to examine whether the means and ability provided by management to panel operators was adequate.

What emerged from the exploration of the leadership issues behind the exception was the following. The manning on the plant (*Means* issue) was enough to ensure safe operations, quality production and the training/coaching of people. The training process was thorough and the pass-out procedure rigorous enough to ensure that operators were not passed out when they were not fully competent (*Ability* issue). The competency process, however, was heavily reliant on the use of coaches who were technically well qualified, but lacked the skills to adequately transfer their technical experience to those they were coaching. The key leadership action, which was highlighted by the exception, was the need to develop the coaching skills of those with technical expertise in the process, so that they could effectively enable others to run the plant independently of themselves.

THE LEADERSHIP DIAGNOSTIC METHODOLOGY

Schuitema has developed a methodology for dealing with exceptions in an organisation, which has become known as the 'Leadership Diagnostic'. As an instrument, the Leadership Diagnostic is designed to identify the command issues, at every level of an organisation, which relate to whatever exception is under scrutiny at the time.

The Leadership Diagnostic has two parts to it. The first part is concerned with establishing who did what to cause the exception/the specific causes which led to the exceptional result. The second part of the Leadership Diagnostic involves the unpacking of the command issues behind every identified root cause. Typically there are a number of causes which account for a single exception.

The Leadership Diagnostic shown below was for a machine shop inspection backlog problem at an aeronautical company. Overall, the inspection team was not able to process the work quickly enough to keep up with current demand, let alone reduce the backlog. The investigation identified four causes at issue in this exception.

Leadership diagnostic – machine shop inspection backlog

PART ONE: Who did what to cause the exception? What are the root causes?

1. **Failure by inspectors to reduce backlog.**
   The causes behind the inadequate throughput by inspectors are primarily Means causes. The current inspectors are very knowledgeable and experienced.

   Although they are demoralised by the backlog problem, they are trying to do their best under the circumstances, despite feeling that management is not giving them the support they need to address the problem.

   The key reasons identified in the diagnostic are:
   - **Measurement** – There is neither planned daily output for the team/individual inspectors, nor review of their achievements against plan. There are no visual specific measures tracking progress against clear targets.
   - **Planning prioritisation** – A planning system based on a 'Work To Do' list and 'Hot List Racks' is not working. Programme managers jump the queue. There is no forewarning from planning.
   - **Documentation** – Inspectors are currently sourcing documentation themselves due to missing and sometimes incomplete documentation. There are delays in authorisation from planning.
   - **Lack of standards** – There are no standard times for different categories of inspection tasks. The stated times on engineering drawings are ignored.
   - **Lack of equipment** – There are delays in calibration of equipment. There are shortages in measuring equipment.
   - **Machines** – The location of machines is not optimal.

2. Design of work.

Inspection receives components which should have been scrapped by production.

There is no self-inspection done by production. The current requirement is for 100% inspection – no sample inspection or focus on critical dimensions only.

Inspectors are bogged down with 'simple' inspection tasks which could be done by less experienced personnel.

3. Failure to appoint inspectors/shortfall in complement.

The estimate of the number of inspector posts which need to be filled urgently varied from 1 to 3. Two people have been retrenched, one has resigned and one has moved into a crew chief role. This is in a context where, with hard data to substantiate it, the workload is increasing. While temporary inspectors are in position (on loan from production), there has not been an appointment of a permanent inspector or temporary inspectors (short-term contract). There is only one person with programming expertise in the team. The age profile of the current inspectors rings alarm bells in terms of medium-term planning.

4. Failure to develop, plan and implement an alternative strategy for inspection.

There are a least two, possible, alternative strategies to inspection. Decentralisation – take the inspectors to the work rather than the work to the inspectors; and/or self-inspection – hand over all or most of the inspection.

L E V E L	Who?: Inspectors WHY? (circle relevant)	Specific Means, Ability or Accountability which needs to be given.
	Did this person do this? If so, he should be **Recognised** or **Rewarded**. If he did not do this, was this a **Means** or an **Ability** problem? If it was not a means or an ability problem, the person should be **Censured** or **Punished**.	The lack of means in terms of measurement, planning of work, documentation, lack of standards, lack of equipment machines currently does not allow Inspectors to make the contribution required of them. Insufficient action has been taken to resolve these issues. It is the crew chief's job to provide the means. He needs to fulfil this critical aspect of his Care and Growth role.

L E V E L	Who?: Crew Chief WHY? (circle relevant)	Specific Means, Ability or Accountability which needs to be given.
	Did this person do this? If so, he should be **Recognised** or **Rewarded**. If he did not do this, was this a **Means** or an **Ability** problem? If it was not a means or an ability problem, the person should be **Censured** or **Punished**.	The crew chief has been in an 'acting' capacity for four months. He is well liked by subordinates but has not established himself in his role. He currently lacks both the Means and Ability to perform a Care and Growth role for his subordinates. He needs to stop doing Inspection work himself. He needs to be formally appointed and given full authority. He needs to understand his role by attending Care and Growth training and through coaching by his manager.

L E V E L	Who?: Production Leader WHY? (circle relevant)	Specific Means, Ability or Accountability which needs to be given.
	Did this person do this? If so, he should be **Recognised** or **Rewarded**. If he did not do this, was this a **Means** or an **Ability** problem? If it was not a means or an ability problem, the person should be **Censured** or **Punished**.	The production leader has been in the role for +/- 9 months. He currently carries all the responsibility and accountability given the leadership vacuum beneath him. Inspection is only 1 of 6 areas reporting to him. He needs to dedicate more time to the problem. He needs to drive an improvement plan for Inspection. He needs to coach the Crew Chief, not do his job for him.

L E V E L	Who?: Manager WHY? (circle relevant)	Specific Means, Ability or Accountability which needs to be given.
	Did this person do this? If so, he should be **Recognised** or **Rewarded**. If he did not do this, was this a **Means** or an **Ability** problem? If it was not a means or an ability problem, the person should be **Censured** or **Punished**.	The manager is also new in the role. He has prioritised the backlog in inspection and asks for progress reports on the issue. He needs to protect the production leader from other demands while he focuses on Inspection. He needs to develop and implement a new structure for the machine shop which separates operational from strategic improvement roles because currently the production leader is struggling to fulfil both roles.

Specific Cause 2: Design of work

L E V E L	Who?: Inspectors WHY? (circle relevant)	Specific Means, Ability or Accountability which needs to be given.
	Did this person do this? If so, he should be **Recognised** or **Rewarded**. If he did not do this, was this a **Means** or an **Ability** problem? If it was not a means or an ability problem, the person should be **Censured** or **Punished**.	*The inspectors currently receive scrap to inspect which should have been scrapped by production.* Production areas which are sending scrap for inspection need to be identified and stopped from doing so.

L E V E L	Who?: Crew Chief WHY? (circle relevant)	Specific Means, Ability or Accountability which needs to be given.
	Did this person do this? If so, he should be **Recognised** or **Rewarded**. If he did not do this, was this a **Means** or an **Ability** problem? If it was not a means or an ability problem, the person should be **Censured** or **Punished**.	*The problem of sending scrap to inspection has been escalated to the crew chief but not resolved.* The crew chief should refuse to accept scrap from production. He should elicit the support of the production leader in this regard/hold other crew chiefs accountable.

L E V E L	Who?: Production Leader WHY? (circle relevant)	Specific Means, Ability or Accountability which needs to be given.
	Did this person do this? If so, he should be **Recognised** or **Rewarded**. If he did not do this, was this a **Means** or an **Ability** problem? If it was not a means or an ability problem, the person should be **Censured** or **Punished**.	*The production leader is not holding production crew chiefs accountable for sending scrap to inspection. Inspection is doing work which should be done by production. Inspectors are doing 'simple' inspection work.* He should hold production team leaders accountable for sending scrap to inspection. He should assign production inspectors to do the 'simple' work. He should introduce self-inspection in production especially since he has authority for that area.

Specific Cause 3/4: Failure to appoint Inspectors / shortfall in complement AND failure to develop, plan and implement an alternative strategy for Inspection.

LEVEL	Who?: Crew Chief	WHY? (circle relevant)	Specific Means, Ability or Accountability which needs to be given.
	Did this person do this? If so, he should be **Recognised** or **Rewarded**. If he did not do this, was this a **Means** or an **Ability** problem? If it was not a means or an ability problem, the person should be **Censured** or **Punished**.		*There is no hard data to determine the manning requirements in Inspection. It is also not clear whether (if the means issues are resolved) more people are required or not.* The crew chief needs to determine the HR needs for his team. He is best placed to do so.

LEVEL	Who?: Production Leader	WHY? (circle relevant)	Specific Means, Ability or Accountability which needs to be given.
	Did this person do this? If so, he should be **Recognised** or **Rewarded**. If he did not do this, was this a **Means** or an **Ability** problem? If it was not a means or an ability problem, the person should be **Censured** or **Punished**.		*It is not clear where in the line the authority to fill appointments resides. A strategy to use temp inspectors from production is in the process of being implemented. Having one person with programming experience in the team is a key weakness.* If he does not already have the authority to appoint people in the workshop he should be given it. He needs to act on the crew chief's recommendations and ensure that the necessary appointments are made.

LEVEL	Who?: Manager	WHY? (circle relevant)	Specific Means, Ability or Accountability which needs to be given.
	Did this person do this? If so, he should be **Recognised** or **Rewarded**. If he did not do this, was this a **Means** or an **Ability** problem? If it was not a means or an ability problem, the person should be **Censured** or **Punished**.		*The current shortages assume a continuation of the current approach that is centralised inspection. Alternative strategies for the future need to be considered and, if appropriate, implemented. The current age profile of inspectors (60% over 50 years) is also a problem in the medium term.* The manager needs to assist the production leader in developing a strategy for the future. He needs to provide him with the means to effect a strategy. Strategic change requires dedicated time and resourcing. It is unlikely that the production leader can effectively implement strategic changes and simultaneously deal with the ongoing management of the workshop. A different structure for the machine shop is possibly required.

PART TWO: Tracking the command issues behind each cause

The second part of the 'Leadership Diagnostic' (tracking the command issues behind each cause) showed quite clearly the leadership contribution which was required, at each level in the line of command, to address the inspection backlog problem. Its effect was to reduce what was a significant business problem to a finite number of Means, Ability or Accountability actions which leaders needed to take with their immediate subordinate(s), as follows:

- **Level 1** (Crew Chief). The crew chief needed to provide the inspectors who reported to him with the means to do their jobs rather than spending 80% of his time doing inspection work himself. He needed to stop accepting scrap from production. Finally, he needed to motivate up the line for the manning levels required to get the job done.

- **Level 2** (Production Leader). The production leader needed to formally appoint the crew chief as the leader of the inspection team and train/coach him in his Care and Growth role. He needed to take action whenever a production team leader passed scrap through to inspection. He also needed to get Production to, as far as possible, inspect its own work.

- **Level 3** (Facilities Manager). The facilities manager needed to shield his production leader from other demands while he focused on the backlog problem. He also needed to develop and implement a new strategy and structure for more effectively dealing with the qualification of work in progress in the factory.

The findings from the Leadership Diagnostic gave each person in the line the opportunity to empower the level below him. Within four months the racks outside the inspection area were virtually empty. The required throughput was being achieved without an increase in the number of inspectors and without excessive overtime being worked.

The inspectors were much happier and more motivated than before, primarily because each level of management above them was doing what was appropriate with those who reported to them directly.

LESSONS LEARNED FROM USING THE LEADERSHIP DIAGNOSTIC METHODOLOGY

Experience over the years, both doing Leadership Diagnostics and coaching managers in doing so (inter alia in the mining, manufacturing, banking and hospitality industries) has produced a number of insights about

LESSONS LEARNED

- Do with benevolent Intent.
- Do on both Positive and Negative exceptions.
- Do both Reactive and Proactive Diagnostics.
- Apply the tool with a specific purpose in mind.
- Apply the tool to a specific incident or result.
- Diagnose by 'Watching the Game'.
- Ask 'Why?' all the way up the line.
- Remedial Action needs to be owned and driven by the line.
- Be wary of excuses – invalid Means and Ability claims.
- Accept that the improvement timeframe will be shorter when Means and Accountability are at issue rather than Ability.

the use of Leadership Diagnostics. They are as follows:

- Leadership Diagnostics should be done with benevolent intent. That is, not as some kind of witch hunt or as an effort to apportion blame. Leadership Diagnostics do in fact have a noble purpose. It is to enable enhanced future contribution all the way up the line. As such, the methodology's primary function is to grow leaders at every level in an organisation.

- Leadership Diagnostics should be done on both positive and negative exceptions. This helps to dispel the myth that a Leadership Diagnostic is essentially punitive in nature, used by management as a means to censure and discipline people. More importantly, doing a Leadership Diagnostic on positive exceptions can help to cultivate excellence in an organisation. Ascertaining what an exceptional performer does (be she a picker in a warehouse or an operations executive) and the *Means*, *Ability* and *Accountability* factors which support her in her excellent performance can yield vital selection and development information for an enterprise. Similarly, determining what each person in the line did to effect an exceptional result (for example, a dramatic improvement in safety performance) can ensure a perpetuation of the positive outcome into the future and/or a replication of excellence in other areas.

- Leadership Diagnostics can be both reactive and proactive. A reactive diagnostic is by definition an analysis of the past. Its value lies in the learning afforded by the event/outcome which has already taken place. A proactive diagnostic on the other hand can be used to improve on past performance going forward. In the case of a proactive diagnosis a stretch goal is set, after which the diagnostic determines what specifically needs to be done by whom (including each person up the line of command) to ensure that the desired outcome is achieved.

- Organisations reap the greatest dividends from the methodology when the tool is used with a specific purpose in mind. An organisation may, for example, elect to do Leadership Diagnostics only on safety incidents (disabling injuries and even near misses) in order to improve its safety performance. Conversely an organisation may decide to do a diagnostic on every complaint it receives from customers because product quality is the burning issue in its business. An aeronautical company undertook a number of Leadership Diagnostics on a variety of exceptions in its business, ranging from 'incorrect stock quantities on the MRP system' through to 'machine downtime in the sheet metal shop due to the unavailability of material'. From the dozen or more exceptions that were analysed over a two-week period it was sufficiently equipped to put together a strategy and action plan to address the core leadership issues in the business.

- The more specific the incident or the result which is chosen for analysis the better. This is because finding solutions to the specific exception per se is actually not the reason for the diagnostic. The specific exception is purely a vehicle for getting to grips with the key command issues which are evidenced by the exception. 'Being appropriate' means addressing each of the command issues which any diagnostic evidences, not fixing the specific exception.

- Leadership Diagnostics highlight the importance of 'watching the game'. A diagnostic is only as useful as the quality of information on which it is based. Quality information can only be garnered by spending time in the field gathering the facts, through direct observation and asking questions of all involved. It is useful, by the way, to get a range of different perspectives when doing a diagnostic. Often, someone who is unfamiliar with the situation, but who knows what *Means*, *Ability* and *Accountability* questions to ask, can provide the most penetrating insights.

- The Leadership Diagnostic needs to be done all the way up the line, preferably to the most senior level in the organisation. This is because what is done or not done seven levels removed from the actions which directly caused the exception, can often constitute the most critical cause. What senior managers do or don't do in a situation is often the 'bull's-eye', the 20% of causes which accounts for 80% of the results. This is confirmed by the fact that remedial actions taken high up in the hierarchy tend to have a far bigger impact than those taken at lower levels. For example, improving the 'haz-op system' on site, in the case of the chemical manufacturer mentioned previously, would have a considerably higher impact than holding the injured operator accountable for not wearing his PVC raincoat.

- In the case of Reactive Diagnostics, concerted and systematic remedial action needs to be taken after the diagnostic. The required remedial actions, based on the diagnostic, must, moreover, be owned and driven by line. Unless this is the case, Leadership Diagnostics may produce some interesting findings but nothing more than that. Sadly there are far more documented Leadership Diagnostics than those which have been acted on. When this is the case, Leadership Diagnostics stand the risk of becoming an academic exercise rather than a means to significantly strengthen an organisation's line of command.

- Not all *Means* and *Ability* issues are valid. Often people proffer Means and Ability issues to avoid being held accountable for their carelessness or deliberate malevolence. When they are in fact 'excuses' they should be treated accordingly.

- Improvements in contribution can be realised most quickly when the issues impeding contribution are *Means* or *Accountability* issues. *Ability* issues, by definition, take longer to address. The machine shop inspection backlog example is a case in point. A dramatic improvement in throughput was realised very quickly, simply by putting the requisite *Means* in place, which would enable the inspectors to do what they were there to do – pass or fail components in the production process.

Responding to exceptions in a business by doing Leadership Diagnostics on them is almost counter-intuitive. Managers typically react to exceptions by taking action to reduce the effect of the exception and, further to this, instituting a control to prevent the exception from coming back again. Management actions have short-term benefits in that the symptom typically goes away, but have no lasting effect. Moreover, management's desire to personally fix the result as quickly as possible often leads to what is referred to as a 'collapsing of the line'. In jumping over the heads of managers/supervisors in the line to get to and fix the result, management effectively disables the line of command below them.

Organisations which have deliberately cultivated the use of the methodology have reaped the greatest dividends from the Leadership Diagnostic methodology in their organisations. They have made the doing of Leadership Diagnostics mandatory and have tasked managers at all levels with reporting back on the findings of their diagnoses on a regular basis. African Explosives Ltd even set a standard for the number of diagnostics done every month on the site and kept score of how well they performed against the standard.

As with everything else, reward follows contribution. Initially doing Leadership Diagnostics seems to be hard work. The benefits which accrue in terms of significant improvements in the calibre of leadership in a business are, however, more than worth it.

SECTION FIVE

The Care and Growth Intervention

So far this book has dealt with each of the specific variables related to unlocking employee contribution at work. In the preceding chapters the practicalities of providing employees with the MEANS to contribute, the ABILITY to do so, and cultivating their will to take ACCOUNTABILITY and be held accountable for their contribution, have been addressed.

It remains to take a step back from the specifics to consider HOW TO implement the Care and Growth model, in its entirety, within an organisation.

This final section (Section Five) consists of a single chapter – *How to implement the Care and Growth model in an Organisation*.

So far this book has set out the principles and practices of the Care and Growth model. These principles and practices can be applied on a DIY basis by small or large businesses, according to their needs. When so applied, they can have dramatic effects, without any involvement by Schuitema.

The final chapter, nevertheless, sets out the methods and tools developed over twenty years to apply the principles of the model. These methods and tools offer expanded insight into how the model can be implemented to best effect. As before, it is for every business owner or manager to decide what elements to take on board.

It does not seek to provide a 'recipe' since one does not exist. Nor does it claim to have the final answer in terms of implementing the Care and Growth model because both the model itself, as well as its implementation, continues to evolve with time.

This chapter begins with what a Care and Growth intervention is and is not. It clarifies the deliverables of this type of intervention as well as those factors which are critical to a successful implementation of the framework. The remainder of the chapter deals with the content and the process of a Care and Growth implementation.

For each of the three areas of content – **Leadership Excellence**, **Team Excellence** and **Personal Excellence** – the three process steps of **establishing**, **diagnosing** and **remediating** against the Care and Growth criteria are explained. Finally conclusions are drawn regarding realising what the model seeks to promote – namely human excellence at the level of the individual, the group and the organisation as a whole.

How to implement the Care and Growth model in an organisation

Knowing the Care and Growth model and *implementing* it are not the same. The former is about understanding the model's basic tenets and what they mean practically. It is a process that takes place in the head. Implementation of the model, on the other hand, is about changing or transforming an organisation. It requires intervention to make it happen.

ORGANISATIONAL TRANSFORMATION

Purpose
(Vision, Mission, Strategy)
Structure
(Work processes,
Organisational design,
Resources)
Culture
(Values, Behaviour, Motivation)
Professional Competence
(Knowledge, Skills)

By definition, therefore, a Care and Growth intervention is NOT a training intervention. Organisational transformation never has, and never will, eventuate in a training room.

A Care and Growth intervention also does NOT equal a leadership development process. Implementing the model in its entirety involves everyone in the organisation, not only those in leadership roles.

As an organisational transformation process it touches all aspects of an organisation: purpose, structure, systems, values, behaviours, motivation and competence. Only business strategy – choice of business model, products and markets – is not within its scope.

THE DELIVERABLES IN A CARE AND GROWTH INTERVENTION

A Care and Growth intervention impacts on employee contribution in an organisation. It does not lay claim to improved business performance, since results can improve for all sorts of reasons extraneous to a transformation of the human side of an enterprise. At the same time there is obviously a connection between people and results. More than that, our experience is that organisations only change when those who work within them change, starting with a transformation of those in charge of the organisation. The cause and effect chain is as follows.

THE CAUSE AND EFFECT CHAIN

Implementation of the model in its entirety realizes the following organisational outcomes.

ORGANISATIONAL OUTCOMES	
AXIOM 1 *Legitimate Power*	• The collective leadership of the enterprise is seen to be legitimate and to have the support of the majority of its employees to being led by it.
AXIOM 2 *Care and Growth*	• There is an inversion of service from 'up' to 'down' the line, which changes the spirit of the average reporting relationship from being boss-centred to subordinate-centred.
AXIOM 3 *Empowerment*	• Individual accountability is cultivated as people take accountability for and are held accountable for their contribution.

AXIOM 4 *Giving*	• The organisation has a noble purpose which engages the will of all who work within it. • There is a commitment by the average employee to give willingly in pursuit of the organisation's objectives.

What enables these outcomes is the cultivation of the intent to serve at the level of the individual, the team and the organisation. At the individual level, the change from *taking* to *giving* is reflected in what

INDIVIDUAL

• **Focus** – from what I can 'get' to what I can 'give' or contribute
• **Concern** – concern with 'rights' to concern with 'duties'
• **Drive** – from 'needs' to 'values' driven

people at work focus on, what concerns them, and what drives their behaviour.

A Care and Growth intervention fosters people at work, whose focus is on what they can *give* or contribute to the organisation and who are concerned with what they owe others, rather than their *rights*, or what they believe they are owed. It cultivates employees whose behaviour is primarily values-driven rather than needs-driven, who do what is right rather than what is expedient. According to Graham Edwards, chief executive of AECI Group, the essence of the intervention in his company *'unleashed a spirit of generosity and courage in our people that we hitherto had not thought was possible.'*

TEAM

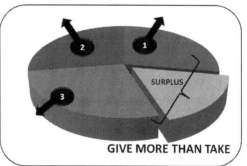

GIVE MORE THAN TAKE

At the team level it cultivates team members' preparedness to subordinate their own interests for the bigger interests of the team. It grows teams where transactions between team members are collaborative, rather than competitive, in nature and where individuals in the team are at least as concerned with setting others up to succeed as they are with pursuing their own shine.

ORGANISATION

4 POSSIBILITIES

1. We value our people √
2. We value our people *and* the contribution they make
3. We value our people *for* the contribution they make
4. We value the contribution made

At an organisational level, the essential change which a Care and Growth intervention effects is a change in what are MEANS and what are ENDS. Employees and customers are now the end, while they were previously the means.

The social contract that an organisation has with its people is fundamentally altered. What the organisation values, people and/or results, is transformed.

A Care and Growth intervention also changes the relationship that the organisation has with its external shareholders. There is a conviction that any enterprise ultimately exists

ORGANISATION

Does Demand exist to serve Supply?

OR

Does Supply exist to serve Demand?

to serve its customers, not itself. As a consequence of this, the primary purpose of the organisation shifts from maximising shareholder value to adding value to the customer, to the community and the environment in which the company operates.

FOR WHOM AND WHEN IS A CARE AND GROWTH INTERVENTION APPROPRIATE

From the above it should be clear that a Care and Growth intervention is applicable in any organisation where employee contribution makes a difference to the excellence of the organisation. Whether a Care and Growth intervention is applicable is not a function of what the organisation does, nor where it is located. The Care and Growth model has been successfully implemented in diverse contexts, both in the public and private sector, and in countries across the globe.

It has made a contribution in organisations beset with industrial conflict and employee distrust and in those where relationships were essentially healthy. It has been applied in highly sophisticated environments as well as in those which are far more basic.

WHEN A CARE AND GROWTH IMPLEMENTATION IS NOT APPROPRIATE

1. The business is broken
2. Incapacity issues
3. Lack of morality at the top
4. Arrogance

There are however four situations in which a Care and Growth intervention has shown itself to be inappropriate. The first instance is when a business is fundamentally broken and is teetering on the brink of collapse. Under these circumstances radical surgery, if not an unplugging of the life support system, is what is called for. Secondly, a Care and Growth intervention cannot gain traction in an organisation staffed with employees who are incapable of performing their jobs to at least a minimum standard. Implementation of the model requires a reasonable match between the work that needs to be done and people's capability to do it.

A Care and Growth intervention also won't succeed when the leadership of an enterprise is morally destitute. The model provides a moral compass for those at work. It simply won't 'fit' in an organisation where the moral quality of those in charge is seriously questionable.

Finally, implementation of the model is not likely to make a contribution in an organisation in which there is an overriding perception of having 'already arrived'. That is, when the leadership of an enterprise is convinced that they currently subscribe to most, if not all, aspects of the model. In this instance, Care and Growth really doesn't have anything to offer.

Over the last twenty years, any of the above four sets of circumstances have been relatively rare. On a few occasions, we have tried and failed to successfully implement the model with organisations where these conditions are present. In retrospect, we either should not have engaged with the particular organisation in the first place, or should have discontinued our services as soon as one of the four realities became evident.

FACTORS WHICH ARE CRITICAL TO THE SUCCESSFUL IMPLEMENTATION OF THE CARE AND GROWTH MODEL

There are three critical factors necessary for a Care and Growth intervention to succeed. They are INSIGHT, COURAGE and PERSEVERANCE by the leadership of the organisation.

- **INSIGHT**

  Many of those in positions of authority who are exposed to the Care and Growth model don't actually 'get' it. The model is seemingly simple and leaders therefore miss what it is arguing for – nothing less than a radical revision of management beliefs and practices. Leaders learn the language of Care and Growth but fail to comprehend what sits beneath the model's vocabulary. They do not perceive what the following statements imply about a change to their leadership.

  Statements from the Care and Growth model

  'Managers only have power by permission'
  'Leadership and power are not concerned with what you can get out of people, but rather with what you can give them'
  'Empowerment is not possible without giving up control over outcomes'
  'Giving is not about being nice, but rather about being appropriate'

  When leaders really 'get' the Care and Growth model they arrive at two key insights. The first, 'that leaders are there for their people, not the other way round', is hard enough to accept. This is because managers, by and large, are measured and rewarded for what they get out of their people not for what they give them.

The second insight is even more demanding. It is that Care and Growth is not even about one's people, but about oneself – that you, not them, are the project'. Repeatedly we have found that the full benefits of a Care and Growth intervention are only realised when there is a personal transformation of those in charge of the enterprise. The successful leadership of others is ultimately only possible from a place of personal maturity as a human being.

- **COURAGE**

  The Care and Growth model is anything but a 'soft and fluffy' thing. To fully implement the model takes backbone and courage.

  ## It takes courage to …

  - Hold people accountable
  - Give up power
  - Shift attention from outcome to process
  - Do what is right

  From experience, most managers find it inordinately difficult to hold people accountable. Consequently, it is the 'soft' rather than the 'hard' mistake which is most prevalent in organisations. Similarly many managers balk at handing over control. They lack the will to let go, to trust others and by doing so to put others in a position to demonstrate their trustworthiness. It also requires courage to shift attention from outcome to process, and even more so to stay focused on contribution when the desired result is not forthcoming.

  Finally, there are always points in any Care and Growth intervention which challenge leaders' capacity for unconditional giving. Situations inevitably arise, which test leaders' preparedness to put themselves on the line, to act on the basis of what is correct rather than what is expedient.

  The essence of the Care and Growth model is benevolence in the heart, but steel in the hand. Without the requisite leadership mettle a genuine implementation of the model is not possible.

- **PERSEVERANCE**

A question that we pose during our Care and Growth workshops is 'Who should change first in the organisational hierarchy?' The first response is always that it is the person at the top who should change first. Until he or she changes, no one will change.

We then divide delegates into groups, with each group being assigned a position in the hierarchy. Each group is then tasked with coming up with a compelling argument as to why they should be the ones to change first. Despite the initial bias in favour of change from the top, convincing arguments are presented in support of change at every level. The conclusion is obvious. The person who can and should change first is ME. More than that, if I don't make the change then the only person accountable is ME.

Clearly it is first prize if the change is indeed led from the top. When leaders at senior levels in the organisation provide the example for others to follow, the implementation process is undoubtedly accelerated. In practice, however, we have found this to be rarely the case. Our experience has shown that it is actually almost impossible to predict where and who in the line will change first.

When Care and Growth was implemented at the explosives factory I worked in many years ago, the person who changed first was a team manager in one of the plants.

Everything in the man's area – productivity, quality, delivery, was a mess. He returned from a Care and Growth workshop and asked the twenty operators in his charge a question that he had never asked them before. It was: 'How can I help you make better connectors (used in explosives)?'

The answer he got was dead silence. This was not surprising, because he previously had only ever exhorted them to give him more and better production.

So he asked them to think about it and in due course they told him. He made it the purpose of his job to remove as many barriers to their delivery as he could. Within ten weeks the results were astonishing.

Care and Growth actually begins in an organisation when one or more individuals, having being exposed to the model, go away and do something with it. The results they accrue from doing so not only personally encourage them to continue, but provide an example for others to follow.

The germination of Care and Growth happens slowly and often takes time to be noticed. At some point, however, it takes root and gathers momentum. Eventually, a point is reached when some sort of critical mass is achieved. Care and Growth is then no longer an exception, it is the norm.

The Blue Cheese Analogy

This has become known as 'the blue cheese analogy'. What begins as a tiny spec of blue advances bit by bit, until a point is reached when at last the cheese becomes 'blue cheese'. This landmark is not necessarily quantifiable, but it can be sensed – it can be seen, felt and smelled – just like a good piece of blue cheese.

Organisations, in other words, do not transform overnight. This is because people are still people, irrespective of advances in technology. Humans, because they are human, require time to respond and adapt to change.

Cultivating an organisation which embodies the principles and spirit of Care and Growth requires patience and perseverance by everyone involved in the process. It should not be contemplated by those who are not in it for the long haul.

Organisations which have reaped the greatest rewards from the model have stuck with the process. Their success has been the sum effect of an on-going series of mini steps made diligently and persistently over a considerable period of time.

CULTIVATING HUMAN EXCELLENCE – CONTENT AND PROCESS

Cultivating human excellence, the intent to serve, in an organisation suggests three areas of content.

Human Excellence – Content

- **Leadership Excellence** – establishing legitimate relationships of power throughout the line of command.

- **Team Excellence** – cultivating interactions between people, which are fundamentally collaborative rather than competitive.

- **Personal Excellence** – enabling personal maturity as a human being by increasing an individual's capacity to suspend his own interests for what is correct in the moment that he is in.

It is possible to work in any of the content areas but, practically speaking, not simultaneously. Most organisations have elected to start in the Leadership Excellence space on the assumption that 'the fish rots from the head'. In the context of an organisation this is a logical place to start.

Content Areas

Those organisations which have gone on to work in the other two areas have typically done so as a result of the following realisations.

The impetus for working with the Team Excellence content is the insight that 'organisations are not so much a function of the people in them, as they are a reflection of the nature of the interactions which take place moment by moment between individuals in an organisation'. For organisations to flourish, the register of the nature of engagement in the organisation must shift from 'what I can get out of this interaction' to 'what I should be contributing'.

The Personal Excellence content is embraced when the insight is gained that 'to truly care for and grow others requires a remarkable degree of maturity and personal mastery by the person doing the caring and growing'. In short, you can't lead others if you are not, in the first instance, in charge of your own life.

Leadership Excellence

The Leadership Excellence content centres around the universal criteria for legitimate relationships of power at work. It translates the Care and Growth criteria into key leadership tasks for those at different points in the leadership hierarchy.

At the first line manager level, the primary Care and Growth tasks are those of knowing and demonstrating concern for individual team members, enabling those who contribute directly to the results to do so, establishing standards of excellence and holding subordinates accountable against them.

What Care and Growth means for...

In addition to the above, managers of managers need to revise their time and attention away from outcomes to building the capacity to achieve outcomes. They also need to develop their ability to coach the first line managers who report to them, learn how to deal appropriately with exceptions in their areas, and acquire the skills to turn victims into masters.

Over and above the coaching, diagnosing and counselling tasks required by middle managers, those at senior levels need to execute the following leadership tasks. They need to establish and teach the benevolent intent of the enterprise to everyone within it, inculcate the Care and Growth values, align everyone in the organisation to a set of measures which gives them feedback on their contribution, create enabling structures and systems and provide a clear line of sight between individual contribution and results.

Implementing the Leadership Excellence content has three process steps: establishing, diagnosing and remediating against the Care and Growth criteria.

- **ESTABLISHING CRITERIA**

    Workshops are the vehicle for establishing the criteria for Leadership

Excellence. The Care and Growth Introductory Workshop (two days) serves the purpose of establishing an understanding of and commitment to the Care and Growth philosophy and principles. The workshop content is the same at all levels in the hierarchy but is adapted to the level of participants at the workshop.

Thereafter a series of Application Modules, or what Business Solutions Group Africa has labeled 'Master Classes', are deployed over a period of time, on a drip feed basis, as half or one day workshops. The Application Modules consist of a suite of workshops. The choice of modules depends on the target population (see above) as well as

Care and Growth Application Modules

- The Meaning of Care
- Living the Care and Growth Values
- Designing Enabling Structures
- Empowering Subordinates
- The issue of Time and Attention
- The issue of Control and Authority
- Coaching for Excellence
- Dealing with Exceptions
- Holding People Appropriately Accountable
- Clarifying Contribution
- Measures and the Team Review Meeting
- Making Masters
- Assessing, Reviewing and Rewarding Contribution
- Dealing with Immature Subordinates, etc

the identification of those content areas most helpful at a point in time. Each module provides a deeper understanding of the particular leadership issue under review and provides practical leadership tools for application in the workplace.

Organisations which have optimised the Application Modules process have done the following:

- Customised the content to their organisation.

- Done a pre- and post-assessment of understanding of the content.

- Required participants to do and then report back on their experience of applying the tools in the workplace.

The best results are achieved when the content is delivered by credible leaders within the organisation and/or when coaches in the organisation have supported leaders in the application of the tools. In one case, a senior manager dedicated over 500 hours to the coaching process, the results of which were significant in terms of entrenching the tools in the organisation.

It should be said that for some individual leaders nothing more than the initial two-day workshop is required. Either they have been intuitively applying the Care and Growth criteria already, or they instinctively know how to do so. Far more often, however, we are approached by those who attend the Introductory workshop with 'this makes absolute sense, but what do I DO to implement it?' The Application Modules are the 'how tos' in terms of leaders' day-to-day leadership practices.

In addition, the implementation of the Care and Growth criteria in an organisation has been facilitated by a further two-step process: diagnosing and remediating against the criteria.

- **DIAGNOSING AGAINST THE CRITERIA**

Diagnosing against the criteria has two functions. Firstly, it stimulates action by holding up a mirror to the collective and individual leadership of how they are currently faring against the criteria. Secondly, diagnosis gives focus in terms of those changes in leadership practice which the diagnostic has highlighted will bring about the most benefits to organisational performance.

There are three possible diagnostic instruments for this purpose: the Employee Opinion Survey, the Leadership Audit, and the Organisation Diagnostic.

The *Employee Opinion Survey* goes beyond providing a thorough understanding of the climate of employee opinion to the 'why' which sits behind employee estimations. It accesses the following vital information as a basis for crafting an effective remedial strategy.

The **Leadership Audit** assesses the degree to which individual leaders and the leadership in total are currently aligned to the Care and Growth criteria.

The deliverable from the Leadership Audit is a profile for each individual leader as well as aggregate profiles for levels, departments and the organisation as a whole. The profiles are compiled from subordinate feedback on the premise that those best placed to measure a leader against Care and Growth are the recipients of it.

Leadership Assessment

SAMPLE SIZES: LEADER: 4		
SCORES FOR:	2010	2011
CARE	1.8	2.2
MEANS	3.0	2.9
ABILITY	1.0	2.5
ACCOUNTABILITY	-2.0	2.2
OVERALL	0.1	2.5

On the scale of 10 to minus 10, a score above five is good, from zero to five is an indication that attention to the relevant aspect is needed and any score below zero is indicative of a serious problem.

The purpose of the profile is to indicate to the leader areas of strength opposite the Care and Growth criteria, as well as focus points for improvement. At Johnson Matthey Catalysts, the Leadership Audit has supported a process for coaching improvements in leadership behaviour. The human resources director summed up the efficacy of the process with the comment, 'the bottom line is that we have better managers now than we did, and most of them are the same people'.

The **Organisation Diagnostic** makes an assessment of the organisational context against the Care and Growth criteria. Its deliverable is a determination of the organisational changes which need to be made to support a sustainable implementation of the Care and Growth framework.

The Organisational Diagnostic goes beyond opinion and perception to an investigation of the organisational variables which enable leadership excellence. Conducted over a number of days at the company's premises, it includes a selection or all of the following types of analysis.

THE ORGANISATIONAL DIAGNOSTIC

- A review of organisational structure to determine how enabling or disenabling structures are to Care and Growth.
- An assessment of the degree to which organisational measures, or scoreboards, evoke employee contribution.
- Attendance at a representative sample of operational review meetings to examine their usefulness in encouraging generous and courageous action.
- The use of leadership diagnostics to determine the command issues behind positive and negative exceptions in the business.
- The shadowing of individual leaders to gain first-hand observation of leadership practices.
- An examination of the use of controls in the organisation's systems and processes.

One or more of the three diagnostic indicators, when done at the start of an intervention, can provide a baseline measure which, if repeated on an interim basis, can be used to track the efficacy of remedial action over time.

- **REMEDIATING AGAINST THE CRITERIA**

Remediating against the Care and Growth leadership criteria is different from one organisation to another. This is because any enterprise's remediation or implementation strategy is informed by both the self-reflection that takes place in the Care and Growth workshops and the findings made by diagnosing against the criteria. The steps taken and their sequence are, by definition, unique.

What is given below is not an exhaustive list, but a selection from what different organisations have done during the remediating phase of the process. The remediation specifics have been dealt with in Sections Two, Three and Four earlier in the book.

IMPLEMENTING THE CARE AND GROWTH LEADERSHIP FRAMEWORK

- **Company Values** – Inculcating values by making explicit what acting consistently with what each value means, integrating values into management practices and holding people accountable against them.
- **Enabling Structures** – Redesigning the organisation to create whole-task work teams and empowering management structures.
- **Time and Attention** – Implementing leadership diaries, which dramatically change how leaders spend their time and what they give attention to.
- **Scoreboards** – Reconfiguring or changing what is used to measure organisational and team success.
- **Goal Alignment** – Instituting an inclusive planning and goal alignment process which engages the will of employees. Then using achievement against goals as the spine of the operational review meeting focused on the 'why' behind the results.
- **Vertical Empowerment** – Defining contribution at different levels in the hierarchy and incrementally devolving decision-making authority away from the centre and down the line.

- **'Snake-killing'** – Systematically removing excessive controls in horizontal business processes.
- **Team Coaching** – Establishing Communities of Practice/ Leadership Forums as vehicles for leaders to learn from each other's experience.
- **Individual Coaching** – Implementing coaching practices where the primary deliverable is a change in the ability of direct reports.
- **Leadership Diagnostics** – Deploying the Leadership Diagnostic Methodology to change the way that exceptions are dealt with in the business.
- **Performance Management Process** – Re-inventing the performance management process and using it to grow leaders

Schuitema's role in the implementation process is to assist in the choice and sequence of implementation activities. It is also to provide a team and individual coaching/consultation service to support leaders in implementing one or more of the above.

Team Excellence

The Team Excellence content is built on the premise that a team succeeds only when the individuals in the team collectively give more than they take. That is, when they subordinate their own interests to the bigger interests of the team. The capacity that people can, and do, have to do this has very little to do with how much they 'have' or how much they 'know'. This capacity to give lies at the level of the will or intent.

Individuals' preparedness to give unconditionally in a group context is, in the first instance, solicited by the leadership of the group. As was argued in the leadership excellence content above, people go the extra mile for leaders of groups who care for and grow them. In addition to this there are four critical variables which account for successful teams.

Firstly, the team has an objective or purpose that solicits the intent to contribute. That purpose has to do with serving the customer. Secondly, each member finds meaning in the job that she does based on an understanding of how her individual role contributes to orchestrating the success of the team. Thirdly, the nature of the interactions between individuals in the team are fundamentally collaborative rather than competitive. For this to happen requires individuals in the team to confirm the significance of other team members. Respect for the contribution of others is the 'gel' which binds team members together. Lastly, the team has an established set of rules of engagement which govern behaviour in the team. Trust, within the team and with outside parties, grows whenever team members demonstrate that they are able to differentiate between what is correct and what is expedient in any situation and then act on the basis of what is correct. In other words, the team puts values first.

Team Excellence

Teams succeed to the degree to which individuals give unconditionally in support of the team's objectives

- Benevolent Intent/ Purpose
- Meaning at the level of the task
- Respect between team members
- Trust by putting values first

From own experience and from witnessing teams in action, these attributes of purpose, meaning, respect and trust do not occur naturally or just because the team has worked together over a period of time. They require a team to step back, to reflect and to deliberately work on how it is functioning as a team.

Schuitema's teambuilding process has been successfully applied both in teams which are essentially toxic and in those with reasonable levels of trust and respect between members. Each teambuilding process is

Team Excellence Process

- Establishing Criteria
- Diagnosing against Criteria
- Remediating against Criteria

constructed in terms of the unique requirements of the team and is therefore based on consultation with team members beforehand. Any Team Excellence process follows the three process steps of establishing, diagnosing and remediating against the Team Excellence criteria.

The above-named criteria are really common sense. They can easily be solicited from team members at the start of a teambuilding process. The current state of the team, in terms of the overall state of the team, can be established by means of metaphor or from peer questionnaires completed prior to the session.

The content of the remediating step is obviously determined by the diagnostic material but may include the following:

- Establishing the team's purpose or benevolent intent. Understanding who the team is here to serve and what value it adds to customers and the world.

- Establishing a line of sight between each individual's role and the overall purpose of the team.

- Establishing the team's values or rules of engagement. Then gaining commitment by team members to behaving in a manner which is consistent with their values.

- Practising gratitude for the unique contribution made by each member of the team.

- Determining what the team needs to do, collectively and individually, to achieve team excellence and deliver on it.

For executive teams, we have developed a process called *Growing by Growing Others* in collaboration with executives from Johnson Matthey Catalysts in the UK. The process is designed to demonstrate the following:

- That every interaction that we have at work is an opportunity to learn and mature, if we chose to use it as such.

- That when the intent to *give* is built into every interaction which takes place between individuals at work, the effect of this is transformative for the organisation, for relationships within the organisation, and for individuals themselves.

The organisational benefit of this is not only that leaders act consistently with the core criterion of benevolent intent or being here to serve, but that relationships between senior leaders at work are essentially collaborative rather than competitive.

The process is broken into three parts:

GROWING BY GROWING OTHERS

1. Establishing the current state of the organisation, the current state of the relationships in the organisation and the connections between the two.

2. Confirming the criteria for excellence for the individual, the group and the organisation.

3. Remediating against the criteria or commitment by each individual to doing what is correct rather than expedient in each of his key relationships at work.

As part of the Leadership Excellence content we argue that the people who matter most in any organisation are those who make a direct contribution to the organisation's results, those who do the work which accounts for the bottom line of the business. If leaders are there to serve their people, then those in the front line are there to serve or add value to a customer.

An intervention is therefore not complete unless the majority of individual contributors are enabled to make their unique contribution to the customer. The vehicle for this is a one- or two-day process which can be applied in both a literate and illiterate context. The process is customised to the organisation and, depending on the numbers involved, can be run by in-house facilitators.

The deliverables from the Service Excellence Process are as follows:

A comment made at the end of the Service Excellence Process, by Tarun Ghoshal, the site manager at Johnson Matthey Catalysts' site in India, was: 'A workplace once characterized by a strong sense of *them* against *us* (the worker/management divide) has now become home to a strong team ethic and commitment to excellence.'

Personal Excellence

The Personal Excellence content is not for all employees in an organisation. Rather it is for key individuals in client organisations whose personal excellence and growth is of paramount importance to the transformation of the business. The aim of the Personal Excellence process is to develop personal mastery; to grow as a human being. The process posits that there is a core variable which accounts for success at the job of being human, which is *intent*. The Personal Excellence process therefore provides a framework for senior people in an organisation to explore and develop their own intent.

During the process participants do the following:

THE PERSONAL EXCELLENCE PROCESS

- Identify what it is that all human beings aspire to and the true source of those things.
- Explore the difference between maturity and immaturity and how an individual's maturity affects himself both personally and in terms of his relationships with other people and the world that he lives in.
- Develop an understanding of the process of the maturation of one's intent from being 'here to get' to being 'here to give unconditionally'.
- Experience how 'right' or generous and courageous action is enabled by the inner equivalents of trust and gratitude. Also, how distrust and resentment impacts on one's capacity to grow as a human being.
- Acquire some powerful tools for engaging with others and with life.
- Determine where the individual is now in relation to her intent, based on what concerns her now, and an interrogation of her biography.
- Leave with a vision – what she chooses to be in the future.

The Personal Excellence Process is run as a five-day intensive residential programme or as a series of one-day sessions over a five-month period. The diagnostic tools used in the process, and afterwards, relate to both reflecting on and silencing one's inner dialogue.

After the initial process, Schuitema assists individuals to further their personal maturation by providing a mentoring service to them.

And finally

The END to which we are committed is clear. It is to enable human excellence, or the intent to serve, at the level of the individual, the team and the organisation in as many contexts as possible.

The MEANS to that end continues to unfold. Nevertheless, the following has become clear to us over the years regarding the efficacy of any Care and Growth intervention.

What promotes success?

1. Start with the current reality
2. Speak to issues in the organisation
3. Avoid the grand plan

Firstly, a Care and Growth intervention must start with where the client organisation is NOW. If those in leadership positions are currently of the view that their job is to achieve results through people, then the starting point is the inversion of Means and Ends in the boss-subordinate relationship in the line. If the average interaction between people in the organisation is self-seeking, then fostering collaborative, rather than competitive, engagements must be the initial focus. If key individuals are struggling with issues of personal security, fulfilment, power and harmony both at work and in their personal lives then personal excellence must be the point of departure.

Secondly, a Care and Growth intervention must be an integral part of, rather than something which runs parallel to, the burning issues in an organisation at the time. The best results have always been realised when the Care and Growth philosophy and practices are applied to the resolution of real issues – be they a lack of employee engagement, product quality, dysfunctional teams, a lack of accountability, an internal focus or any other issue.

Finally, organisations should resist the temptation to lay out and follow a grand plan to implement the Care and Growth framework. The implementation process is undoubtedly far better, even if it seems counter-intuitive, when it is taken one step at a time in the right direction, trusting that the next step to take will become apparent as events unfold and life happens.

References

Achor, R (2010). *The Happiness Advantage*. Virgin Books, a Random House Group Company, USA.

Buckingham, M (2004). *Now Discover Your Strengths*. Pocket Books, UK.

Buckingham, M (2006). *The One Thing You Need to Know*. Pocket Books, UK.

Collins, J (2001). *Good to Great*. Random House Business Books, UK.

Covey, SR (1992). *Seven Habits of Highly Effective People*. Simon & Schuster Ltd, London.

Crotty, A and Bonorchis, R (2006). *Executive Pay in South Africa – Who Gets What and Why*. Double Storey Books, a division of Juta & Co Ltd, South Africa.

Csikszentmihalyl, M (1990). *Flow: The Psychology of Optimal Experience*. Harper and Row, New York.

Gladwell, M (2008). *Outliers – The Story of Success*. Penguin Group, London.

Hamel, G (2007). *The Future of Management*. Harvard Business School Publishing, Massachusetts, USA.

Hamel, G (2010). *The Hole in The Soul of Business*. Wall Street Journal, USA.

Handy, C (1995). *The Empty Raincoat – Making Sense of the Future*. Arrow Books Limited, UK.

Kets de Vries, MFR (2001). *The Leadership Mystique*. Pearson Education Limited, UK.

Pink, DH (2009). *Drive – The Surprising Truth About What Motivates Us*. Penguin Books Ltd, USA.

Semler, R (2003). *The Seven-Day Weekend*. Random House Group Ltd, USA.

Schuitema, E (1994). *Beyond Management – Towards Establishing Ethical Business Leadership*. Southern Book Publishers Pty Ltd, South Africa.

Schuitema, E (2004). *Leadership – The Care and Growth Model*. Ampersand Press, Cape Town.

Southey, J (2011). *Carbon Fibre, Sweat and Management Theory*. Article on Schuitema Blog

Welsch, J (2005). *Winning*. Harper Collins Publishers, USA.